Unit 2: Participating in society — 152–165

Your activity: what's the choice?	154
Making the choice	156
Planning the activity	158
Developing your skills: advocacy and representation	160
Participation in action	162
The impact of your action	164

Unit 3: Citizenship in context — 166–239

Option A: Environmental change and sustainable development — 168–189

Making ethical decisions	170
Global warming – the perspectives	172
What can you do?	174
Not in my backyard?	176
Do targets work?	178
Sustainability: local or national?	180
The same rules for all?	182
Trade or aid?	184
Environmental change and sustainable development: the exam	186–189

Option B: Changing communities: social and cultural identities — 190–211

Making ethical decisions	192
Why come to Britain	194
Can we stay?	196
Coming and going	198
A melting pot?	200
Are we really equal?	202
Attitudes to immigration	204
Working together	206
Changing communities: social and cultural identities: the exam	208–211

Option C: Influencing and changing decisions in society and government — 212–239

Making ethical decisions	214
Influencing change	216
Political change	218
Changing democracy	220
Crime: fact or fiction?	222
What's the point of prison?	224
Criminal or civil?	226
What's happening to freedom?	228
Who's listening?	230
Can we control the economy?	232
Influencing and changing decisions in society and government: the exam	234–239

Unit 4: Citizenship campaign — 240–257

Your campaign: what's the choice?	242
Which campaign?	244
Developing your skills: questionnaires	246
Developing your skills: spreading the message	248
Developing your skills: planning a protest	250
Planning your campaign	252
Participation in action	254
What was the impact?	256

Unit 1: theme 1

Rights and

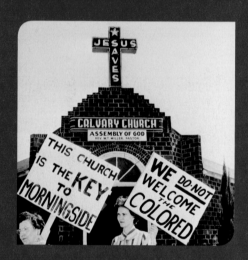

1.1 Communities and identities — 6–15

What is a community?	6	Religious understanding	12
A national culture	8	Identities	14
Where are your roots?	10		

1.2 Human, legal and political rights — 16–27

What are human rights?	16	Discrimination and legal rights	22
Legal rights	18	Rights with responsibilities	24
Meeting barriers	20	Political rights	26

responsibilities

1.3 Development and struggle   28–31

Rights for all?   28   We want to vote!   30

1.4 Rights and responsibilities of consumers, employers and employees   32–7

Protecting the customer   32   Responsibilities in the workplace   36

Fair play at work   34

Rights and responsibilities: the exam   38–41

What is a community?

Getting you thinking

1 How many of these communities do you belong to?
2 What other communities do you belong to?
3 How many of these communities do you share with people of different ages and/or interests?
4 If you don't belong to some of these communities, do you know people who do? How do you know these people?
5 What do these communities give you and what do you give them?

Belonging to a community

A **community** is a group of people who are connected in some way. Most people belong to several communities. Someone your age, living in the UK, could be a member of all these communities: school, the local neighbourhood, the country, the **European** Union, a religious group and others.

Neighbourhoods

There is a lot of overlap between different communities.

A **neighbourhood** community refers to those people who share local interests because of where they live.

It might be the whole of a village or small town, but in a city the neighbourhood can be more difficult to identify. For example, someone living in Whitechapel in London might think of the neighbourhood as 'London', 'Whitechapel', 'the East End' or even just their own particular street.

You will discover the meaning of community and understand how you can belong to more than one community at the same time.

'I belong to ...'

As well as belonging to a neighbourhood, people are also connected by their lifestyle, religion, ethnicity or nationality.

The Chinese community

The Chinese community in the UK dates back to the mid-1800s. They live in all parts of the UK and there are well established 'Chinatowns' in Birmingham, Liverpool, London, Manchester and Newcastle. There are over 400 Chinese organisations that serve the needs of the Chinese community in the UK, including language schools, women's groups, and art and business associations. Chinese New Year, food, martial arts, medicine and Feng Shui have all become part of British life.

The Christian community

There are almost 49,000 Christian churches in the United Kingdom across more than ten different denominations, ranging from Church of England and Roman Catholic to Methodist and Greek Orthodox. As well as involving people in the wider Christian community, many churches are a focus for local people, offering facilities and events open to Christians and non-Christians alike.

Irish travellers

There are about 1300 Irish travellers in Northern Ireland. They are a centuries-old ethnic community that travels around in mobile homes. They have their own culture, customs, traditions and language.

The Muslim community

Almost all of the Muslim population in Britain are descendants of the families of people who came to Britain in the 1950s, 60s and 70s. However, Islam has been followed in Britain for centuries. At least 300 years ago, Indian–Muslim sailors, recruited by the East India Company, settled in port towns. The first mosque in Britain probably opened in Cardiff in 1860. Today, there are Muslim communities all over Britain.

Check your understanding

1. Explain why people can belong to more than one community and why there is an overlap between communities.
2. Describe what each of the communities shown has in common. What makes each one a community?

... another point of view?

'It is easier to feel part of a community if you live in a village or small town rather than a city.'

Do you agree with this statement? Give reasons for your opinion, showing you have considered another point of view.

Key Terms

community: a group of people who are in close contact and who share common interests and values

neighbourhood: a local area within which people live as neighbours, sharing living space and interests

A national culture

Getting you thinking

1 Many people who visit Britain have a very traditional vision of the country. How would you describe it?

2 If you had to describe British culture to people, what would you include?

3 Do you think other people might have a different picture? How might their vision differ from yours?

What does it mean to be British?

This is a difficult question and it has many possible answers. Do you think it means that:

- you share a geographical boundary with other British people?
- you share a history that links the separate parts of England, Wales, Scotland and Northern Ireland?
- you share a common language?
- you identify with many common habits, values and pastimes?
- you have the right to have a British passport so you can move freely in and out of the United Kingdom?

A national identity is often easier to describe when you are in a different country. How might you feel if you went abroad on holiday? In Spain, for example, you would come across a different language, a different kind of diet, different kinds of schooling and different games played by children and adults.

A sense of belonging

A sense of belonging comes from growing up and living in a particular place. Parents, schools and the media pass on common ideas of British culture. Different generations are also influenced by their own personal experiences. People who have fought in wars for their country are likely to feel a different sense of belonging from those who only feel British when they are away on holiday.

Which community?

People may also identify with different kinds of national community. People from ethnic minorities may feel more comfortable with members of their own ethnic community than with other **British nationals**. Similarly, people from various regions such as the Midlands or the South West might identify more with people from their own region than with people from other regions.

It is possible to belong to many different communities at the same time. Sports fans may feel quite comfortable supporting a British team in one competition, an English or Welsh team in another, and their local team in a third.

You will explore the meaning of national identity and culture, and discover that Britain community is very diverse.

A multicultural community

Population of Great Britain by ethnic group (millions)

White	42.7
Black Caribbean	0.6
Black African	0.6
Indian	1.2
Pakistani	0.8
Bangladeshi	0.3
Chinese	0.3
Other groups	0.3

Source: Social Trends 2008, ONS

The ethnic mix of the national community has changed steadily over the years to include a significant number of people of Afro-Caribbean, African and Asian descent. In some areas, the majority of the local population is now of one of these groups. Many of them have developed a sense of belonging and feel British, as the graph on the right shows.

In a **multicultural community:**

- a local school may serve a community with several different home languages and different festivals to celebrate
- welfare services often provide information printed in several languages
- hospitals and clinics work with a variety of traditions and expectations surrounding births and deaths
- local councils have to take account of different community needs for shops and religious buildings
- businesses may have staff and customers from a range of cultural backgrounds.

Who feels British?

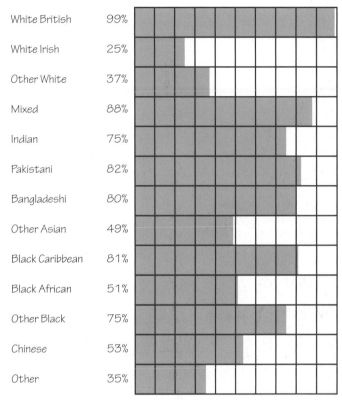

White British	99%
White Irish	25%
Other White	37%
Mixed	88%
Indian	75%
Pakistani	82%
Bangladeshi	80%
Other Asian	49%
Black Caribbean	81%
Black African	51%
Other Black	75%
Chinese	53%
Other	35%

Source: ONS

Action

What do your friends and family mean by 'being British'? Share your findings with the class.

Check your understanding

1 What does it mean to say that Britain is a multicultural community?
2 List as many different aspects of British culture as you can that you think help define British national identity.

... another point of view?

'The region I live in is more important to me than my national culture.'
Do you agree with this statement? Give reasons for your opinion, showing you have considered another point of view.

Key Terms

British nationals: citizens of the United Kingdom

multicultural community: a community made up of people from many different cultural or ethnic groups

Where are your roots?

Getting you thinking

Whose genes?

1 Many of us know where our grandparents lived and perhaps out great grandparents. Where did yours come from?

2 Do you think it is important for you to know your roots? Explain your answer.

I live in Cheddar in Somerset. My DNA tells me I'm related to a man who lived here 40,000 years ago.

I live in London and I know my family came from Yorkshire. My DNA tells me I have relations who were Mongolian, Brazilian, a Russian and a woman who lived near the Mediterranean 117,000 years ago.

I thought I was British but my DNA tells me I'm descended from Native Americans. They must have been brought here as slaves.

'To forget your ancestors is to be a tree without roots.' Chinese proverb

3 If we know we have lots of different roots, does it help us to understand others?

A pick-and-mix people

Throughout its history, people have settled in Britain from many different countries. They bring their language, ideas and customs, all of which have mixed together to make up the country's culture.

Warlike invasions of Romans, Saxons, Vikings and Normans were followed by peaceful migrations from Europe and many former British colonies. Just look in the dictionary, phone book or map to find words and names from many languages.

➤ In the past 250 years, about six million people have come from Ireland in search of a better life. Many came to the UK during the potato famine of the 1840s.

➤ In 1860, one-quarter of the population of Liverpool were Irish migrants.

➤ Poles have lived here ever since the reign of Queen Elizabeth I, but the majority of UK Poles settled here after World War II when Poland was occupied first by the Nazis, and then by the Soviet armies.

➤ There has been a Jewish population in the UK for hundreds of years, but most arrived in the 1930s and 40s. They came to the UK to escape from religious and racial persecution in Russia and Europe.

➤ In the 1950s, many people from British colonies in Africa, Asia and the Caribbean settled in the UK looking for work, as there was a shortage of manual and semiskilled employees in Britain during this period.

➤ In the 1970s, thousands of Ugandan Asians arrived here after being expelled from Uganda.

➤ As more countries have joined the European Union, people from Eastern Europe, including Poland, have come to the UK to work because there are more opportunities.

Immigration today is more restricted for people from many parts of the world.

In the same way that people from other countries come to Britain, people emigrate from Britain to go and live in other countries. The table below shows some reasons for **immigration** and **emigration** in Britain.

Why do people come and go? (thousands)			
	Immigration	Emigration	Balance
For work	103.4	92.8	10.6
With a partner	77.2	51.1	26.1
For study	91.2	13.7	77.5
Other	164.6	99.3	65.3
No reason	27.7	49.2	−21.5
All reasons	464.0	306.0	158.0

Source: Office of National Statistics

You will find out about the diverse communities that make up the UK.

Ethnic minorities in each region

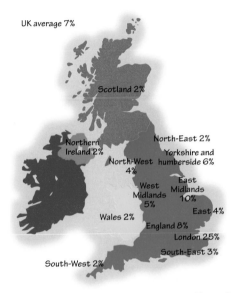

UK average 7%

Scotland 2%

Northern Ireland 2%

North-East 2%

North-West 4%

Yorkshire and humberside 6%

West Midlands 5%

East Midlands 10%

Wales 2%

East 4%

England 8%

London 25%

South-West 2%

South-East 3%

Source: 2001 Census, Office of National Statistics

Leicester: a lesson in racial understanding

Many people living in Leicester have non-white roots, and the city is proud of its **cultural diversity**. When rioting has taken place in other cities, Leicester has remained calm. However, in the 1970s, it was labelled one of the most racist cities in Britain. There were adverts in the local papers telling immigrants not to come to Leicester and racial tension was high.

The city council took the lead by outlawing racism. It promoted Leicester as a city that welcomes everybody. The council created Britain's first-ever race relations committee. A public education programme made people aware of others' hopes and fears. Since then, various groups have worked hard to promote good race relations in the city.

There are now over 1,500 Asian businesses in the city, and many Asian councillors on the city council. Festivals such as Diwali now attract over 25,000 people to the city.

Action

Research the background and culture of any immigrant groups that have settled in your local area. Find out why they left their homelands, and to what extent they have been able to retain their language and culture. Present your findings to the class

Check your understanding

1 Suggest two reasons why the UK is a culturally diverse society.
2 Why did many immigrants come to Britain in the 1950s?
3 Why do people immigrate and emigrate?
4 In which regions, outside London, would you find the most culturally diverse communities?
5 Describe two things the council did to improve race relations in Leicester.
6 Why do you think there have been no riots in Leicester when there has been trouble in other cities?
7 Do you think other regions of the UK will become more culturally diverse in future? Give reasons.
8 What do you think can be done to bring different ethnic groups together?

... another point of view?

'Immigration benefits a country.'
Do you agree with this statement? Give reasons for your opinion, showing you have considered another point of view.

'Immigration benefits a country' (-12 Mark)

- Different Reasons for Immigration
- Promotes Cultural Diversity
- Less Racist
- More Racist?
- Learn Different things
- Mv view.

Religious understanding

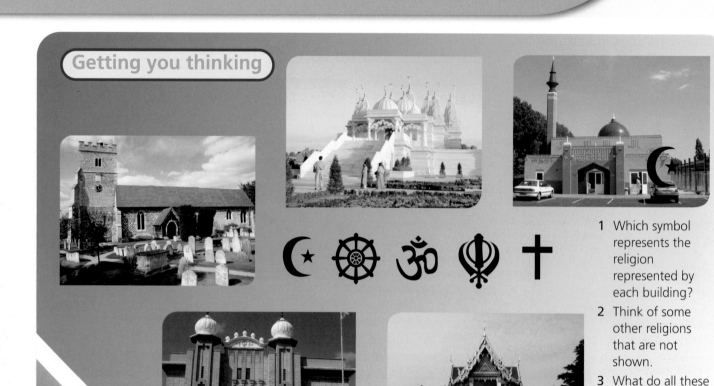

Getting you thinking

1 Which symbol represents the religion represented by each building?

2 Think of some other religions that are not shown.

3 What do all these religions have in common? List as many as you can.

Diverse views

Although most UK citizens would probably claim to be Christians, there are many other diverse religious groups in the UK. The majority of these are found in large cities, such as London, Birmingham, Manchester and Leeds, where most of the UK's ethnic **minority** communities live. This religious diversity is the result of people settling here over many years, mostly from former British colonies.

The main ethnic minority groups and their religions are:

- **Bangladeshis:** Mostly Muslim (small number of Hindus)
- **Indians (Punjabis):** Mostly Sikh, some Hindus
- **Indians (Gujeratis):** Mostly Hindus, some Muslims
- **Pakistanis:** Muslim
- **Chinese:** Christian, Confucian and Buddhist
- **Afro-Caribbeans:** Christian and Rastafarian.

Within many religions there are different 'branches'. Anglicans, Methodists, Quakers and Catholics are all part of the wider Christian tradition but practise their religion in different ways. In the same way, Orthodox and Reform Jews share many beliefs but worship in separate synagogues.

Sometimes an individual's clothes, the food they eat or the language they speak gives you a clue to their religion. But this is not always the case. Think about all the UK citizens with Indian roots. Some of them are Sikhs, but what about the others?

UK citizens with Indian roots: different religions

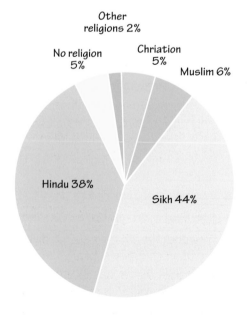

Other religions 2%

No religion 5%

Chriation 5%

Muslim 6%

Hindu 38%

Sikh 44%

Source: www.statistics.gov.uk

You will find out about the religious diversity of the UK and why religious tolerance is important.

Religion in conflict

Threatened for converting

A Bradford man who faced threats and harassment for converting to Christianity from Islam was told by police to 'stop being a crusader and move to another place'.

Nissar Hussein and his wife, Qubra, converted from Islam to Christianity in 1996. They were subsequently alienated from family and friends.

As news of the couple's conversion spread, their Bradford home was vandalised and their car was set on fire. In 2001, one man told Mr Hussein that if he did not return to Islam, he would burn down his house.

I go to an Asian church

I go to church with my family every Sunday. We can wear our Indian clothes and meet other Asian and English friends that we may not see during the week. Going to an Asian church means we worship God in both the English and the Indian traditions.

During the service, one person usually stands up at the front and leads the service. We sing in different languages, including English, as many of the church members are Asian, although people from other nationalities sometimes come along.

We also have Indian instruments to help with the singing and worship. People pray in different languages too. Both men and women pray. In most Asian churches the men and women usually sit on separate sides. The young people sit on both sides, depending on their age, and whether both of their parents come to church.

1 Why do you think Nisssar and Qubra's friends and family disliked them converting?
2 The Asian church is a Christian church. How is it trying to bring people together?

Everyone's right

The United Nations (UN), an international organisation to which most countries belong, put together a Declaration of Human Rights (see page 17). This Declaration includes a section on religion, which states that everyone is free to follow any religion or to choose to follow none. Everyone has the right to join an established religion, or to start a sect or cult of their own. Nobody should be prevented from following the religion of their choice.

... another point of view?

'It is always important to be **tolerant** of other people's religious beliefs.'
Do you agree with this statement? Give reasons for your opinion, showing you have considered another point of view.

Check your understanding

1 Why does the UK have such a diversity of religions? Can you name any other countries where you find the same religious diversity?
2 What does the Universal Declaration of Human Rights say about your religious freedom? Is this always observed?

Key Terms

minority: a small part of a larger group of people
tolerant: open-minded, accepting

Identities

Getting you thinking

I've got Asian roots. I love sport, have loads of mates and I'm always having fun.

I come from Brighton. My parents are divorced. I've got one brother and two half-sisters. I like watching TV and listening to music. I spend loads of time at the beach with my friends.

I'm from Newcastle. I'm 15, an only child and a huge fan of EastEnders and reality TV shows.

1. What has contributed to the identity of each of these people?
2. How do you think these factors have affected them?
3. How much does your identity depend on where you live, on your family's roots or on your religion?
4. If you had been asked the question 'Who are you?' when you were five years old, what would you have said? How would you answer this question now?
5. Make a list of factors that will shape your identity as you get older.

Who am I?

In some countries, such as France, all citizens must carry an **identity card**. There are plans to introduce one in the UK. This card gives details such as your name, address and date of birth. But the word '**identity**' has another, broader meaning. The identity of a person is a combination of where they come from and the influences on their life.

Your identity develops and changes as you develop and change. Can you remember how you felt when you first went to school? You've learned a lot about yourself in the ten or more years since then. You now have a better understanding of your good and bad points; you are more self-aware and better aware of how other people see you. Looking back, that five-year-old 'you' will seem like a very different person.

Your identity will continue to develop further as you grow older and as you become an employee, a parent, partner/wife/husband and so on.

An identity card obviously can't show all this information about you. However, some governments like them because it means that people can be easily identified.

You will discover the meaning of identity and some of the factors that determine it.

Conflicting loyalties

Britain has one of the highest rates of mixed-race relationships in the world. By 2010, it is estimated that London will be made up of more **dual heritage** and black people than white. While most people would agree that cultural diversity is a good thing, the mixing of races and nationalities can occasionally produce conflicts.

> If, for example, your mother is Chinese, your father is Irish, you were born in Paris but you live in London, how would you answer the question: 'Where are you from?'

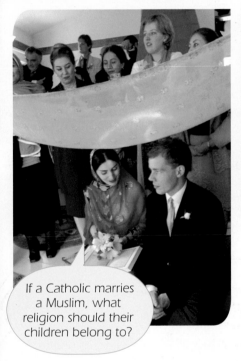

> If a Catholic marries a Muslim, what religion should their children belong to?

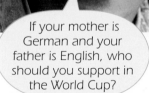

> If your mother is German and your father is English, who should you support in the World Cup?

> How do you react if someone tells you you're not really black and you're not really white?

1 In your own words, describe the conflicting loyalties felt by each of the people.

2 Which person has the most difficult situation to resolve, and why?

3 Suggest other situations that involve conflicting loyalties.

Check your understanding

1 What does 'dual heritage' mean?
2 Describe how dual heritage can sometimes lead to conflicts of identity.

... another point of view?

'People are more alike than different.'

Do you agree with this statement? Give reasons for your opinion showing you have considered another point of view.

Key Terms

dual heritage: people with parents or ancestors of different origins

identity: who or what someone or something is

identity card: a card that establishes someone's identity

What are human rights?

Getting you thinking

1 What are these children deprived of?
2 Make a list of the things you think every child should have.
3 Use your list to write a statement of children's rights.

Human rights

People all over the world suffer because their basic needs are not met. Some people's freedoms are limited by the country in which they live. Nobody should live without these basic **human rights:**

- the right to education
- the right to work
- the right to fair conditions at work
- the right to travel
- the right to food and clothes
- the right to healthcare
- the right to meet with friends
- the right to own property
- the right to follow your religion
- the right to marry and have children
- the rights of minorities to be treated the same as the majority.

1 Which of the rights listed above are the most important to you? Why?
2 Can you think of some situations where any of your rights might be threatened?
3 What examples are there in the news of people's human rights being threatened?

The case of A versus the United Kingdom

A nine-year-old boy was beaten with a cane by his stepfather. When taken to court, his stepfather claimed that his actions were within English law, which allows parents to use 'reasonable force' to punish a child. He was found not guilty. The boy's lawyers took the case to the European Court of Human Rights, which decided that the boy had suffered 'cruel, inhuman and degrading punishment'.

The boy was awarded £10,000 in damages and the UK government agreed to change the law to give better protection in future.

There has still been no change in the law. Parents can still use 'reasonable force'.

You will find out about human rights and how they affect us.

The United Nations and human rights

The United Nations is an international organisation. It was set up in 1945 and most countries in the world now belong. Together, these members have developed two important statements of human rights. The Universal Declaration of Human Rights was created in 1948 and the Convention on the Rights of the Child was agreed in 1981.

The Convention on the Rights of the Child (CRC)

This **Convention** requires governments all around the world to think about the needs of young people and to consult them about matters that affect them, such as education, family life, law and order. Millions of young people do not have relatives to look after them: those caught up in civil wars in Africa, for instance. The CRC recognises this and says that young people must have rights of their own – rights that don't depend on parents or other adults.

There are still 250 000 children serving as soldiers around the world. The CRC states that 'Governments should not allow children under 15 to join the army.'

Action

Collect newspaper reports and internet articles concerned with human rights. Discuss the effects that being deprived of these rights can have on people.

Check your understanding

1. Why was the Universal **Declaration** of Human Rights written?
2. What is the main difference between the scope of the Universal Declaration of Human Rights and that of the European Convention on Human Rights?
3. What can European citizens do if they feel their human rights are being denied?
4. Does everyone have the rights that are set out in these two statements of rights? Give examples.

They set out standards for everyone, everywhere; but in many parts of the world people's human rights are still abused. The Declaration offers guidance for countries but cannot be enforced legally if a country's laws do not take it up.

Universal Declaration of Human Rights (UDHR)

The UDHR was drawn up by world leaders after the Second World War. They wanted to prevent such terrible things happening again. It states that everyone has a right to life and liberty, freedom of speech and movement, a fair wage, a fair trial, education and many other basic human rights.

Huang Qi was arrested. He had been involved in assisting families to bring a legal case against the local authorities. Their children had died when school buildings collapsed in the earthquake

... another point of view?

'People should learn to look after themselves rather than being protected by Declarations and Conventions.'

Do you agree with this statement? Give reasons for your opinion, showing you have considered another point of view.

Key Terms

Convention: an agreement (often between governments)

Declaration: a document setting down aims and intentions

human rights: things that people are morally or legally allowed to do or have

United Nations: an international organisation that tries to encourage peace, cooperation and friendship between countries

Legal rights

Getting you thinking

1 What do these photographs tell you about human rights in USA in the mid-1900s?

2 Which basic human rights were being denied?

3 Do you think you would see sights like these in the USA today? Give reasons.

What are legal rights?

When law protects a human right, it becomes a **legal right**. For example, everyone has the right to go to public places such as parks, hotels and restaurants. The Race Relations Act makes it illegal for anyone to be refused entry to any public place because of his or her ethnicity.

The **Act** also applies to employment and education. For example, it is illegal for an employer to tell someone, 'You can't have the job because you're black.' Similarly, it would be illegal to set up a school that accepted only black students. The Race Relations Act is just one law among many that protect people's rights.

The Universal Declaration of Human Rights says you have a right to a fair wage. The 1998 Minimum Wage Act made this a legal right, so all adult workers in England and Wales must be paid the minimum wage. The Universal Declaration of Human Rights also says you have a right to 'equal pay for equal work'. The Sex Discrimination Act made equal pay a legal right

You will discover how the law is used to protect people's human rights.

Turning human rights into legal rights

The right to education
The right to work
The right to fair conditions at work
The right to travel
The right to food and clothes
The right to healthcare
The right to meet friends
The right to own property
The right to follow your religion
The right to marry and have children
The rights of minorities to be treated the same as the majority
The right to life
The right to freedom
The right to privacy
The right to fair trial
The right not to be tortured or punished cruelly
The right to vote

1 Can these human rights all be turned into legal rights? Give reasons.
2 Suggest what these laws might say.

Legal rights and age limits

Everyone has basic rights. Some are limited by law.

Some of your legal right in the UK

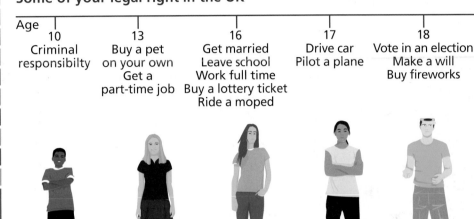

Age	10	13	16	17	18
	Criminal responsibilty	Buy a pet on your own Get a part-time job	Get married Leave school Work full time Buy a lottery ticket Ride a moped	Drive car Pilot a plane	Vote in an election Make a will Buy fireworks

1 Why does the law impose age limits like these?
2 Which of these age limits would you change? Explain why.
3 Whose human rights are being protected by each of these age limits?

Find out more about legal rights

Human rights and legal rights are a theme throughout this book. You have already explored religious rights and the laws that protect them. The Race Relations Act and The Disability **Discrimination** Act help to protect minorities (page 22). Later in the course, you will find out about laws to protect you at work (page 35) and how your privacy is protected (page 50).

Action

Research at what age and under what conditions young people have a legal right to drink alcohol. Carry out a survey to find out what your group thinks about these rights and age limits. How easy is it to police these laws?

Check your understanding

1 What is the difference between a human right and a legal right?
2 Name one law that makes a human right a legal right.
3 What does the phrase 'sex discrimination' mean? Give an example.

... another point of view?

'Legal rights just protect people from themselves.'
Do you agree with this statement? Give reasons for your opinion, showing you have considered another point of view.

Key Terms

Act: a law passed by Parliament

discrimination (racial, sex and disability): treating someone less favourably because of their colour, ethnic origins, gender or disability

legal right: a right that is protected by law

Meeting barriers

Getting you thinking

Some children were playing on the beach when an old 'bag lady' came along. She was talking to herself and picking things up off the beach as she walked. Parents called their children over and told them to stay close by, until the old woman had moved on. The following day, they discovered that the old woman came to the beach every day, picking up bits of glass so children wouldn't cut their feet.

1 Why did the parents call their children over? What is the moral of the story?

2 Have you ever misjudged somebody because of their dress or behaviour? Have you ever been misjudged?

3 Think of individuals or groups who are misjudged in this way, and say why they have been misunderstood.

Prejudice and discrimination

People treat each other badly for all sorts of reasons. Such unfair treatment can mean that people don't get jobs or are kept out of clubs, as well as many other things. The case studies on the next page show some strategies used to overcome prejudice and discrimination. Think about how each person's human rights are being affected.

The pyramid of discrimination

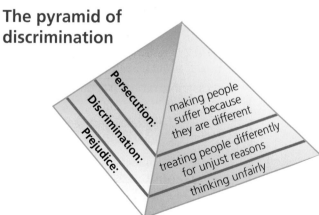

Persecution: making people suffer because they are different

Discrimination: treating people differently for unjust reasons

Prejudice: thinking unfairly

Part of the 'rough and tumble' of school?

Lancaster Youth and Community Service set up a group for gay and lesbian young people, to help them cope with the homophobic bullying they encountered in schools and colleges. One young man who belongs to the group said, 'I love coming here. It's the only time in the week I feel completely safe. It's the one place I can be myself.'

1 What does the young man's comment tell you about homophobic bullying?

2 What can schools do to reduce homophobic bullying?

You will find out about discrimination and consider how it affects people and how it might be overcome.

'Education is the answer'

Although there are many black and Asian football players and they are accepted by football fans everywhere, there are still problems with racial prejudice and discrimination. Some fans have been known to call out racist comments and make monkey noises when black players are on the pitch.

Sir Alex Ferguson, Manchester United's manager, is a supporter of football's anti-racism campaign 'Kick It Out!'. This is what he says:

'I think it's all down to education and how people are brought up. I was brought up in a family where there was never any prejudice. I think education from family and school is the most important thing. If parents are saying to their kids "Don't play with that Charlie down the road because he is black," what message does that give? I think education is the secret.'

The situation today is better than it was 20 years ago, and 20 years ago it was better than 30 years ago. So progress eventually eliminates a lot of what is going on.

1 Do you agree with Sir Alex that 'it's all down to education'? Give reasons.

2 Why do you think things are improving?

3 Why do you think all top clubs and star football players in the UK support the Kick It Out! campaign?

Young and Powerful

Young and Powerful is a group of young disabled and non-disabled people supported by Comic Relief. They all go to mainstream schools and campaign for **inclusive education**. They believe all children need to be taught together, so they can learn from each other.

1 What does the phrase 'inclusive education' mean?

2 What kinds of physical barriers would a wheelchair-user face if they came to your school? Would they face any other kinds of barriers?

Action

Use the Kick It Out! website, www.kickitout.org, to research what your local football clubs, professional and amateur, are doing to combat racism.

Check your understanding

1 What is prejudice? Why are some people prejudiced against others?

2 What is discrimination? Give some examples.

3 Look at the different cases on these two pages and say whether the people or groups described could have experienced prejudice, discrimination or persecution.

4 How are the people in each story overcoming prejudice?

5 How does discrimination affect people's human rights?

... another point of view?

'Discrimination is the result of ignorance.'

Do you agree with this statement? Give reasons for your opinion, showing you have considered another point of view. You might think about fear, ignorance, upbringing, insecurity or bad experiences. Refer to the groups or individuals mentioned on these two pages to support your answers.

Key Terms

homophobic: fearing or hating homosexuals

inclusive education: schooling that involves everyone, regardless of disability or non-disability

racism: the idea that some people of different origins are not as good as others

Discrimination and legal rights

1 What message is the poster giving?

2 What other forms of discrimination take place at work?

3 Why do people need protection against discrimination?

4 How do you think the law can help?

Fighting discrimination with the law

Everyone deserves a fair chance to be successful in life. Poster campaigns and other public awareness programmes try to educate people to think beyond prejudice. These campaigns are just one way of dealing with **discrimination**. There are also legal ways of tackling prejudice and discrimination. There are three important anti-discrimination laws:

The Sex Discrimination Act

Sex discrimination generally works against the interests of females, and particularly in the workplace. It can be difficult to ensure that women have the same opportunities for promotion as men, when many have time away at some point to have children. Although the Act usually protects women, if a man is unfairly treated because he is a man, he is also protected by the Act.

The Race Relations Act

The Race Relations Act makes it an offence to treat a person differently on the grounds of race, colour, nationality, and national or ethnic origin. In practice, most racial discrimination in Britain is against people from ethnic minorities, but people from every nationality are protected by the law.

The Disability Discrimination Act

This Act aims to end discrimination against disabled people. A disability should not stop a person from being employed unless it stops them doing the job. Employers must help their staff. A deaf employee working in an office should be given a videophone to allow them to work like everybody else.

You will discover how legal rights protect people against discrimination.

How has the law helped?

Look at these cases where the anti-discrimination Acts have helped people.

Maintenance manager wins sex discrimination case

Laetitia Booth had been a maintenance manager on the railways. When the company was reorganised she was given a lower status job. She sued the company for sex discrimination and unfair dismissal and won.

1 Do you think that maintenance managers on the railways are mainly men or women?
2 Do you think this had any effect on the company's decision?
3 How did the law protect her?

Deaf man wins damages

Keith Wynn is profoundly deaf. He applied for a job with Multipulse Electronics Ltd. He was well qualified as he had held a similar job in another company for 25 years. Multipulse cancelled his interview because they had not organised a sign language interpreter. He heard nothing more. He challenged them in court and won considerable damages.

1 What did Multipulse Electronics do wrong?
2 How did the law protect Mr Wynn?

£2.8 million compensation for suffering racial discrimination

Balbinder Chagger from Hayes, Middlesex, worked as a £100,000-a-year trading risk controller for Abbey until he was made redundant in 2006. He claimed he lost his job because of racial discrimination. A woman with a similar performance history got the job.

The court heard that Chagger would never find equivalent work again and should be compensated on the basis that he would lose 75 per cent of earnings for the rest of his working life.

Abbey is planning to appeal.

1 Why did Mr Chagger think he should have had the job?
2 How does the law protect people from racial discrimination?
3 Why do you think Abbey appealed against the amount of damages?
4 How does the law protect people from racial discrimination?

Action

What does your school do to ensure equal opportunities for all students and staff?

Contact Scope or look on their website (www.scope.org.uk) and find out about their Schools Access Initiative.

Check your understanding

1 List the Acts that protect people from discrimination. Think of some situations when people might need to use these laws.
2 What is the connection between human rights and these legal rights?

... another point of view?

'Public awareness campaigns are enough to deal with the problem of discrimination.'

Do you agree with this statement? Give reasons for your opinion, showing you have considered another point of view.

Key Terms

compensation: making amends for something; something given to make good a loss

discrimination (racial, sex and disability): treating someone less favourably because of their colour, ethnic origins, gender or disability

Rights with responsibilities

In 2005, more than 980 people were injured by fireworks. Some were seriously hurt

1 You must be over 18 to buy fireworks, and yet over 50 per cent of all injuries were to children under 18. Who do you think is to blame for these accidents:

- companies that make fireworks
- shops that sell fireworks
- parents
- people who organise public displays
- the police
- the children themselves?

    1 Give reasons for your answer.
    2 What would you do to reduce the number of accidents with fireworks?
    3 Turn your suggestions for question 2 into a firework safety code.

Firework injuries in the UK
Age groups of people injured

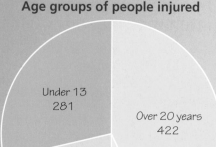

Under 13 281

Over 20 years 422

13–17 213

18–20 69

Place where accident occurred

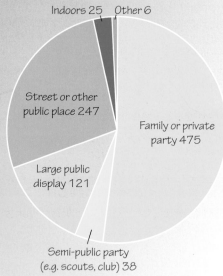

Indoors 25 Other 6

Street or other public place 247

Family or private party 475

Large public display 121

Semi-public party (e.g. scouts, club) 38

Source: Firework injury statistics 2005, BERR

Rights and responsibilities

Everyone over 18 has a right to buy fireworks. This right, like many others, brings with it certain responsibilities. You must follow the firework code: never throw a lighted firework at anyone, and never set them off in the street, where they might disturb elderly neighbours who have a right to peace and quiet, or alarm pets. The age limit for buying fireworks is set by law at 18 because this is the age at which the law expects people to be responsible enough to handle fireworks.

Rights and responsibilities are best thought of as two sides of the same coin. You have a right to own a bike and ride it down your street, but you also have a **responsibility** to ride it carefully so you don't endanger pedestrians or other road users. For example, if you ride without lights in the dark, you could cause a motorist to swerve and crash while trying to avoid you. Even if no one is hurt in the accident, there could be financial consequences for the driver if they need their car to do their job.

You will find out about the link between rights and responsibilities.

All children also have a right to an education, as expressed in the Convention of the Rights of the Child (CRC), but students have a responsibility not to disrupt lessons so others can't learn. You have a right to be respected, but you must also **respect** others. For example, you have the right to follow a particular religion and would expect your religious views to be respected. In the same way, you must respect the religious views of others.

Needs and wants

What you have a right to and what you want are not the same thing. For instance, the Convention on the Rights of the Child states that you have the right to 'clean water and healthy food'. You might say, 'I don't like drinking water. I want cola or coffee!' But the CRC focuses on the most basic human rights and needs, which are denied to millions of people all over the world: it isn't about 'wants'.

As living standards rise and countries become richer, people's 'wants' increase too. Most UK families would say that televisions, washing machines, central heating and fridges are 'basic' household items, but our great-grandparents would have considered them luxuries.

Action

Discuss why people in less economically developed countries (LEDCs) do not have their basic needs satisfied. How are their human rights affected?

Check your understanding

1 List some responsibilities that go with the following rights:
- the right to an education
- the right to drink alcohol
- the right to own and drive a car.

2 Sort the following into two lists: 'Wants' and 'Needs'.

- healthy food
- 'A' levels
- holidays
- fashionable clothes
- a good job
- friends
- healthcare

- pocket money
- TV in your room
- clean air
- free travel to school
- sex education
- parents/adults who look after you

3 Now add five or six more items to each list.

... another point of view?

'People should never have rights without responsibilities.'
Do you agree with this statement? Give reasons for your opinion, showing you have considered another point of view.

Key Terms

respect: to have a good opinion of someone

responsibility: something it is your duty to do or to look after

Political rights

Getting you thinking

1 Do you think we can influence any of these issues?
2 Explain how we can do so.

You can make a difference!

In the UK we have **political rights**. This means that people can have their say and make a real difference. Just as the United Nations has set down everyone's human rights, it has done the same for political rights. We are all entitled:

'to vote and to be elected at genuine elections which shall be held by secret ballot'.

International Covenant of Political Rights

This means that we live in a **democracy** in which almost everyone over the age of 18 can **vote** and can also stand as a candidate in an **election**.

Who can we vote for?

- **Locally**

  Whether you live in a town or a rural community, you can vote for people to represent your area. These people are known as **councillors** and are your first source of help if you are concerned about a local issue.

- **Nationally**

  Every part of the country is represented by a **Member of Parliament**. Most people decide to vote for a candidate who has views they agree with.

- **Internationally**

  The European Union has a parliament, which represents all members of the European Union. We elect **Members of the European Parliament** to have a say in the plans that are developed for Europe.

  You will learn more about these organisations, voting and elections later in the course.

You will find out about your rights to have an effect on the way the country is run.

A group of young people in Aldbourne got together to campaign for a BMX track in their village. After raising funds and representing their views at the Parish Council, they achieved their objective – and won the Philip Lawrence award for Good Citizenship. This was just the beginning of their activities. They have become an official Youth Council, which is elected by the young people in the area.

Speakers' corner – everyone can have their say

Freedom of speech

In the UK we are free to say what we like as long as we don't break the law by discriminating against others or inciting violence. There is even a special place in London where people go to express their views.

People can also organise campaigns and meet to protest against activity they don't like. Without these freedoms, our political rights would be meaningless because it would be very difficult to oppose the government or protest against the activities of other organisations.

The UN and political rights

Article 21 of the UN Declaration of Human Rights says 'Everyone has the right to take part in the government of his country, directly or through a freely chosen representative.'

Key Terms

councillor: a member of a local council, elected by people in the area

democracy: government by the people, either directly or through elected representatives

election: selection of one or more people for an official position by voting

Member of Parliament: a person who has been elected to represent a part of the country in Parliament

Member of the European Parliament: a person who has been elected to represent a part of the country in the European Parliament

political rights: rights to take part in elections and other democratic activities

vote: to choose a candidate in an election

Check your understanding

1 What is meant by political rights?
2 How can we use our political rights?
3 How would the UK be different without these rights?
4 What cause have people protested for or against recently?
5 Why are freedom of speech and the freedom to campaign important if people are to put rights into practice?

... another point of view?

'We don't need political rights. The government can decide what happens to us.'

Do you agree with this statement? Give reasons for your opinion showing that you have considered another point of view.

27

Rights for all?

Getting you thinking

UK 1900

Egypt

1 How is the life of these children
   a the same
   b different?
2 How has life for children in the UK changed since 1900?
3 How do the lives of children in the UK and Egypt match the requirements of the UN Declaration on Human Rights and the Convention on the Rights of the Child? See page 17.

Human rights in Europe

After the UN created the Universal Declaration of Human Rights, the countries of Europe adopted it and developed systems to enforce it. The UK has more recently included it in our laws through the Human Rights Act. This means that the UN Declaration has become part of the legal rights of people who live in the UK.

1950 The European Convention on Human Rights (ECHR)
This sets the framework for European countries. If the residents of one country don't think they have had a fair response from the courts, they can take their case to the European Court of Human Rights.

Getting better ...

In the last 20 years:

- the number of children who die before the age of five has fallen from 13 million to 9.7 million (that's nearly 25 per cent)
- more than 1.2 billion people have gained access to improved drinking water
- about 1.2 billion people have gained access to improved sanitation.

In the past four years, the number of children working in hazardous jobs has fallen by 26 per cent.

1998 Human Rights Act (UK)
Since 2000, the UK has had its own laws on human rights, which say that all organisations have a duty to protect the rights of all individuals (as set out in the ECHR). The Human Rights Act protects everyone in the UK.

You will discover how human rights have developed and that many inequalities still exist.

... but there's more to do

- Nearly 50 million births are unregistered every year. Nearly half of them are in countries in southern Asia such as India and Bangladesh.
- About 1.2 million children are trafficked worldwide every year.
- More than 250,000 children are currently serving as child soldiers.
- About 72 million children are out of school; many of them are girls.
- About 771 million adults are illiterate.

Children miss school for many reasons, but the main one is poverty. They often have to pay for uniforms and books and even school fees. Communities may not have the money to run a school – or children may simply live too far away. Governments need to be persuaded that education is important.

Check your understanding

1 What is the main difference between the scope of the Universal Declaration of Human Rights and that of the European Convention on Human Rights?
2 What can European citizens do if they feel their human rights are being denied?
3 In what ways has the move to improve human rights been successful?
4 Why is more improvement needed?
5 What effect would such improvements have for:
   a the individual
   b the country where they live?

... another point of view?

'Each country should be able to set its own rules about the rights of its citizens.'

Do you agree with this statement? Give reasons for your opinion, showing you have considered another point of view.

Freedom?

Mani said she was sold into slavery at the age of 12 for about £325, and was regularly beaten and sexually abused. In 2005, two years after Niger passed a law forbidding slavery, Mani was freed. This proved to be worthless, as she was immediately forced into a form of marriage.

When she fled and married another man, her master had her arrested and charged with bigamy. She was imprisoned for two months on remand.

The court of the Economic Community of West African States ruled that Niger failed in its obligations to protect Mani and awarded her £12,000 damages.

The UN's view

A highly critical report published by the United Nations Committee on the Rights of the Child has slammed the UK government as failing to meet international standards on the treatment of children. In a number of vital areas – from juvenile justice to the rights of disabled children, from the protection of young asylum seekers to the right of children to privacy – the government is failing to meet its obligations under international law.

Key Terms

asylum seeker: someone who has applied for protection as a refugee and has not yet been told whether he or she will be accepted

We want to vote!

Getting you thinking

who can vote?

1 How many years ago did more men start to get the vote?
2 What had happened before these changes took place?
3 In what year did some women get the vote?
4 What had happened before any women got the vote?
5 In what year did all adults get the vote?
6 Do you think people should be able to vote at 16?

In 1819 in Manchester the army massacred people protesting for the vote

In 1905 women were arrested for campaigning for the vote

VOTES AT 16

Before 1832
1 in 10 men

1832
1 in 5 men
over 21

1867
1 in 3 men
over 21

1884
2 in 3 men
had the vote

1918
votes for all
men and
women over 30

1928
all men and
women over 21
have the vote

1970
voting aged
reduced to 18

2010
voting
age 16?

The struggle

Being able to vote is very important. If you can't, you have no say in what goes on in the country where you live. If only the rich have the vote, they may not choose to look after people who need support. Both healthcare and education for all were introduced in the UK after everyone could vote.

It's not very long since landowners were the only people who could vote. It has been a long struggle to have the freedoms that we have today. In 1819 many protesters were killed and injured when troops were sent in to break up the 50,000 people demonstrating in Manchester. This became known as the Peterloo Massacre. This was just one example of the campaign to give ordinary people representation in Parliament.

You will discover just how hard people have fought for the right to vote.

Votes for women

Once most men were able to vote, the focus shifted to women. The suffragettes, as they were known, took to the streets. Many were arrested and locked up. Some went on hunger strike and were force fed so they would not die and become martyrs for the cause of women's votes. They chained themselves to the railings of Downing Street, where the Prime Minister lives. One died when she threw herself under the King's horse at the races. Many men didn't really want women to vote, as this cartoon shows.

Eventually women over 30 were given the vote. It took another ten years for women to catch up with men and be able to vote at 21. The UK at last had universal **suffrage**.

Britain was the first country in the world to lower the voting age to 18 and there is now a fierce debate about whether to reduce it to 16.

Election Day!

Other countries' struggles

• Gender

In the UK, gender was the main issue when it came to gaining a vote. This has been the case in many countries. In Switzerland women didn't get the vote until 1971. In some countries it depends on who is in power. Afghan women were able to vote from 1965 until 1996 but then lost the right until 2001. They still have to vote in separate areas from men.

• Race

Some countries have not allowed people from ethnic minorities to have the vote. In the USA, the constitution says everyone should be free to vote; but all sorts of rules were used to stop African Americans voting until the 1960s, when the government passed a law putting an end to such practices.

In South Africa, black people were not allowed to vote until 1994. In the first election, when Nelson Mandela became President, people queued for hours to cast their vote.

In South Africa, voting was so important people waited in line for hours

Afghan women voting

People round the world have been fighting for their right to take part in the government of their country – as stated in the UNDHR.

... another point of view?

'People have fought so hard to get the vote, it is irresponsible not to use it.'

Do you agree with this statement? Give reasons for your opinion, showing you have considered another point of view.

Check your understanding

1 What does suffrage mean?
2 Why is it important to have a vote?
3 When did men and women get the vote in the UK?
4 What did they have to do to achieve it?
5 Why have people been prevented from voting in other countries?

Key Terms

suffrage: the right to vote

suffragette: person who campaigned for the right of women to vote

Protecting the customer

A new head of hair in two weeks

INSTANT HAIR RESTOR

INSTA...AIR

1 Match these questions to the situations. Can I get my money back? Can I get compensation? Can that be true?

2 Who do you think is at fault in each of the examples: the retailer, manufacturer or consumer? Explain why.

3 Have you ever had to complain about something you have bought? How did you go about it? What was the result?

Consumer Rights-
- *Trade Descripton Act*
- *Sale and Supply of Goods Act*
- *Food Safety Act*
- *Consumer Protection Act*

...rder or over the ...nsumer, you have ... pay someone, such as ...to provide a service.

...sumers' rights include:

...minal offence to make ...example, 'Was £200. ...ever been sold at the ...ur service, this must be

...cerned that goods sold ...urpose they are sold

...preparation and selling of food and drink in both shops and restaurants. The Act makes it an offence to sell or serve food or drink that is unsafe.

- the **Consumer Protection Act**, which means that consumers can claim for damages if they are injured as a result of using faulty goods. If a child is hurt by an unsafe toy, the manufacturers can be prosecuted.

Is it safe?

You will find out about laws that help consumers get a fair deal.

How can you enforce your rights?

If you have bought goods or services and you are dissatisfied with them, you have a right to claim your money back, to make an exchange or to have a repeat of the service.

1. Contact the trader with details of your complaint, say what you want done and give them a chance to put the matter right.

2. If you are not happy with the outcome, you can seek advice from the **Citizens Advice Bureau** (CAB). They can help with a wide variety of problems, including shopping complaints.

3. The Citizens Advice Bureau may recommend you go to a **Trading Standards Department**. They can investigate complaints about misleading descriptions or prices, and the safety of consumer goods. They can take action against people who break the law.

4. The **Office of Fair Trading**, a government office, can also take action against traders who break consumer laws.

Action

Working in pairs, think about why traders and businesses prefer to sort out complaints themselves.

Check your understanding

1. If you bought a CD at a reduced price because the CD cover was damaged, would you be able to take it back to the shop and claim a refund? Give reasons for your answer.
2. If you bought something from a shop and it was faulty, but the shop refused to refund your money, what could you do?
3. What extra rights do you have when home shopping or shopping over the internet, compared with when you buy something from a shop?

... another point of view?

'Consumers should look after themselves.'

Do you agree with this statement? Give reasons for your opinion, showing you have considered another point of view.

Sellers have rights too

In certain situations consumers cannot claim refunds or demand exchanges. If you bought a shirt in a sale and you knew it.had a defect, you would not be able to claim your money back, because the seller didn't hide the problem from you when you bought it.

Sellers do not have to exchange goods, but most will do so as long as they have not been used. So, if you have bought some clothes and you change your mind about them later, you will find most shops are happy to exchange them, even though they don't have to by law.

Home shopping and the internet

When you buy over the internet from a company trading in the UK, you are covered by more or less the same legislation as that which covers shop purchases:

- the goods you've bought should be of satisfactory quality
- they should be fit for the purpose they are sold for
- they should be as described by the seller.

Key Terms

Citizens Advice Bureau (CAB): an organisation that offers free advice on consumer and other legal matters

consumer: a person who buys goods or services for their own use

Office of Fair Trading: a government office that can take action against traders who break the law

Trading Standards Department: an official body that enforces consumer-based law

Fair play at work

Getting you thinking

1 What sorts of problems do you think people might face when at work?

2 How do you think an employer might make their staff's working life better?

3 What effect do you think a happy workforce has on a business?

4 What do you think the law should have to say about working conditions?

Why do we need employment laws?

Employment laws exist to protect employees and make sure businesses carry out their responsibilities towards their staff. Without these laws, people's human right to fair conditions at work could be harder to protect.

Exploiting people

Before laws were introduced to protect people, some employers treated their staff unfairly. Employees suffered though:

- long hours
- dangerous and unhealthy working conditions
- poor pay
- not being treated as individuals with individual needs.

There was no government support in terms of unemployment benefit or sickness pay, so employees could not afford to argue with their employers, nor could they afford to be ill.

Unions

Employees began to form **trade unions**. They negotiated with employers to reach fairer agreements on pay and working conditions. Over the years, these agreements have led to huge improvements in the rights of employees.

By trying to persuade employers and Parliament to adopt fairer and safer working practices, the unions proved to be effective **pressure groups** in looking after the interests of their members. A group of people bargaining together is more powerful than individuals working alone.

Unions protect the rights of their members

You will find out about laws that protect employees.

How does the law protect?

The **Equal Pay Act** means that men and women in jobs that require the same effort, skills or responsibility should be paid the same amount.

The **contract of employment** is an agreement between employer and employee setting out the pay and conditions, including holiday entitlements.

The **Sex Discrimination Act** and the **Race Relations Act** protect individuals from being treated differently because of their sex, nationality or ethnicity.

The **Employment Equality Regulations** protect people from discrimination on the basis of age, religion and sexual orientation.

The **Disability Discrimination Act** means that people who are disabled must be given equal opportunities.

Health and safety laws are designed to reduce accidents. Employers must provide a safe working environment and train employees to work safely.

European regulations

Some **European Union** members have signed up to a Social Chapter. The Chapter sets employment rights, such as maternity and paternity leave, so that everyone has guaranteed working conditions.

The UK has not signed the Chapter because higher wages and better conditions would push up business costs. UK businesses would therefore become less competitive as prices would rise and it would be harder to sell their products. This might mean that the number of jobs in the UK would fall.

Action

1. Find out what unions provide for their members.
2. Produce a union recruitment poster giving reasons why employees should join. You can get ideas from www.tuc.org.uk or www.unison.org.uk.

Check your understanding

1. Who do unions represent and what are they trying to do?
2. What areas do the main employment laws cover?

... another point of view?

'The UK should sign the EU's Social Chapter.'

Do you agree with this statement? Give reasons for your opinion, showing you have considered another point of view.

Key Terms

employment laws: laws passed by Parliament and by the European Union law-making bodies that set out the rights and responsibilities of employers and employees

European Union: a group of 25 countries that work together in fields such as the environment, social issues, the economy and trade

pressure group: a group of people that tries to change public opinion or government policy to its own views or beliefs

trade unions: organisations that look after the interests of a group of employees

Responsibilities in the workplace

Getting you thinking

1 Explain each of ASDA's rules.
2 Why does ASDA expect its staff to have a responsible attitude to their work?
3 ASDA expects its staff to be responsible. What should the staff expect from ASDA?

What ASDA expects from you

Attendance

If you don't come to work, your work has to be done by your colleagues and it reduces our opportunity to offer good customer service. However, sometimes absence from work is unavoidable. If you can't come to work, please contact the store no later than two hours before the start of your shift.

Punctuality

Customers expect us to be available to give them the service they want, so all colleagues must avoid lateness.

Appearance

Colleagues must wear the uniform provided by the Company and adhere to the dress standards.

Friends and relatives

Colleagues must not serve relatives or friends at either counters or checkouts.

Mobile phones

Colleagues are allowed to make personal calls during their break times from pay phones provided in store. Colleagues may not carry or use personal mobile phones whilst working.

Your responsibilities as an employee

Just as employers have responsibilities towards their employees, so the employees have responsibilities towards their employer.

Employees must carry out their responsibilities as set out in the **contract of employment**. Employees should receive this within eight weeks of starting a new job. This contract sets out what the employer and the employee are expected to do. This is important: there are two sides to the contract and both the employer and employee must do what they have agreed to. If the employee fails to do this, they can be dismissed. If the employer doesn't keep their side of the contract, the employee can take them to an **employment tribunal**.

A contract should include the following:
- names of employer and employee
- entitlement to sick pay
- date of starting
- pension details (if any)
- rate of pay and working hours
- complaints and disciplinary procedures
- place of work
- conditions for ending the employment contract
- holiday entitlement.

You will understand that both employers and employees have responsibilities in the workplace.

What if it goes wrong?

People can be dismissed if they are unable to do the job properly or have been involved in any misconduct, such as fighting, discrimination, deliberate damage or theft. A minor misconduct, such as bad timekeeping, usually results in a verbal **warning**. If the misconduct continues, there will be a written warning and, if there is no further improvement, it can lead to **dismissal**. A major misconduct, like theft, can lead to instant dismissal.

Dismissal is different from **redundancy**. Redundancy occurs when the job has ended and no one is being taken on to replace you. It is the employer's responsibility and the employee will receive a payment at least equivalent to one month's pay for every year employed by the business.

Disagreements over dismissal

There might be a disagreement between the employer and the employee over a dismissal. If it can't be sorted out, the case can be taken to an employment tribunal. This is a type of court of law that has the power to fine the business and make it pay damages to the employee if it finds that the employee was not to blame. If the dismissed person belongs to a union, they can seek advice from it and the union can represent them at the tribunal. Sometimes tribunals come out in favour of the employer and sometimes in favour of the employee.

An industrial tribunal: a more informal court of law

Action

Look in a local or national paper to see if there are any reports of an industrial tribunal. What was the issue? Who won? Why? Had one side acted irresponsibly? If so, explain how.

Check your understanding

1 What is the contract of employment for?
2 What reasons can be given for dismissal?
3 What is the difference between dismissal and redundancy?
4 What can an employee do if they feel they have been mistreated?

... another point of view?

'Rights at work are more important than responsibilities.'
Do you agree with this statement? Give reasons for your opinion, showing you have considered another point of view.

Key Terms

contract of employment: a document that details an employee's and employer's responsibilities for a particular job

dismissal: when employers end an employee's contract of employment (sometimes called 'sacking')

employment tribunal: a type of court dealing only with disagreements over employment laws

redundancy: when a person loses their job because the job doesn't need to be done anymore

warning: written or spoken warning given by an employer to an employee if the employer thinks the employee has been breaking the contract of employment

Jamie Oliver has blasted mums for selling junk food to kids through the school fence

Two mums in Rotherham say pupils have the right to choose – and reject – the healthy meals served up after Jamie's campaign to transform school dinners. The two mums take orders from kids during the morning break. They then return with pies, burgers and fizzy drinks from nearby takeaways and hand the food through the fence. They say that the school's food is disgusting and the kids are not allowed out to get food they enjoy.

Jamie says the pair were daft to claim junk food was better for their children. 'Thanks to parents like these, kids just aren't getting the nutrition they need to grow healthily.'

The school says that all its food is freshly prepared and meets the Government's healthy eating guidelines. Healthy food campaigners claim that what these women are doing is shameful.

Leave margin blank

1. Explain one right that the two mums are claiming for the children at school. *(2 marks)*

   The mums claim that the children do not have the right to choose what they want to eat as they are not free to leave the school at dinnertime.

   > Remember that if the question asks you to explain – and is worth two marks – you need to do a little more than just writing down a fact.

2. Explain one right that Jamie is claiming for the children at the school. *(2 marks)*

   Jamie says that the mums are stopping the children eating properly and growing up to be strong and healthy. Everyone has the right to an adequate standard of living.

3. Identify two other rights that the children in the pictures do not have. *(2 marks)*

A home

Education

> As it says 'identify' you only need to give a simple answer. Medical care would have been a good answer too.

4. What is the role of the United Nations Universal Declaration of Human Rights? *(2 marks)*

It has been agreed by all member countries of the UN. It cannot be enforced but it sets the standard for all countries.

5. Why does the Government set up guidelines for healthy eating? *(1 mark)*

To stop people becoming obese.

6. Which of the following laws protects people's rights at work? *(1 mark)*

☐ A. The Sale of Goods Act

☐ B. The Trade Descriptions Act

☐ C. The Disability Discrimination Act

☐ D. The Consumer Protection Act

Extended writing

'In multicultural Britain, people should not try to live separate lives.'

Do you agree with this point of view?

Give reasons for your opinion, showing you have considered another point of view. You should support your argument with examples wherever possible.

To answer the question above, you could consider the following points and other information of your own.

- Why might people from different cultures want to live separate lives?
- Do people have a human right to live their lives in whatever way they choose?
- Why does it matter if people from different cultures choose to live separate lives?
- What are the advantages of people from different cultures going to the same schools and living in the same neighbourhoods?

(12 marks)

Source: Edexcel 2007

Leave margin blank

I agree that people should not try to live separate lives but for some people it is hard to do.

> A good start. The student has set out a point of view and has started to show another one.

People who have come to Britain from another country sometimes want to spend time with people who speak their language and have the same customs. It is easier than speaking a foreign language and they might be homesick.

> This shows that the student is using the bullet points to build the argument – but make sure the bullets are woven into the argument and are not just answered by themselves.

The United Nations Declaration of Human Rights says that people have the right to their religious beliefs and a right to privacy so they can meet people from their own culture if they want, as long as they don't hurt anyone else. If they do decide to just live in their own community, it is difficult to make the country multicultural.

> This shows that the student has a good understanding of the content of Citizenship. There are also links between the main question and the bullets.

If people live separate lives, we never learn about each other and people are afraid of things they don't know. This can cause trouble if people are suspicious of each other. We have lots to learn from each other that can make all our lives better. There are lots of multicultural events round the country. The Notting Hill Carnival is a good example of ways we can learn about different cultures.

> The example is just right. It shows the student understands the argument.

Children who go to school together get to know about each other better and stop being scared of people who are different. Their mums and dads can meet up at the school gate as well. The children learn English at school and can help their families to learn it too. Some schools run English lessons for parents too. This means that they can fit into the whole community and know what's going on. They are more likely to be able to get a job too so they meet other people too.

If they are asylum seekers they might want to go home when things calm down so they might not think it is important to learn English or join in the community. If they want to stay, it is important to learn the language and try to join in.

> The student has identified some good reasons why people should go to school together. More could be said about living together but there are hints at it in the sentence on learning English and getting a job.

If people do not lead separate lives, the community is likely to be happier and everyone wins but I know some mums who do not speak English and it is hard to learn when you get older so they find it hard to join in.

> A good summing up using an example from the student's own community.

Unit 1: theme 2 Power, politics

2.1 How the media informs and influences public debate   44–51

What is the media?	44	Why should the press be free?	48
What news?	46	Legal, decent, honest and truthful?	50

2.2 How the media informs and influences public opinion   52–5

Whose views?	52	What influence?	54

2.3 The justice system   56–63

What's the point of law?	56	Who puts the law into practice?	60
Civil and criminal law: what's the difference?	58	Criminal courts	62

and the media

2.4 The voice of democracy 64–75

Taking part	64	What does the council do?	70
Who represents us?	66	Talking to the council	72
How does the council work?	68	Putting on the pressure	74

2.5 The role of democracy 76–85

Getting elected	76	A louder voice	82
What does an MP do?	78	The impact of public opinion	84
How are laws made?	80		

2.6 Does democracy work? 86–91

More democratic?	86	Not the only way?	90
Vote, vote, vote!	88		

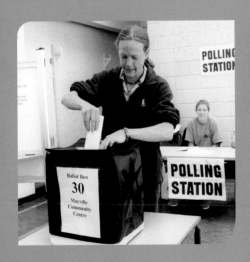

What is the media?

Getting you thinking

Let's all chill out together this evening.

Let's plan a holiday.

Let's find out if my team won.

Let's find out the latest news.

Let's choose which new car we want.

Let's have a quiet night at home.

Let's find out about fair trade.

1 Choose two different types of media that you might use for each activity. Explain your choices.
2 Put them into groups that show their main use, for example 'entertainment' and 'information'.
3 Do you believe or trust more of what you learn from one kind of media than from another?
4 How do you decide what to trust?
5 What effect does reading, seeing or hearing material that you don't trust have on your views?

Mass media

The media has become a massive industry during the last 50 years. One hundred years ago, newspapers were the only form of information about what was happening in people's locality, the UK and beyond. In the days when many people couldn't read, they only knew what they were told by other people.

Today, there is information everywhere. Newspapers and magazines are widely available. You could watch television 24 hours a day. Cable television and the digital revolution have changed things even more. They provide news, entertainment and education whenever you want it, even from your mobile phone.

Viewers, listeners and readers

Habits change. A hundred years ago, politicians could expect to speak to a packed hall at election time. There was no television, so it was the only way people could ever see who they were voting for. Today, the numbers watching party political broadcasts are in decline. Perhaps there is so much exposure that people are no longer curious about who governs them.

As new methods of communication arrive, people move on. When radio was introduced, families would sit together listening carefully. When television broadcasts started, radio listening declined. Now we have over 50 television channels, so each company has to work extra hard to attract our attention. With more families having the internet at home or on the road, television watching may take different forms. What will come next?

You will develop an understanding of the scope and influence of the media.

Who does what?

Despite all the changes, people still buy newspapers, books and magazines, listen to the radio and watch television. The choice of media means that we select the ways of finding out information that suit us best. Although the patterns change, most people use most media most of the time. They simply adjust the amount of time they spend on each one.

The internet

Political parties use the internet to provide information and organise online surveys of public opinion. People might want to vote if they can join in debates and have easier access to information.

Products for people

All forms of media aim to provide what the customer wants. There are television channels that are aimed at young people and others aimed at an older population. There is also a growing number aimed at people with specific interests, ranging from music to gardening, from cooking to history.

Adult participation in selected leisure activities (%): by age							
Age	16–19	20–24	25–29	30–44	45–59	60–69	70 +
Watching TV	100	99	99	99	99	99	99
Listening to radio	92	93	93	92	89	82	76
Listening to CDs	98	97	95	91	83	71	57
Reading books	63	67	66	65	67	64	64

Source: Social Trends

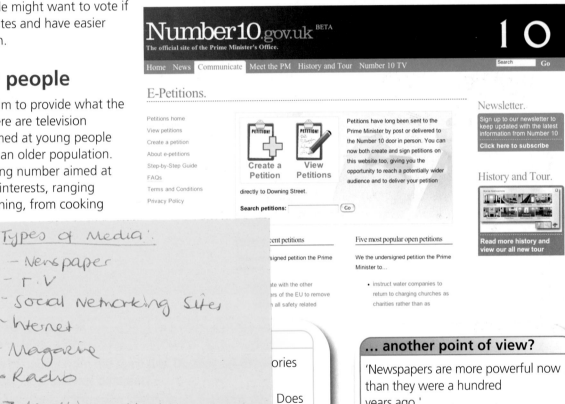

Handwritten note:

Types of Media:
- Newspaper
- T.V
- Social Networking Sites
- Internet
- Magazine
- Radio
→ Anything that is addressed to more than one person.

Action

1 Look at a rang[...] [st]ories in different w[...]

2 Watch the ne[...] Does each channel [...] a different appr[...]

3 Do you prefe[...] [te]lling the story? Do [...]

Check your understanding

1 What is meant by the media?
2 How has the media changed over the last 100 years?
3 What does the media provide?
4 Why is the media powerful?

... another point of view?

'Newspapers are more powerful now than they were a hundred years ago.'
Do you agree with this statement? Give reasons for your opinion, showing you have considered another point of view

Key Terms

media: ways of communicating with large numbers of people

public opinion: the popular view

What news?

Getting you thinking

More than just the papers

1 Which media company owns the most papers?
2 Which companies also have a share in television companies?
3 If the people who run the companies have strong views, what effect might this have on the news in the papers and on television?
4 Do you think a media company could affect decisions made by the government?
5 Why do you think the government limits the number of papers and television stations that can be owned by one company?

News Corp
The Sun, News of the World, The Times, The Sunday Times, Sky TV

Trinity Mirror
The Mirror, Sunday Mirror, The People

Guardian News Group
The Guardian, The Observer, 37 radio stations, interest in Auto Trader and many trade magazines

Daily Mail & General Trust
Daily Mail, Mail on Sunday, London Lite, Metro, 20 per cent interest in Independent Television News

Barclay Brothers
The Daily Telegraph, The Telegraph on Sunday

Where does the power lie?

A newspaper or television news programme can choose the stories it wants to tell. It can also decide how to tell the story. The owners of a paper appoint an **editor** to run it for them. The editor has the power to make these decisions. Often, an editor is chosen because they have the same points of view as the owners. This means that the way the news is presented reflects the owner's point of view. Television news has editors too. They put the programme together in just the same way.

Most newspapers belong to companies that are owned by shareholders. The objective is to make a profit, so sales are a top priority. Lots of sales means lots of advertising and selling advertising helps to increase profits. Businesses that want to sell their products will buy space in papers with many readers.

All these factors combine to make newspapers and television very powerful.

Who buys what?

Most people read a paper that agrees with their own views. Conservative voters often buy The Daily Telegraph or the Daily Express, while Labour voters might buy The Guardian or Daily Mirror. The way the news is presented depends on the views of the papers' owners and editors. The cartoons are often the give-away. They are always ruder about the party they don't support!

You will explore how media ownership can influence our opinions.

The influence of advertising

Advertising pays for commercial television and the papers. If you were the editor, what would you do if you were faced with a story that showed one of your main advertisers in a bad light? Would you:

* run the story?
* hold it for a day when there were no adverts from that business?
* rewrite the story so it was less critical?
* just ignore it?

It's a tough decision to make.

In a spin?

Politicians often want to be at the top of the news and shown in a good light. Political parties employ **spin doctors** who write the stories and work hard to get them in the news. A common story is about new government spending on health, education or other areas that people care about. When **journalists** look carefully, however, they often find that the spending has been announced several times before! This is the work of spin doctors.

Whose views?

Everyone has a point of view, and often it is hard to hide. If, as a reader or viewer, you are aware of the **bias** of a television programme or newspaper, you can take it into account. If not, you may just believe it all. In a country where only one point of view is permitted, people are unlikely to know what is really going on.

Under control

Every time one media company wants to take over another, the plans are reviewed. If the takeover puts too much power in too few hands, it won't be allowed to go ahead. News Corp, a company listed in both Australia and America and run by an Australian, owns media businesses in 100 countries and 30 languages. It covers newspapers, books, films and digital media. If it wanted to buy another UK newspaper, it would be investigated by the Office of Fair Trading.

A few of News Corp's titles

Twentieth Century Fox · Sky TV · National Geographic Channel · HarperCollins · MySpace · News Corp · The Times · The Sun · thelondonpaper · News of the World · The Sunday Times

Action

Compare articles about the same story or event in two different newspapers. Is there a difference in the way the stories are told? Is there any bias?

Check your understanding

1 What does an editor do?
2 Why are media owners powerful?
3 What factors influence the contents of a newspaper?
4 How is media ownership controlled?

... another point of view?

'The media must always be free to express a point of view.'

Do you agree with this statement? Give reasons for your opinion, showing you have considered another point of view.

Key Terms

bias: to favour one thing over another unfairly

editor: the person who is responsible for the content of a newspaper or television or radio programme

journalist: a person who gathers news and produces reports for the media

spin doctor: someone who tries to get certain stories into the public eye and to make bad news sound better

Why should the press be free?

Getting you thinking

Journalists protest in Namibia about the clampdown on press freedom in Zimbabwe, the country next door. They would have been arrested if they had protested in Zimbabwe

ZIMBABWE
Laws passed that:

- only allow foreign journalists into the country to cover specific events
- only allow registered journalists to work
- require media organisations to be registered
- stop people criticising the President
- limit publication of important information
- stop stories that discriminate against a political party
- only allow demonstrations that have government approval.

International journalist arrested

The Independent newspaper's Zimbabwe reporter has been arrested under new laws. His house had been ransacked and he was told that the order for his arrest had come from the highest level in the government.

'The worst-ever attack on the liberties of the people.'

A member of the Zimbabwean parliament

Zimbabwe was about to have an election when these laws were passed.

1 What did these laws prevent?
2 Why do you think the government brought them into force?
3 What effect do you think this had on the results of the election?

4 Explain why the laws were seen as 'the worst–ever attack on the liberties of the people'.
5 Why is it important for the media to be free to report on events?
6 Do you think there should be any limit on what the media can say?

What is freedom?

'Everyone has the right to the freedom of opinion and expression; this right includes freedom to hold opinions without interference and to seek, receive and impart information and ideas through any media, regardless of frontiers.'

Universal Declaration of Human Rights

One of every human being's rights is to have their say. If they don't like the government, they should be free to say so. If people think the government should spend more or less on health, education or defence, laws should not prevent them from saying so. If people want to know what is going on, they should be free to find out. Information and data should not be kept secret unless there is a good reason. In a democracy, people need to be able to hear others' points of view and know what is going on if they are to use their vote effectively.

You will understand the importance of a free press.

Why control the press?

If information is kept from people, they will find it hard to decide whether the government is keeping its promises or breaking the law in order to stay in power. If a government is determined to stay in power, preventing people from knowing the truth can be very effective. **Censorship** means that people will only know what you want them to know.

Press freedom is often the first thing to go when the government of a country wants to prevent democracy working. A country that controls the press cannot really be democratic. There are examples throughout history. In the last century, the Soviet Union controlled all forms of media. Even today, there are no television channels that are free from government control in Russia (as part of the former Soviet Union is now known). China also has strong controls on what the people are told. There are examples of press control throughout the world.

A voter in Zimbabwe reading a government-owned paper, which accuses the opposition party of terrorism. All media output is controlled by the government

In Russia the government controls all television output

Is it ever right to control the media?

When the UK was fighting Argentina over the Falkland Islands in 1981, there was a complete news blackout. Every night a government spokesman appeared on the television and gave a report. He read a message in a slow, serious manner, telling us what the government thought we should know.

When people are caught spying, very often much of the information that is provided in court is not published.

These are both examples of occasions when national security is thought more important than press freedom. Sometimes, by telling people everything, you may be giving the game away. There is, however, always a debate about how much information should be given out.

Check your understanding

1 What does the Universal Declaration of Human Rights have to say about press freedom?
2 Why might a government that wants to be re-elected decide to control the press?
3 Why can democracy not work effectively if the press is controlled?
4 Are there reasons why press freedom should sometimes be limited? Explain your answer.
5 Draw up a list of issues that you think the press should be free to discuss and any that you think it should not be allowed to print stories about. Use your list to draw up a law on press freedom.

... another point of view?

'The media must always be free to express a point of view.'
Do you agree with this statement? Give reasons for your opinion, showing you have considered another point of view.

Key Terms

censorship: limiting the information given to the general public
press freedom: the ability of the press to give information and express opinion

Legal, decent, honest and truthful?

Getting you thinking

1. Identify the different sorts of people in these pictures.
2. What sorts of thing does the press do to give people cause for complaint?
3. Do you think that these complaints are always justified?
4. Make a list of things you feel the press should not do.
5. Make suggestions about how to stop the press doing this sort of thing.

What are the rules?

Anyone in the public eye can be pestered by the press. People find themselves being looked at through the long lens of a camera and on the front page the next day. Ordinary people who have had some good luck or experienced misfortune are just as vulnerable as the famous.

The Press Complaints Commission attempts to prevent this invasion of privacy but it is not always successful. It has drawn up the **Press Code** as guidance for journalists working in the media. Although it can look at complaints and decide if the code has been broken, it can do little to prevent its happening again.

The wrong side of the law?

Sometimes it's a question of invading people's privacy, but on other occasions the media gets its facts wrong. When this happens, a paper or television channel can find itself in court facing a **libel** or **slander** case.

Laws prevent anyone from making public statements about people that are not true. Footballers have challenged people who said they fixed a game, politicians have challenged newspapers that said they received money for asking particular questions in Parliament. Private Eye, the magazine that takes a satirical look at the world, often finds itself in court because it has pushed the limits too far.

The Press Code

Newspapers:

- must not publish inaccurate, misleading or distorted information or pictures
- must give a right to reply to any inaccurate reporting
- must respect people's private and family life
- must not harass people for information
- must not intrude on grief or shock
- must not intrude on children during their schooling
- must not use hidden bugs to find things out
- must avoid prejudice
- must not make payments to people involved in criminal cases
- must not profit from financial information
- must not identify victims of sexual assault
- must protect confidential sources.

You will find out how rules about what can and cannot be published are enforced.

Popular or quality?

People buy four times more popular papers than quality papers. The quality press tends to take a more serious view of the world and its headlines reflect this. In contrast, on days when dramatic world events are taking place, popular papers have been famous for headlining footballers, sex and money.

Average sales of daily newspapers in the UK

	Daily sales	Percentage change
Sun	3,045,899	-0.72
Daily Express	752,181	-6.39
Daily Mail	2,193,715	-4.98
Daily Mirror	1,400,206	-7.56
Daily Star	714,192	-8.32
Financial Times	448,532	-0.68
The Times	636,946	-3.04
The Guardian	358,379	-4.24
The Independent	201,113	-8.29
Daily Telegraph	835,497	-3.95

1 Which is the largest selling quality paper?
2 Which is the largest selling popular paper?
3 Why do you think newspaper owners might be worried?
4 What do you think has happened to the way people find out about the news?

Action

1 What decisions has the Press Complaints Commission made recently? Do you agree with their findings? Why?
2 Look at the headlines on a range of newspapers on the same day. How do the popular and quality papers compare? You will find newspapers on the internet as well as in newsagents.

Check your understanding

1 How should people's privacy be protected?
2 How effective do you think the Press Complaints Commission is?
3 Can you think of any examples when their rules have been broken?
4 Why is it important for journalists to protect confidential sources of information?
5 How do quality papers differ from the popular papers?
6 How does the law limit what newspapers can print?

... another point of view?

'Celebrities work hard to attract media attention but they should be protected when the press invades their privacy.'

Do you agree with this statement? Give reasons for your opinion, showing you have considered another point of view.

Legal limits

Just like anyone else, the media has to obey laws about decency. Discrimination is against the law and some parts of the media have to be very careful not to overstep the limits. The popular papers find themselves in front of the Press Complaints Commission or in court more often than the quality press. But who is responsible? After all, the more sensational the story, the more we want to buy the paper.

Key Terms

libel: writing incorrect things about people

Press Code: guidelines for the media and journalists about the information they gather and how they obtain and use it

slander: saying incorrect things about people

Whose views?

Getting you thinking

My friends think...

I found it on the internet...

But Dad, I read it in the Sun...

But I saw it on TV...

1 How are all these people making decisions?

2 What problems are there in making decisions in these ways?

3 Do you think there are better ways of making decisions?

4 Draw some bubbles with statements that you think might help them to make more informed decisions.

Subject to persuasion?

We are all subject to persuasion, but we need to look in the right places to be persuaded. People very often read the newspaper that agrees with their views and switch channels on TV when they hear messages that contradict their own ideas. They don't even hear the other side of the story.

There are all sorts of decisions that are made about where you live, your school life or your social life. If councils are to make sensible decisions about these issues, they need to take a variety of points of view into account.

The stories that surround these sorts of decisions are often reported in the local paper. Can you imagine what it would be like if the press could only report the council's point of view and nobody was allowed to challenge it? What effect would this have on people's views?

What information?

More and more information is available to us. The government collects masses of data that are put together by the Office of National Statistics. You'll find lots on its website. The Freedom of Information Act also allows access to a wide range of information about people, businesses and government.

The **Data Protection Act**, however, prevents information that is stored on computers being given out freely. The Human Rights Act limits the information that can be published about people.

There is a balance between helping people to find information and limiting the information that is available, to protect privacy or the national interest.

You will investigate how people are influenced.

Opinions for the public?

The media is full of **opinion polls**. Questions are asked about all sorts of topics, from love to politics. When elections are looming, pollsters are out in force and the results of their surveys are published almost daily. 'Are voters changing their minds?' is the first thought of many journalists.

The use of opinion polls has been questioned. If one party, according to the polls, is very popular, its supporters might not vote on election day because they may assume enough people will vote anyway. The party that is behind often fears that more voters will desert the sinking ship. If a poll shows that the parties are very close, it can be because it is hard to get it exactly right.

In some countries, these fears have led to the publication of opinion polls being banned in the last weeks before an election.

medical staff and patients

tax payers

Keeping a balance

Whenever people have to come to a decision, they need to listen to a variety of points of view. These are often called the views of **stakeholders** or people who have an interest in the decision. If you ask, 'Should the government spend more on health?', you have to think about the patients and medical staff, as well as the people who will receive less funding or the tax payer who will pay more tax. They are all stakeholders.

A search through the media often provides the material you need to decide for yourself.

Action

Find an opinion poll that has been carried out recently. What are the results? Does it influence your views? Explain why or why not.

Check your understanding

1 If the local council wants to build a new road to bypass a local shopping area, who should it consult?
2 How does restricting press freedom affect people's views?
3 What is an opinion poll?
4 Why can opinion polls be a) helpful, b) misleading?
5 Why do you need to consider the views of stakeholders?

... another point of view?

'I know what I think and no one will change my mind.'
Do you agree with this statement? Give reasons for your opinion, showing you have considered another point of view.

Key Terms

Data Protection Act: a law that limits the way in which information stored on computers can be used

opinion poll: questioning a sample of the population to build a picture of the views of the public on a particular topic

stakeholder: someone who has an interest in a decision that is being made

What influence?

Getting you thinking

Sarah's Law

When eight-year-old Sarah Payne was abducted and murdered, the News of the World campaigned for the law to be changed. It wanted lists of known paedophiles to be published so everyone knew where they lived – and actually published its own list.

The campaign led to vigilantism when people were persecuted because they were suspected of being offenders. A paediatrician, a doctor who looks after children, was even chased by protestors who didn't know the difference between the two words.

The News of the World closed down its campaign but still claimed the credit when eight years later the government introduced a six-month pilot scheme in four parts of the country.

It's victory for Sarah

Government Minister said

'This would not have happened without the campaign of the paper. It's a very good beginning and I welcome it.'

The pilot

Concerned parents and carers can seek from their local police details of the background of friends, neighbours and relatives who have unsupervised access to their children. But they must sign a legal agreement not to misuse any information they receive.

1 What effect do you think this campaign had on sales of the News of the World?

2 What immediate effect did the campaign have?

3 What was the long-term effect?

4 Why do you think the government decided to pilot the scheme rather than make it law for everyone?

5 If the pilot becomes law, what effect do you think it will have on voters?

What's the message?

Newspapers have one key motive – to make a profit for the owners. Making a profit means selling more papers. Selling more papers means advertisers want to buy space because they will reach more potential customers.

In times when newspaper sales are falling because people get their news from other sorts of media, competition is fierce. The editor of the News of the World was well aware that the Sarah's Law campaign would attract customers.

Customers are not innocent players, because they tend to buy more papers when the headlines are dramatic.

The government has responded to this campaign but has not met its demands. There is no public list of offenders, but individuals can be given information in confidence. Voters may be tempted to support a party that it thinks listens to public opinion – but the ideas often have to be moderated in order to work in practice.

You will find out how the media and pressure groups influence government policy.

Fox hunting

The Campaign for the Protection of Hunted Animals and the League Against Cruel Sports joined forces to campaign against fox hunting. Both pressure groups had been campaigning for years because they wanted the law to change.

Public relations

Many organisations feel they need help to get their message over. Even the Girl Guides use a public relations company to help get their image right and let the public know what they are doing.

Businesses all use public relations experts to help them. When Gap was challenged over child labour, its public relations team quickly put out a campaign to explain the situation.

Organisations that can afford such support may have more impact when influencing the public or the government.

Check your understanding

1 What is the first motive of a newspaper?
2 How can this affect the stories it highlights?
3 What is a pressure group?
4 What is the objective of a pressure group?
5 How can the use of public relations experts affect our views of an organisation?
6 Why is the media powerful?

... another point of view?

'Government should be the only source of information and pressure groups should be banned.'

Do you agree with this statement? Give reasons for your opinion, showing you have considered another point of view.

The Mirror says

'So it was only ever about ripping animals apart in the name of sport. And most British people don't agree with that. So we rely on our MPs to stop it.'

Fox slaughter banned at last

North West League Against Cruel Sports
'Every Saturday during the hunting season we will be out monitoring the activities of one of our local hunts. We do this so that we can gain evidence of the cruelty which is involved in hunting and we use this evidence to inform the press, television and radio who can bring these cruelties to a wider audience.'

1 What did the League Against Cruel Sports wish to achieve?
2 How did it go about it?
3 Why did it think it was in the right?
4 Why do you think the government decided to ban fox hunting?

A source of power?

Giving people information can be a source of power. The decision about what to tell and what not to tell means that you can affect the way people think. When people vote in an election, they are making decisions that affect the country for the next five years. How do they make their voting decisions? Very often, they are based on information from the media. The media therefore helps people to make decisions. If the information is not accurate, the effect can be very damaging. If the media presents what it wants people to know, rather than the whole truth, it is difficult for people to make informed decisions.

The following pages explore reasons why the media does not always present the whole truth and why the freedom to communicate is important for democracy.

What's the point of law?

Getting you thinking

At the beginning of Year 11, Annie, Sanjay, Mikael, Deb, Steve and Al know that they have a hard year ahead if they are to get the GCSEs they want. They are dreaming of the summer when they know it will all be over. The plan is to go on holiday together – somewhere in the sun. It will not be cheap but they are cleaning cars together at the same time as saving up on their own.

1 Why might the friends fall out before July?

2 What rules might they need to set up to stop themselves from falling out?

3 Who sets your school rules?

4 Are people more likely to keep the rules if they have been involved in setting them?

5 What problems would there be if there were no laws?

Why do people obey the law?

Law-abiding citizens obey the law for a variety of reasons: they may have strong religious or moral views about breaking the law; they may be afraid of being caught and arrested; they may fear the shame that going to prison would bring on them and their family; they may be worried about damaging their 'good name' (their reputation).

In some situations it is obvious why a law is needed. If drivers drove through traffic lights on 'stop', they could be seriously injured or killed, or cause injury or death to someone else.

Why do we need laws?

The short answer is, try imagining life without them! Your life would be chaotic, and the most vulnerable members of society, such as the very young, the elderly, the ill and some minorities, would suffer most. What would happen to children, for example, if there were no laws on divorce?

For laws to work properly they need the support of the majority of the population. Most people agree that child abuse is a

Breaking the law can damage your good name

shocking crime and abusers must be punished. But public opinion is more divided on euthanasia. Some think it wrong to treat doctors as criminals if they help terminally ill patients in pain to die. Others would argue that this is morally wrong as well as unlawful.

You will understand why we need laws.

Who's the loser?

A shoplifter who has stolen a couple of T-shirts might argue that their actions won't put a big company like Marks and Spencer out of business. But:

- if everybody stole from them it would push up prices for everyone else who shops there, because Marks and Spencer had to pay for the T-shirts

- if you steal from Marks and Spencer, you steal from the people who own the business, so it's just like stealing a mobile phone or a car.

In the same way, if people don't pay income tax when they should, the government will have less money to pay for schools and hospitals. Many people are therefore affected indirectly by tax evasion.

Action

1. In groups, think about your usual daily routine and list how many times during the day you come across a rule or law. Why do you choose to obey or not to obey these rules and laws?

2. You sometimes hear people say 'But it's a bad law.' Make a list of your reasons for laws being good or bad. Be ready to explain your ideas.

3. Find out what new laws have been passed recently. Why do you think they are necessary?

Check your understanding

1. In your own words, give four reasons why people obey the law. Suggest one more reason not mentioned on these pages.

2. Make a list of crimes that have immediate consequences for the general public. List others that may have long-term and less immediate consequences.

3. Why do you think it is important that the majority of citizens support a particular law? Suggest one law that probably has majority support. Suggest one that probably doesn't, and give a reason.

… another point of view?

'You should never break the law.'

Do you agree with this statement? Give reasons for your opinion, showing you have considered another point of view.

Why do laws change?

There are laws to cover a vast range of activities, including adoption, marriage and divorce, terrorism, discrimination, motoring, banking, sex, drugs, theft and assault. New developments, such as cloning or the internet, often require new laws.

Civil and criminal law: what's the difference?

Getting you thinking

Grant Raphael, a cameraman, made fake entries on his old school friend Mathew Firsht's Facebook profile. The entries were not very polite! Mathew sued his old friend for libel and misuse of private information. He was awarded £22,000 damages against his friend, who had to pay the cost of the case as well.

Biker's murderers jailed for life

1 Which case is a private issue?
2 Which case involved the police?
3 Which case is more worrying for the general public? Why?
4 Can you think of some other examples of private issues and of some which involve the police?

Two kinds of law

Over many centuries of law making, two separate but related branches of the law have evolved to meet changing circumstances: **civil law** and **criminal law**.

Most civil cases are about disputes between individuals or groups, and very often these arguments are about rights. Examples include company law, adoption, accidents at work and consumer rights.

Criminal law deals with offences such as murder, theft and drug dealing. In a criminal case, the conflict is between the government (acting for all citizens) and the lawbreakers.

Who's right?

The person who brings a case to a civil court is called the claimant. The person accused of doing wrong is called the defendant. In some civil cases, the claimant sets out to **sue** the defendant. If the claimant wins, the defendant will have to give them money, which is known as damages.

Katie Price and Peter Andre won large libel damages after they took action over claims they were uncaring parents. They sued the owners of the newspaper after the story appeared in the News of the World. It was based on an interview with former nanny Rebecca Gauld. In a new development, the newspaper's solicitor apologised and accepted the allegations were untrue, adding that the couple were decent and responsible parents who cared deeply for their children.

1 Who is the claimant in this case? Who is the defendant?
2 Why was this case heard in a civil court?

You will find out about the difference between civil and criminal law.

A civil court

A judge sitting without a jury decides almost all civil cases

Criminal courts

There is a separate system of courts to deal with criminal cases. Less serious offences are dealt with in magistrates' courts. Serious offences are dealt with in crown courts before a judge and a jury

What happens in a civil court?

Most civil cases are heard in a **county court**. Because a court case can be very expensive, most people try to settle the dispute before it gets to court.

A small number of civil cases are heard in a **High Court**. These courts deal with complex family disputes and other complicated financial and legal matters, such as bankruptcy and large claims for damages. Any case involving £50,000 or more is heard in the High Court.

If a civil case involves a claim of less than £5,000, it will be heard in a **small claims court**. About 90,000 cases a year are heard in these courts.

Key Terms

civil law: this covers disputes between individuals or groups. Civil law cases are often about rights

county court: a local court that has limited powers in civil cases

criminal law: this deals with offences such as murder and drug dealing. These cases are between the Crown Prosecution Service (acting for all citizens) and the offender

crown court: courts held in towns in England and Wales where judges hear cases

High Court: the court where judges hear cases on serious crimes

judge: a person who decides questions of law in a court

jury: a group of people who decide if someone is guilty in a court of law

magistrates' court: a court held before two or more public officers dealing with minor crimes

small claims court: a local court, which hears civil cases involving small amounts of money

sue: to make a claim against someone or something

Action

Make a list of the different kind of cases that appear in civil courts. Which human rights are involved in each type?

Check your understanding

1 What are the main differences between civil and criminal cases?
2 What is a) a claimant, b) a defendant and c) a small claims court?
3 What type of crime is dealt with in either the magistrates' or crown courts?
4 Why are most civil cases settled before they reach court?

… another point of view?

'Neighbours should sort things out instead of going to court.'

Do you agree with this statement? Give reasons for your opinion, showing you have considered another point of view.

Who puts the law into practice?

Getting you thinking

1 You've broken the law and have to appear in court. Which of the following would you prefer as your 'judge and jury', and why?
   - Your teachers
   - Your classmates
   - Your parents
   - The police
   - Other young people who've been in trouble themselves
   - The victims of your crime
   - A group of people chosen at random, who do not know you

2 Which group do you think the victim would prefer? Give reasons.

3 Which group do you think would give the fairest outcome? Give reasons.

The criminal justice system

The criminal justice system is large and complex. These are the roles within it.

Judges

The judges who work in both criminal and civil courts are known collectively as the **judiciary**. Most judges have worked for at least ten years as a barrister, but a few solicitors also become judges. In a jury trial, it is the jury that decides if the accused is guilty or not, but the judge who determines the sentence.

Senior judges (who sit in the higher courts) are very powerful. They don't make laws: Parliament does that. You'll find out about how laws are made on page 81. But if there is an argument about how a law should be interpreted, it is the senior judges who decide.

Magistrates

Full-time magistrates are called district judges and are paid for their work. They are usually barristers or solicitors with at least seven years' experience. They sit alone.

Part-time magistrates come from all walks of life. They are not legally qualified and are not paid. They work with other magistrates.

Jury

A jury is made up of 12 adults, who sit in a crown court and decide whether the accused person is innocent or guilty. A jury is made up of members of the public chosen at random.

You will find out about the various roles of people who work within the criminal justice system.

Police

The police do not make laws, they enforce them. Their job is to protect the public, arrest lawbreakers and bring them before the courts.

Solicitors

All **solicitors** must pass law exams because, among other things, they can give legal advice to people who have to go to court. Some solicitors also speak in court on behalf of their clients.

Barristers

Barristers undergo a long legal training too, but they spend most of their time in court representing their clients. They are the only lawyers qualified to speak in any type of court.

Probation officers

If an offender is given a community sentence, they will work with a local probation officer. **Probation officers** are professionally qualified. They write court reports on offenders and supervise them in the community when they've been sentenced.

A new uniform has been designed for judges in civil cases. It aims to make them less remote from the public. Do you think it works? If so, explain why

Action

1   Research the entry requirements (that is, age, qualifications, etc.) of either a police officer or a solicitor.
2   Interview a probation officer to find out about the work they do with offenders in the community. You may wish to research a specific aspect of their work. For example, probation officers often work with young offenders who have problems with alcohol and other drugs.
3   Research who can be called for jury service and what serving on a jury involves.

Check your understanding

1   What do judges do in trials where there is a jury?
2   What powers do senior judges have?
3   What is the most important difference between the role of the police and the role of judges?
4   What is the difference between a barrister and a solicitor?
5   What skills and personal qualities do you think you need to be a good magistrate?
6   Can you think of any reasons why people don't apply to be magistrates?

Key Terms

barrister: a lawyer who represents and speaks for their clients in court

judiciary: all the judges in a country

probation officer: someone who writes court reports on offenders and supervises them in the community

solicitor: a lawyer who gives legal advice and may speak for their clients in court

Criminal courts

Getting you thinking

1 Which of the two courtrooms above is the most 'child-friendly' and why?
2 Should courts be made more 'adult-friendly'? Give reasons.
3 Is it good idea that courts are open to the public? Give reasons.
4 The results of court cases are published in the paper. What effect might this have on people who think about committing a crime?

Two types of court

Courts are formal places. Everyone involved must take the process very seriously. In some countries, youth courts are more informal because people think young people are more likely to tell the truth in a more relaxed environment.

There are two types of court for criminal cases: magistrates' courts and crown courts.

A magistrates' court

Over 95 per cent of all criminal trials take place in magistrates' courts. Specially trained magistrates also run youth courts for offenders aged between 10 and 17. Magistrates, who sit in court with at least one other magistrate, also deal with a small number of civil cases.

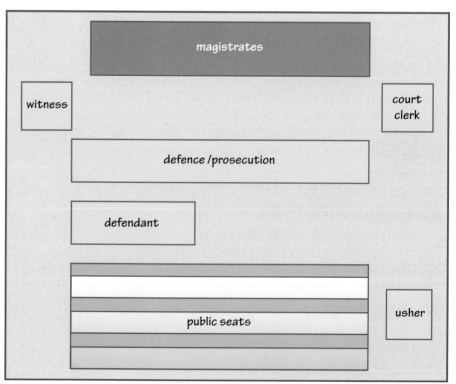

A magistrates' court

You will find out about the differences between a magistrates' court and a crown court.

Mitigating factors

There is no jury in a magistrates' court, so magistrates must be absolutely sure 'beyond reasonable doubt' that the accused is guilty. They must also take into account any **mitigating** factors. If, for example, a woman stole from a supermarket because she had no money to buy food for herself and her children, magistrates would take this into account and might give her a lesser sentence.

A crown court

The most serious criminal cases are heard in a crown court. The atmosphere is more solemn and the proceedings are more formal than in a magistrates' court. The judges and barristers wear wigs and gowns. A jury decides if the defendant is guilty or not (unless the defendant pleads guilty, in which case no jury is involved).

Crown court judges can have different powers. Only High Court judges, who sit in the larger courts, can try very serious cases, such as murder and rape. Others, known as circuit judges and **recorders**, try less serious cases such as theft, for example.

Crown court judges and juries must also take into account any mitigating factors, in the same way that magistrates do. The maximum sentence in a crown court is life imprisonment.

What sentences can magistrates give?

Magistrates have the power to give the following penalties:

- prison: up to a maximum of six months
- community sentences
- Antisocial Behaviour Orders (ASBOs)
- fines: of up to a maximum £5,000
- discharge: conditional or absolute

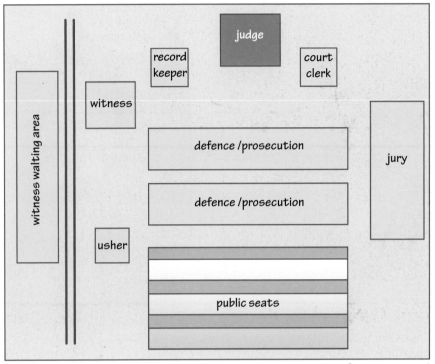

A crown court

Check your understanding

1 What are 'mitigating factors'? Support your answer with an example.
2 What kinds of mitigating factors might influence magistrates' decisions when sentencing young offenders?
3 List the differences between a magistrates' court and crown court.
4 What is the maximum sentence each type of court can impose?
5 When is a jury used in a crown court case?

... another point of view?

'Courts should be friendlier places.'

Do you agree with this statement? Give reasons for your opinion, showing you have considered another point of view.

Key Terms

mitigating: making something less intense or severe

recorder: a barrister or solicitor of at least ten years' experience, who acts as a part-time judge in a crown court

Taking part

Getting you thinking

1. How are these young people participating in school life?
2. Do you take part in school life in other ways?
3. One of them has a complaint. What could they do about it?
4. Do you think participating in school life affects the way students think about the school?

Joining in

All schools have different ways in which students can join in. For example, there are stories of students painting the social areas of their school or making an environmental garden, and many schools run projects where students work together to combat problems such as bullying.

All these ways of joining in help people to have more respect for the school and their fellow students. If you have created and looked after something, or have worked hard to make the school a better place, you want it to stay like that. If you see others spoiling it in some way, you will probably want to stop them.

A school where there is lots of participation is likely to have many students who have a sense of belonging and, therefore, respect its way of life.

Students and staff during a school council meeting

You will investigate how and why people participate in the life of the school in order to understand how democracy works.

Having a voice

There are other ways in which students can help to run the school. Do you have a **school council**? In most cases where these operate, every class and year group has a representative on the school council. Sometimes there may be year-group councils, because younger students can find it hard to be heard when in meetings with older students. The school council will discuss things that they want changing, or comment on proposals from the staff.

When all students in school feel that they have a voice, they are likely to be happier about the decisions that are made.

Choosing the representatives

When classes have to choose a member of the school council, they usually do it by holding an **election**. Students can volunteer to stand, or they might be put forward by their friends. They are often asked to make a speech about their views, after which an election is held. In the election, everyone in the class can vote for the person who they want to be the class representative. The one with the most votes will join the school council. This representative will be responsible for listening to their classmates' opinions and standing up for these views in school council meetings. There are too many students in every school for every individual opinion to be heard, so having one person to represent a group is a practical system.

This process of choosing and electing representatives is known as **representative democracy**, a system in which people have a chance to vote for someone who they want to represent them. This happens in schools all over the country, but it also happens in elections in your local area and the whole country.

The level of involvement of the council can vary, but many are consulted when important decisions, such as teacher appointments, are made. One newly appointed deputy head-teacher said, 'The toughest part of the whole interview was the one with the students.' It was tough because he respected the students' views and knew that these were the people he had to be able to influence if he was to have a successful future. It's much easier to work with people if they respect you.

Choosing a representative in a national election

Action

Does your school have a school council? If it does, what has it discussed recently? If it doesn't have a council, do you think it should? Why?

Check your understanding

1 In your own words, say why it can be useful to have a school council.
2 What does 'representative democracy' mean?

... another point of view?

'It's easier to work with people if they respect you.'

Do you agree with this statement? Give reasons for your opinion, showing you have considered another point of view. Think of examples of situations in which working together could be made easier if those taking part had more respect for each other.

Key Terms

representative democracy: a type of democracy where citizens have the right to choose someone to represent them on a council or in Parliament as an MP

school council: a group of people who represent the classes and year groups of the school. It gives students the opportunity to participate in decision-making

Who represents us?

Getting you thinking

Can do! I

The public loos had been a mess for years. There were always people hanging out nearby and vandalising them. No one wanted to use them!

Steve, Emma and Akari decided to work out what could be done. They got a group of friends together to think about it.

The local community could do with a loo, but it would have to be indestructible. There would be plenty of space left in the building once modern, new facilities had been installed. All the local kids complained there was nothing to do in the evening. Many sat at home and watched the telly or played computer games – but they never had the latest ones. So they came up with the idea of setting up an internet café in the rest of the space. It could be used by all sorts of people who didn't have a computer or wanted to learn – and it would be a good place to get together.

It would take some work and they'd have to persuade people that it could be done – and they'd need some help.

The local councillor had been into school recently to judge a Citizenship competition. While she was there, she'd explained that the council was a group of people who were chosen to represent different parts of the town – so this was their starting point.

1 The internet café was for everyone to use. Who do you think should make decisions about it? Explain why.

2 It is difficult for everyone to have a say on every topic. How might it be made simpler?

3 What sorts of decisions do you think should be made locally? Explain why.

Representing everyone

Akari, Emma and Steve had an issue that they wanted to discuss. The loos were a waste of space – which could be put to a better use. They needed to find the right people to talk to. They knew who the local councillor was – so this was the place to start.

The local council is made up of local people who make decisions about local services. These **councillors** represent different parts of the town, called wards. They are chosen in an election by the people who live in that **ward**.

In many areas, local elections take place every four years. **Political parties** put forward candidates for people to choose between. Each party will have already decided on a list of plans, called a **manifesto**. These plans will be put into practice if the party wins enough seats on the council.

You will find out how decisions are made about your local area.

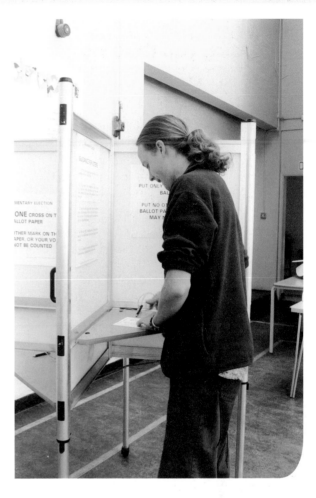

Sometimes there is a long list of people to choose from at an election. Some will represent the well-known political parties such as Labour, the Conservatives and the Liberal Democrats. Others will represent smaller groups like the Green party, or people who are independent of a party and are campaigning on a local issue. Most councils are a mix of political parties, but the party with most councillors takes overall control.

Almost everyone who is aged 18 or more can vote in these elections. Just like with the school council, the process is democratic because everyone can take part. Each year a form is sent to every house in the area to check who is entitled to vote.

Your vote is always secret, so nobody can check on your decision. Has your school or village hall ever been used as a **polling station** on election day?

Action

1 Find out who represents your area on the local council.
2 What is the mix of political parties that makes up your local council?
3 Find out about an issue that the council is discussing at the moment. What are the different points of view? Follow it up and find out what happens in the end.

Check your understanding

1 Who is on the local council?
2 How were these representatives chosen?
3 Why are most councils a mix of political parties?
4 Why do you think it is important that your vote is secret?

... another point of view?

'Local decisions should be made by local people.'

Do you agree with this statement? Give reasons for your opinion, showing you have considered another point of view.

Key Terms

council: a group of people who are elected to look after the affairs of a town, district or county

manifesto: a published statement of the aims and policies of a political party

political party: an organised group of people with common aims who put up candidates for elections

polling station: a place where votes are cast; often a school, library or village hall

ward: an area that forms a separate part of a local council

How does the council work?

Getting you thinking

Can do! II

Steve, Emma and Akari set about finding out how to contact the people at the council who could help. They rang the main council switchboard and asked to talk to someone who could help them. They were put through to the Environment and Amenity Services and explained their plans.

They were told that it would cost quite a lot and the council had responsibilities to provide all sorts of other services and that money was short. They were told they should talk to the person who was responsible for community development.

They should also talk to the members of the council's **cabinet** responsible for public toilets and community development. An email or letter might be the best way to make contact because being a councillor is a spare-time job; they will be at work during the day. With the help of their local councillor, they set up a meeting to explain the plans.

1 Who makes decisions about local leisure and recreation issues?
2 What differences are there between the councillor and the person who works in the Environment and Amenity department?
3 Why do you think the council has to make choices between spending money on developing the public toilets and on services for the elderly?
4 Why do you think the council listens to people who come to them with ideas about developing their community?

How is the council organised?

Every area of the country elects a councillor. When the council first meets after an election, it elects a leader and the members of the cabinet. The leader and cabinet all come from the political party that won the most votes: they have the **majority**.

Each member of the cabinet will have responsibility for one area of the council's work; for example, education, social services, finance, and leisure and recreation.

Apart from electing the cabinet, the council also elects Overview and Scrutiny committees to make sure the council is run properly.

Being a councillor carries a lot of responsibility, but the role is mainly voluntary. Councillors are paid travel expenses and an attendance fee for meetings, but they don't usually receive a salary.

How does the council do its work?

All the councillors meet to put together the plan for the year. They set the budget for each area of spending. The Overview and Scrutiny committees then make sure this plan is followed.

There are some areas, such as planning for things like housing and road building, that the council as a whole controls. Planning decisions are made according to laws laid down by central government, so the council sets up a committee to make sure that the rules are followed.

All councillors, whether they are members of the cabinet or not, must represent their ward in council decisions. They have a vote in council meetings and must use it in a way that serves their ward best.

As most of the people on the council have full-time jobs, they cannot run the services as well. A **Chief Executive** is appointed to take responsibility for this. In each department, people who are experts in their field are employed to make sure it all runs smoothly.

You will find out how the council does its work.

The structure of the council
This is the most common structure for councils in the UK.

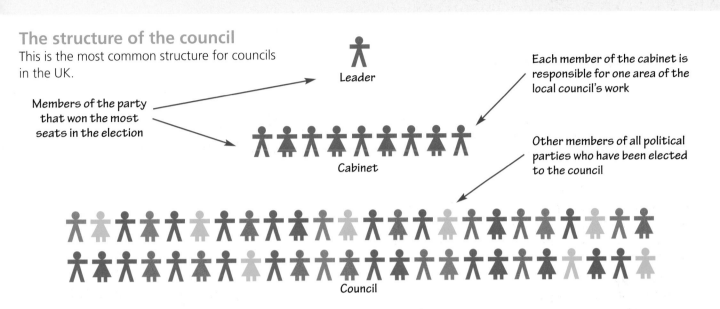

Leader

Members of the party that won the most seats in the election

Each member of the cabinet is responsible for one area of the local council's work

Cabinet

Other members of all political parties who have been elected to the council

Council

Committees

These people make recommendations to the cabinet about developments they would like to see in the area. The Scrutiny Committee checks up on the work of the cabinet.

Action
Have a look at your local council's website. Two example addresses are:

www.suffolkcc.gov.uk

www.hullcc.gov.uk.

1 How is your council organised? Is there a cabinet and leader?
2 Which political party, if any, has control of your local council?
3 Find out about the work a councillor from your ward does.
4 Who would Steve, Emma and Akai have to talk to if the public loos were in your area?

Check your understanding
1 What does the council's cabinet do?
2 Who decides how much money to spend on each part of the council's work?
3 What do councillors do for their wards?
4 What's the difference between a councillor and a Chief Executive?

... another point of view?
'The public loos should be converted.'

Do you agree with this statement? Give reasons for your opinion, showing you have considered another point of view.

What is a mayor?
In most places, a **mayor** has little power but takes part in local ceremonies. When the Queen or other famous people come to visit, the mayor puts on the chain of office and meets them. In May 2002, elections for directly elected mayors were held in a number of towns for the first time. Elected mayors have a great deal of power, as London's mayor has shown.

Key Terms
cabinet: the main decision-making body of the council

Chief Executive: an employee of the council, responsible for the smooth running of services

majority: the party with a majority has won a bigger proportion of the votes than the others

mayor: a member of the council who is selected to be its representative on ceremonial occasions. In some areas they are the elected leader

What does the council do?

Getting you thinking

1 Which one would you spend more money on? Explain why.

2 If you spend more on your choice, which services would you cut? Explain why.

3 If you decide not to cut anything, where would the money come from?

4 Why do councils often not want to spend more?

What does the council do?

Your local council is responsible for a range of services for your community, including education, social services, leisure, planning and transport, housing, fire and the police.

The amount of spending will depend on many different things. Here are some examples:

- If the population of the area is very young, they will need lots of schools.

- If there are many old people, they may need help from social services.

- If there are lots of people, there will be lots of refuse to collect.

A brand new sports centre, for example, is a very expensive item that has to be paid for. The council will work out how much it needs to spend in the coming year and then calculate how much money it must raise.

The council funds schools, which are free. It runs sports centres, which are usually cheaper than private clubs. The council provides these services because many people would not be able to afford to pay for them otherwise.

Sometimes councils work together with private businesses to run their services. Council houses can be sold to private housing associations, and councils can use the money to repair remaining council property or to build new council housing. Councils often pay businesses to run leisure facilities for them.

Central government sets a limit on how much money each council can spend. So the council has to work out its priorities. It never has the money to provide everything it would like to provide. When you vote in local elections, you are helping to decide what happens where you live.

You will discover which services are provided by local government and how the money is raised to provide them.

A local council's income and expenditure (in £ million)

Expenditure

Social services £37.4

Fire and plice £8.6

Planning and transport £12.8

Leisure £8.8

Housing £4.5

Other £6.7

Education £62.3

Income

Business rates £45.3

General government grant £26.1

Council tax £68

Tax surplus from last year £1.8

1 Make a list of services provided by this council. Put them in order according to how much they cost.

2 Why does the council spend money on these services?

3 If the council decided to spend more on leisure, where might the money come from?

Where does the money come from?

In order to pay for these services, the local council raises money from residents and businesses in the area. A large part of its spending comes from central government.

Council tax is paid by all the residents of the area. The amount that each person pays will depend on the value of the house they live in. People who live in bigger houses will pay more than those who live in smaller houses.

Business rates are paid by all the local businesses. The amount that is paid depends on the rent that could be charged for the office, shop or factory that the business uses.

Central government contributes a major part. The amount it contributes depends on the needs of the specific area and on how much can be raised locally. Poorer areas tend to receive more from central government than richer parts of the country.

Central government helps poorer areas more because it is harder for them to raise money locally. If many people are unemployed, houses will tend to have a lower value, so the council tax will only bring in a relatively small amount of money. Spending in these areas often needs to be greater because people who live there often need a lot of help from Social Services.

Action

How does your local council raise and spend its money? You can find out from the town hall, council offices or the library. The council might also have a website with the information.

Check your understanding

1 What sorts of services do local councils provide?
2 Where do local councils get their money from?
3 Why does central government give more money to some councils than to others?
4 Why is it important to vote in local elections?

... another point of view?

'Local taxation should be based on how much you earn instead of the value of your house.'

Do you agree with this statement? Give reasons for your opinion, showing you have considered another point of view.

Key Terms

business rates: a form of tax paid by all the businesses in an area. The amount a business pays depends on the rent that could be charged for their premises

council tax: a tax paid by everyone who lives in an area. It is based on the value of their house

Talking to the council

Getting you thinking

Warrington Youth Council

Warrington Youth Council is an action group. They have previously looked at issues affecting young people, such as accessible and affordable public transport, bullying, recycling in schools and the council's budget.

The strong influence of Warrington Youth Council was demonstrated in January 2007, when the group met the Strategic Director of Children's Services and an executive council member about the intended 100 per cent increase of transport fares in Warrington. The Warrington Youth Council group managed to negotiate a 50 per cent rise instead.

Warrington Youth Council members are even asked to interview candidates applying for important jobs at the council.

The Youth Council produces a manifesto that sets out what they want to see happen in future years. It includes:

- health
- transport
- young people and the police
- things to do and places to go
- the media
- the environment.

1 What issues has Warrington Youth Council dealt with?
2 What has been their greatest success?
3 Why is it useful to set out your plans for the future?
4 Why do people below the age of 18 need to have people to represent them?
5 Is there a youth council where you live? Find out from your local council's website (these are easy to find – they are www.name of council.gov.uk).

Your views count

In Warrington, the council takes young people's views seriously. It even changes its plans when the Youth Council puts it under pressure. They have frequent meetings with the official who is responsible for everything to do with young people.

Communicating with the council

Everyone's first line of communication with the local council is at the election. Almost all the population aged 18 or over has a vote. The actions of the council between elections will affect people's decisions when it comes to voting.

The way you go about talking to the council depends on the issue:
- If you want to influence a decision, you need to get to the decision-making process at an early stage. Talking to your councillor is a good start as you can ask advice on how to put across your point of view.
- If you want to find out what is going to happen in the future, ask to look at the **Forward Plan**, as this will set out the general aim of the council's plans.
- If you want to find out about a decision that has been made, have a look at the **minutes** of the cabinet meeting.
- If something has gone wrong, you will want to complain. You will probably need to talk to the people employed by the council, but your local councillor will be able to help. If all your complaints fail and you really think the council is in the wrong, you may have to turn to the **ombudsman**. This is the last resort and you need to have done all you can to get the council to sort out the problem.

You will find out how people can raise issues with the local council.

Protesting to the council in person

Talk to your local councillor

Find out about the council members and officers

Have a look at the papers from council or cabinet meetings

Go to a cabinet meeting

Want to raise an issue with the council?

Complain to the council

Look at the Forward Plan

Complain to the ombudsman

Go to a council meeting

More effective?

A lone voice can sometimes seem too quiet to be heard. A group of people who all have the same views can be more effective than one person campaigning alone. The campaign might be about aircraft noise, wanting a by-pass, not wanting a by-pass, the opening of a new supermarket, the lack of facilities for young people or many, many other issues.

Action

Look at your local council's website. What does it tell you about getting in touch with people at the council? Does it have a young people's section? If not, ask them why!

Check your understanding

1 How often are council elections held?
2 In what ways could you contact the local council in the following situations?
   - You notice that the paving stones in your street are becoming cracked and uneven.
   - You disagree about plans to build a new supermarket.
   - You want to know how much money is going to be spent on education.
   - You've heard that a youth centre is going to close down.

... another point of view?

'The local council should take more notice of the views of young people.'
Do you agree with this statement? Give reasons for your opinion, showing you have considered another point of view.

Key Terms

Forward Plan: a document that sets out the aims of the council in the long term

minutes: a formal record of what has been said at a meeting

ombudsman: a person who investigates complaints against the government or a public organisation

youth council: a group of young people who meet to discuss what is going on in the local area and put their ideas to the council leader

Putting on the pressure

Getting you thinking

I will never forget the day when Jay, a boy from the village, was killed. He wasn't the first person to be hit by a car that was speeding through the village. The council seemed to think that 40mph was quite slow enough, but drivers always thought they could get away with more. What we really needed was a 30mph limit and some rumble strips so everyone noticed.

When Jay died, I realised it was time to act. I started a petition. There were copies in all the local shops, in the pub, and with all the local organisations. Soon we had over 5,000 signatures and we were ready to make our mark.

I took the advice of our local councillor, who suggested that I should go to the council meeting to make my point. I sent a letter and the petition in advance so they would be prepared. At the meeting I stood up and explained what we were asking for. The council members listened carefully.

The council members understood what we wanted and why we wanted it. Within a few months, we, like other villages, had the 30mph limit that would make our lives safer.

Why was it a good idea to:

1 organise a petition
2 talk to the local councillor
3 send a letter and the petition before the meeting
4 go to the meeting in person?

Pressure groups

People who have a message that they want to get across often form a **pressure group**. A group of people who want something to change often has more effect than a single person. Pressure groups want to influence people in government – local, national and even international.

Pressure groups come in all shapes and sizes, but they are usually concerned with one issue or area of policy. For example, the petition for a 30mph limit was started by one person, but in order to put pressure on the local council other people got involved. They formed a small pressure group, which had one objective. Once the work was done and the group had succeeded in getting the 30mph limit, they could then stop campaigning.

Many pressure groups work on a much larger scale. Major pressure groups such as Greenpeace and Shelter have objectives that often lead them to put pressure on national government and big businesses, as well as organising activities at a local level.

You will find out how pressure groups can influence the actions of the council.

Getting your voice heard

The key to getting your voice heard is to put together a campaign that reaches as many people as possible.

Is there a group of people who care about the issue?
Organise the group and give people responsibilities.

Is the message clear?
Make sure that everyone understands what you are trying to achieve.

Who do you need to talk to?
Find out who is responsible for the things you want to change.

Have you got good evidence?
Do you need a petition to show that lots of people care about the issue? Have you got the facts and figures right?

How do you get the message across?
You might give out leaflets in the high street, put out a press release so the local media know what is happening, campaign in public about the issue or prepare a presentation for the council. You will need to fit the method to the audience that you are trying to influence.

Can you make your argument more persuasive?
Look at all the material you have. Test it out on people. Make sure that the key points are very clear. Are there any key issues that will make people take notice? Use them!

Is there a local radio station or newspaper?
Local radio stations and papers are always looking for news. How do you get in touch with them?

Action

Is there a local issue that you really care about? Work out what you would do in order to change things. If you are doing the full GCSE, this will be good preparation for your Campaign in Unit 4.

Check your understanding

1 What is the aim of pressure groups?
2 How can members of a pressure group get their voices heard?
3 Why might a pressure group only exist for a short length of time?

... another point of view?

'A pressure group is usually more effective than a single person at getting things changed.'

Do you agree with this statement? Give reasons for your opinion, showing you have considered another point of view.

Getting elected

Getting you thinking

1 What made Jo decide to become an MP?
2 How did Jo decide which political party to join?
3 Why does Jo think people should have their say?
4 What issues do politicians deal with?
5 What could happen if you don't bother to vote?

'Politics has an impact on every aspect of our lives. From protecting our environment, to the quality of your education or how much you get paid for your Saturday job: all of these things are affected by politicians. I decided to stand for election because I wanted to change things, and not just complain about what I didn't like.

I first became interested in politics when I took part in a Parliamentary debate at my secondary school. We took the parts of the government and opposition parties, and throughout the day we debated various issues such as education, health and defence. It was fast and furious. It brought politics to life for me.

The issues that I felt particularly strongly about were education and trying to change the way the electoral system works. I joined the Lib Dems when I was a student, mainly because of these two issues. Over time I became interested in other issues such as civil liberties, the environment and the way businesses work with the community.

For a long time I was determined to take up a career in business and keep politics as an interest for my spare time. But when I was first persuaded to stand for Parliament, I began to realise that politics was my real passion. I decided to follow my ambition to represent my home seat in Parliament. Lots of young people don't seem to be interested in politics. But it's all about everyday life, so it's important to vote and play a part. If you don't, you can't really complain about what happens. Becoming an MP means I can really have my say.'

Becoming a Member of Parliament

There are 646 **Members of Parliament**, or MPs. They have all been elected to represent a part of the country known as a **constituency**. Most MPs were chosen by one of the political parties to be its candidate at an election. If they win the election, they then become the MP who represents everyone in the area.

A few people stand as independents and therefore do not go through the party system. This was the case with a doctor, Richard Taylor, who was furious that the local hospital was to be closed; he stood as an independent and won the seat.

Fighting an election

You have all seen posters everywhere at election time. The campaign starts the minute a **general election** is declared, if not before. The current government tries to choose the best moment to 'go to the country', which is another way of saying 'calling an election'.

To attract voters, the political parties and candidates will:

- send out leaflets telling people what they have done in the past and plan to do in future
- go **canvassing**
- attract press coverage
- hold public meetings.

Jo Swinson campaigning

You will discover how an MP gets elected to the House of Commons and learn how the electoral system works.

Who shall I vote for?

Whether you decide to vote for the Conservatives, Labour, the Liberal Democrats or one of the smaller parties, all sorts of factors will affect your decision.

Which paper do you read?
Newspapers, radio and TV let people know what's going on, but they can also affect the way people think. Some newspapers always reflect the ideas of one of the political parties, while others take a wider view.

What's your age, gender and ethnicity?
More young people and ethnic minorities vote Labour. More women used to vote Conservative but the balance has now shifted.

Which social class are you in?
Upper and middle class people have tended to vote Conservative and working class people to vote Labour. However, this divide has become less rigid as the parties' policies have become more alike and society has become less class-based.

Do you like the party's policies and image?
People tend to vote for the party as a whole rather than their local candidate. The image of the party and its leader has become increasingly important as the role of the media has increased.

What do your friends think?
People's decisions on who to vote for are often affected by their friends and family.

What's your religion?
Religious beliefs can persuade people to vote for the party that holds views in line with their own.

Where do you live?
Political parties often have strongholds in certain areas. For instance, in the South East more people have traditionally voted Conservative.

When people have taken all these things into account, they will decide who to vote for. Whoever is elected MP is then responsible for representing all the people in their constituency in Parliament, whichever party they belong to.

Action

1 Who is your local MP? Which political party do they belong to?
2 How many candidates were there at the last election in your constituency? Which parties did they represent? How many votes did each candidate win?

Check your understanding

1 How many MPs are there in the House of Commons?
2 What is the name for the area represented by an MP?
3 Do all candidates represent one of the main political parties? Explain your answer.
4 How do candidates try to attract voters?
5 What affects the way people cast their vote?

... another point of view?

'I vote for a candidate because my friends and family do.'
Do you agree with this statement? Give reasons for your opinion, showing you have considered another point of view.

Key Terms

canvassing: when people try to persuade others to vote for their party in an election

constituency: the area represented by an MP

general election: an election for a new government. In the UK, these take place at least every five years

What does an MP do?

Getting you thinking

'Entering the House of Commons for the first time was really exciting. I'd worked so hard throughout the election, so winning my seat was great.

As an MP I hope to make a difference in two ways. Firstly, I can help the 65,000 people who live in my constituency. They raise questions and ask me to help sort out their problems at my regular surgeries. They also contact me by letter, telephone or email. I take a keen interest in local issues and get involved in supporting community initiatives.

Secondly, in the **House of Commons**, we all debate new laws and changes to existing ones. The detailed work on new laws is carried out in committees and not all in the chamber of the House of Commons, which you tend to see on television. There are also committees that check up on the work of government departments such as education and health.

I think being an MP is the best job in the world because I can really have an effect on the future of the country.'

1 Why was Jo so excited when she entered the House of Commons for the first time?
2 What might you think if you had become an MP and entered the House of Commons for the first time?
3 What did Jo expect to do once she had become an MP?
4 If you had just become an MP, what would you like to change?

Jo Swinson enters the Houses of Parliament for her first day in office

Taking your seat

For a new MP, taking your seat in the House of Commons is an exciting event. After what might be years of wanting and waiting to be elected, joining the body that runs the country is a big moment.

MPs debate new laws and policies in the House of Commons. Sometimes debates become furious and the **Speaker** has to act very firmly to keep things in order. On occasion, an MP can be temporarily thrown out of the House of Commons if things get out of hand. MPs generally vote with the party to which they belong, but sometimes they follow their conscience.

Starting work

MPs have a range of responsibilities.

Their first responsibility is to the people who elected them. There is often a lot of mail from the constituency, which must be dealt with. An MP will hold a frequent 'surgery' in the constituency to listen to people's ideas and worries. They take part in debates in the House of Commons and will usually vote with their political party.

If they have a post in a government department, they will be busy working on government policy and working out new laws.

They might sit on a committee that keeps a check on the activities of the government departments.

You will discover what Members of Parliament do.

The Speaker is an MP, chosen by the rest to organise business and keep order.

Backbench MPs, who don't have jobs in the government or opposition, sit on benches at the back.

The government benches: the **Prime Minister** sits at the front, surrounded by the **Cabinet**.

The opposition benches: the Leader of the **Opposition** sits at the front, surrounded by the **Shadow Cabinet**.

MPs who don't belong to the main party or largest opposition party also sit on the opposition bench.

Into power

When a political party wins a general election, it forms a government. The leader usually becomes the Prime Minister. His or her first task is to choose the members of the Cabinet. This is the inner circle of people who run the government departments. These departments include:

- the Treasury, which runs the finances
- the Home Office, which is responsible for protecting the public
- the Foreign and Commonwealth Affairs Office, which is responsible for the UK's interests abroad.

Other departments cover:

- health
- defence
- justice
- children, schools and families
- culture, media and sport
- business and enterprise
- environment, food and rural affairs
- transport
- international development.

Wales, Scotland and Northern Ireland also have their own departments. The people who lead these departments are known as **Secretaries of State**. They have assistants who are called **Ministers of State**. There is also a range of other jobs for non-cabinet MPs in the departments.

After the election, MPs wait for a call from the Prime Minister's office, in the hope of getting a job in the government. Getting the first job in a government department is a step to becoming a Minister.

Check your understanding

1 What is the responsibility of every MP?
2 What does a Secretary of State do?
3 What do government departments do?
4 Who is in the Cabinet?
5 What is the role of the Cabinet?

… another point of view?

'MPs should always vote with the party they belong to.'

Do you agree with this statement? Give reasons for your opinion, showing you have considered another point of view.

Key Terms

Cabinet: a group of MPs who head major government departments. It meets weekly to make decisions about how government policy will be carried out

House of Commons: the more powerful of the two parts of the British Parliament. Its members are elected by the public

Minister of State: an assistant to the Secretary of State

Opposition: political parties who are not in power

Prime Minister: the leader of the majority party in the House of Commons and the leader of the government

Secretary of State: an MP who is in charge of a government department such as health or defence

Shadow Cabinet: MPs from the main opposition party who 'shadow' MPs who head major government departments

Speaker: the MP elected to act as chairman for debates in the House of Commons

How are laws made?

Getting you thinking

Climate change law: reduce greenhouse gas emissions by 80 per cent by 2050

The Community Rehabilitation Order aims to:

- ensure the young person takes responsibility for his/her crime.
- help the young person to resolve any personal difficulties that may have contributed to his/her offending.
- help the young person become a law abiding and responsible member of the community.

Smoking ban: no one can smoke in enclosed public places

School-leaving age: from 2013 everyone will have to stay in education or training until 17

1. Why do you think the government wanted to make laws like these?
2. What, in your opinion, would happen if the government passed laws that the population did not like?
3. Why do people, in general, keep the laws that are passed by Parliament?

Power

Parliament passes laws that determine how we live our lives. By electing a government, we give it the power to do this. If people break the laws, they can be punished. The government is given authority (a mandate) because the population accepts that an election is a fair way of deciding who will hold power for a five-year period.

The government is **accountable** because it has to answer to the voters. If voters do not like what is happening, the government will not be re-elected.

How are laws made?

Laws go through several stages before coming into force. The government often puts out a **Green Paper**, which puts forward ideas for future laws. Once the ideas have been made final, a **White Paper** is published. This lays out the government's policy. To turn policy into law, the proposals are introduced to Parliament in the form of a **bill**. To change the school-leaving age, for example, the government would have to introduce an Education Bill. Having gone through the process shown in the diagram on the page opposite, the bill becomes an **Act** of Parliament and, therefore, part of the law of the country. The government is accountable to the population so it needs to be sure that everyone has had an opportunity to comment.

It is important that laws are carefully put together, or 'drafted', because there are always some people who want to find a way of avoiding them. If a law can be interpreted in a different way, it will be very hard to enforce. The law to ban hunting, for example, is proving difficult to enforce.

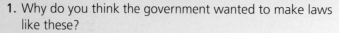

You will understand the process that a bill goes through before it becomes law.

The debate

Most bills are introduced by the government. Sometimes the two parties are in agreement and all goes smoothly, but often the opposition seriously disagrees either on the policy as a whole or on aspects of it. This leads to lengthy debate when the opposition tries to persuade the government to accept changes – or amendments – to the bill.

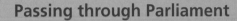

Passing through Parliament

First reading
The bill is introduced formally in the House of Commons. Before it reaches this stage, it has been worked on by a Drafting Committee to make sure that it is correctly put together. A bill can be many pages long. At this stage there is no debate.

Second reading
A few weeks after the first reading stage, the bill is debated fully in the House of Commons. A vote is taken and, if the majority of MPs approve of the bill, it is passed.

Standing committee
A group of 16 to 20 MPs look at the bill carefully and make any alterations that came up at the second reading, or which they now think are appropriate.

House of Lords
The bill goes through the same process as in the Commons. If the Lords want to change anything, the bill is returned to the Commons.

Report stage
The committee sends a report to the House of Commons with all its amendments. These amendments are either approved or changed. Changes are made when there is a lot of opposition to the bill or if there is strong public pressure to do so.

Third reading
The amended bill is presented to the House of Commons. A debate is held and a vote is taken on whether to approve it.

Royal assent
Once the bill has passed all its stages in the Commons and the Lords, it is sent to the Queen for her signature. This is really a formality, as the Queen would never refuse to sign a bill that had been through the democratic process. The bill then becomes an Act of Parliament and part of the law of the country.

Action

Choose a new law that you would like to see passed. Put your proposals into a 'bill'. Work out what the opposition is likely to say and prepare your arguments.

Check your understanding

1 What is the difference between a bill and an Act?
2 What sort of things do committees have to pay attention to when making amendments to bills?
3 Why do you think there are so many stages before a law is made?

Key Terms

accountable: if you are accountable for something, you are responsible for it and have to explain your actions

Act: a law passed by Parliament

bill: a proposal to change something into law

Green Paper: this puts forward ideas that the government wants discussed before it starts to develop a policy

White Paper: this puts government policy up for discussion before it becomes law

A louder voice

Getting you thinking

What's happening to identity cards?

The government says it wants to give people a sure-fire way of proving they are who they say they are. It argues ID cards will boost national security, tackle identity fraud, prevent illegal working and improve border controls.

NO2ID is a campaigning organisation. They say 'We are a single-issue group focused on the threat to liberty and privacy posed by the rapid growth of the database state, of which ID cards are the most visible part. We are entirely independent. We do not endorse any party, nor campaign on any other topic.'

Liberty, the human rights pressure group, expressed concern about the government's ability to safeguard the individuals' intimate details on the National Identity Register after government departments last year lost 30 million pieces of personal data, including those of 25 million child benefit claimants.

It's been delayed. Under the original plans the first British citizens would have been issued with ID cards in 2008, with the widespread roll-out taking place in 2010. This has now been put back to 2012. Even then, people applying for passports will no longer be forced to have an ID card whether they want one or not, although their details will still be entered into a central identity database.

1 Why does the government think identity cards should be introduced?
2 Why does NO2ID disagree?
3 What does it mean to be a 'single issue' group?
4 Do you think there is a connection between the actions of the pressure groups and the delay in the introduction of identity cards?
5 How strong do you think the connection is between public opinion and government policy?

What do pressure groups do?

Pressure groups often work to promote a cause such as looking after the environment, like the World Wide Fund for Nature and Friends of the Earth, or by helping relieve housing problems, like Shelter. Trade unions and other organisations are pressure groups that work to protect the interests of their members.

How do pressure groups work?

Pressure groups look for the best ways to get their message across and find support. They might:

- use adverts, press releases, special days or media stunts to put an issue in the public eye
- **lobby** MPs by writing to them, meeting them, organising petitions and trying to involve them in the work of the organisation
- try to influence changes in the law
- sponsor MPs and finance political parties.

People often say 'they' when referring to government, big business and other organisations that they don't think they can affect: 'They must do something about ...'.

An increasing number of people want to make their voice heard. Have a look at the Number 10 e-petition website: http://petitions.number10.gov.uk/. Anyone can start a petition on a topic of their choice. If there's something you feel strongly about, why wait for someone else to do something about it?

You will understand how and why people participate in political parties and pressure groups.

The pros and cons of pressure groups

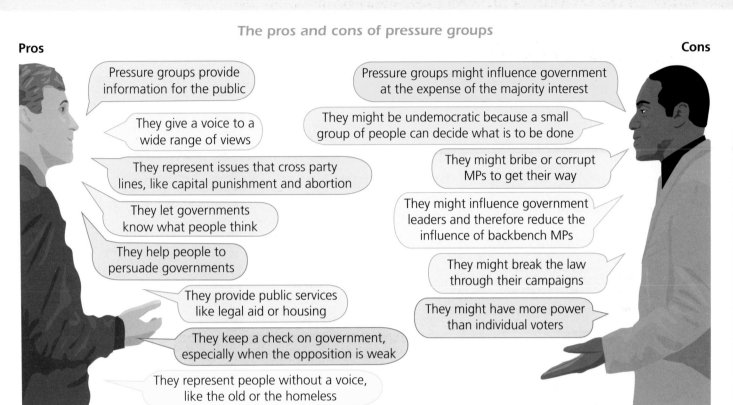

Pros

Pressure groups provide information for the public

They give a voice to a wide range of views

They represent issues that cross party lines, like capital punishment and abortion

They let governments know what people think

They help people to persuade governments

They provide public services like legal aid or housing

They keep a check on government, especially when the opposition is weak

They represent people without a voice, like the old or the homeless

Cons

Pressure groups might influence government at the expense of the majority interest

They might be undemocratic because a small group of people can decide what is to be done

They might bribe or corrupt MPs to get their way

They might influence government leaders and therefore reduce the influence of backbench MPs

They might break the law through their campaigns

They might have more power than individual voters

Action

1 Find out about political youth sections from political party websites.
2 Find out about the work of a national or international pressure group. What are their current campaigns? What successes have they had in the past? How do they encourage individuals to join in with their work?
3 What issue would you want to support? Explain why.
4 Which political party might you decide to join? Explain why.

Check your understanding

1 What can individuals do if they want to help shape the way things are done?
2 Why could it be argued that pressure groups help democracy? Why could it be said that they harm democracy?
3 Why are political parties interested in attracting young members?

... another point of view?

'An individual can have an effect, but you can make a bigger difference if you work with others.'

Do you agree with this statement? Give reasons for your opinion, showing you have considered another point of view.

Political parties: why should you join?

If you are interested in politics, you might decide to join the party that holds views closest to your own. The major political parties all have youth sections. Organisations encourage young people to take part because they want people to stay committed to their party later on in life. If you want to find out about them, have a look at their websites, where you will find their manifestos and information about their youth sections.

Key Terms

lobby: to try to persuade MPs to support a particular point of view. This used to happen in the 'lobby', or hallway, on the way into Parliament

The impact of public opinion

Getting you thinking

Western extension to London's Congestion Charging zone stopped after consultation

The **public consultation** on the congestion charging zone ran for six weeks and attracted nearly 28,000 responses. 69 per cent of individuals and businesses supported the removal of the western extension. 19 per cent stated that they wanted the extension kept as it is, and 12 per cent supported changing the scheme to improve the way that it operates.

What do we mean by campaigns?

'You might call it influencing, **advocacy** or campaigning but it is all about change. Whether you are trying to save a local community centre from closing or lobbying government, you are trying to produce a change.

NCVO is a highly effective lobbying organisation and represents the views of its members, and the wider voluntary sector to government, the European Union and other bodies.'

National Council for Voluntary Organisations

Making a difference

'Our mission is to drive the change to make our society the first in which disabled people achieve equality. Human rights are a powerful tool to achieve this change through our campaigning.'

Scope

1 Why did the Greater London Council decide to scrap the western extension of the congestion charging zone?

2 Why do organisations campaign?

3 Whose opinion does the National Council for Voluntary Organisations want to change? Explain why.

4 How could they go about campaigning?

5 What is Scope's mission?

6 Why do they think human rights are a powerful tool?

What is public opinion?

Public opinion sums up the views of the population. It can give the government strong messages about people's views on current issues. This can affect how laws are changed. Governments aim to be re-elected and therefore generally take public opinion into account when they make decisions.

Opinion polls are often held in order to find out what people think. They may be organised by people who want their views to be heard and think some hard evidence of people's views will help to persuade the government to listen.

Newspapers are always running opinion polls to find out which political party has most public support.

You will find out how voluntary organisations and consultations affect decisions made by the government.

Should we change the clocks in April and October?

There is often discussion about whether we should have British summer time all the year round.

Here is what people thought:
Yes – keep a standard time all year: 60.40%
No – change clocks twice a year as now: 36.89%
Don't know: 2.71%

1 Did people want to change the clocks?
2 How might this help to persuade the government to change the time?
3 Can you think of reasons why people might want to stop changing the clocks?

What is a voluntary organisation?

Voluntary organisations are usually run by people with a mission to change something. Scope (see 'Getting you thinking') wants to make life better for people with disabilities. There is a close link between voluntary organisations and pressure groups – they both want to change aspects of life.

Because voluntary organisations have a mission, they work hard to persuade the government to make changes to accept their proposals. They also want to influence public opinion in order to encourage the government to listen.

Why consult?

The government and local councils consult people on a range of issues. Local government is required to do so. There are a variety of benefits of doing so:

- Consultation allows people to have their say and can lead to more democracy.

- People may come up with innovative ideas.

- If the services provided are what people want, more people will use them.

If consultation comes up with answers that oppose the government's view, it can be difficult to handle. As with the School Council, if students are asked their opinion, the headteacher must be prepared to accept their views or have a very good reason to explain why they are not possible!

Check your understanding

1 What is public opinion?
2 What are voluntary organisations? Give some examples.
3 What is advocacy?
4 Why does government carry out public consultations?
5 What influence can voluntary organisations have on public opinion?

... another point of view?

'The government always knows best and looks after people so we don't need voluntary organisations.'

Do you agree with this statement? Give reasons for your opinion, showing you have considered another point of view.

Key Terms

advocacy: arguing on behalf of a particular issue

public consultation: involves asking the public about their opinions on changes in the law, policies or large-scale developments

voluntary organisations: bodies whose activities are carried out for reasons other than profit, but which do not include any public or local authority

85

More democratic?

Getting you thinking

"But why doesn't Cornwall have a parliament? It's just as different from London as Wales and Scotland."

"I voted for my MP but I wouldn't have voted for that new law that's just been passed!"

"Why should people sit in the House of Lords and make decisions about our future, when they haven't been elected?"

1 Do you think that other regions of the country should have parliaments? Explain your views.

2 Why do we vote for MPs rather than everyone voting for every law that is passed?

3 Do you think that the people in the House of Lords should be elected? Explain your views.

How democratic?

Democracy originated in ancient Athens, Greece, where all citizens voted on every issue. This was less democratic than it sounds because only a small proportion of the population was classed as 'citizens'. Women and slaves, for example, were excluded.

In the UK, we elect MPs to represent us, because the country is too large for everyone to have their say on all occasions. However, MPs vote, in general, according to the policy of their political party. MPs can't vote in a way that suits all their constituents, because some voted for another political party and hold different views.

When a **referendum** is held, every voter can make a direct contribution to a decision. In the UK, they are held on topics that have great long-term implications for the country, such as joining the Euro. The outcome may be binding or may just be used to advise the government.

Sometimes MPs are given a 'free vote', which means they don't have to vote with their party. Free votes are usually taken on matters of conscience, such as abortion. MPs will often be lobbied hard by pressure groups that want their support. Constituents may also want their MP to vote in a particular way.

You will discover that there are changes taking place in the way democracy works.

Real democracy?

The House of Lords has always had the role of checking and challenging bills as they pass through the system to become law. It has always included **hereditary peers**, who were only there because they had inherited the role. This was not really a good reason for being involved in ruling the country. There has been pressure to reform the House of Lords for a long time.

Life peers, who have been appointed by the government or opposition, also sit in the House of Lords. The number of new life peers is controlled by the government. A number of **people's peers** have also been appointed and there are plans for further change. But the House of Lords is still not really democratic, even though there are now fewer hereditary peers.

Devolution

The Scottish Parliament and Welsh **Assembly** were both set up following referenda. There had been lengthy campaigns for **devolution** in both countries. People wanted devolution because it shifted some power and authority from London to their own capital cities. Scotland voted strongly for its Parliament, which has the ability to raise taxes and pass laws. There are constant debates about how much power the Parliament should have.

The Welsh voted by a narrow margin of 0.6 per cent for their Assembly. The Welsh Assembly can spend the UK government's allocation of money to Wales, but it cannot set taxes and make laws because it is not a parliament.

Since the formation of Northern Ireland in 1921, there have been many attempts to create some form of government there. The current Assembly has powers to control education, health and local government, but the Assembly has often been suspended because of disagreement among Irish politicians.

The Powers of the Scottish Parliament
Agriculture, Fisheries and Forestry
Economic development
Education
Environment
Food standards
Health
Home Affairs
Law – Courts, Police, Fire Services
Local government
Research and statistics
Social work
Sport and the Arts
Tourism
Training
Transport

There are calls for regional assemblies in the rest of the UK too. Many people in regions such as Cornwall feel that their part of the country is distinctive and has different needs from the rest of the UK. People in the North East, however, rejected the idea when a referendum was held. The cost of running a regional assembly was one factor in their decision.

Check your understanding

1 What is the purpose of a referendum? When are they held?
2 What kind of issues are MPs allowed a free vote on? Why?
3 Who can influence MPs when they have a free vote?
4 What's the difference in the amount of power held by the Scottish Parliament and the Welsh Assembly?
5 Why do some people want to have regional governments?

… another point of view?

'Devolution means that better decisions are made for a region because they are made locally.'
Do you agree with this statement? Give reasons for your opinion, showing you have considered another point of view.

Key Terms

assembly: a body of people elected to decide on some areas of spending in a region

devolution: the transfer of power from central to regional government

hereditary peers: people who inherited the title 'Lord' or 'Lady'

people's peers: people who are selected to sit in the House of Lords

referendum: a vote by the whole electorate on a particular issue

Vote, vote, vote!

Getting you thinking

In England and Wales:

We make a valuable contribution to society – but we can't . . .

vote

Join **Votes at 16** now

For further information contact
E-mail info@votesat16.org.uk and www.votesat16.org.uk

The National Youth Agency
www.nya.org.uk

'Young Labour has listened to the excellent campaigns organised by the British Youth Council, UK Youth Parliament, the Votes at 16 Coalition and other youth organisations – Young Labour was keen to spearhead votes at 16 within the Labour Party.'

In Scotland:
You can go to war for your country, legally have sex, get married or be held responsible for a crime.

Now the Scottish Government has called for the voting age to be lowered to 16 and demanded the powers from Westminster to implement the change in Scotland.

In Jersey:
You can vote in the elections when you are 16 and 17.

1 What are the successes of the Votes at 16 campaign?
2 What changes does the Scottish Government want in its powers?
3 What else can you do at 16 that indicates that you should be able to vote?
4 Draw up a list of pros and cons for people being able to vote at 16.

Threats to democracy?

In the 2005 General Election, only 60 per cent of the **electorate** voted. The Labour Party won 55 per cent of the seats in the House of Commons with only 35 per cent of the votes. Some say that this means the United Kingdom is no longer a very democratic country.

Making your vote count

'First past the post' is the system used for general elections in the UK. People have one vote in one constituency and the candidate with the most votes in each constituency becomes the MP for that area. If you added all the votes in the country together, sometimes the winning party does not have the most votes. In each constituency, the candidate with the most votes wins, whether the majority is small or large. If the party that wins the most seats has lots of small majorities, the total vote count may be smaller than that of the opposition.

When all the constituencies in the country are taken together, the proportion of the votes each party won might not be the same as the proportion of seats each party has in the government. This also makes it hard for small parties to win any seats.

You will develop an understanding of the ways in which people might be encouraged to vote in the UK.

A new system of voting?

Proportional representation, or PR, means that every vote counts. Northern Ireland uses the single transferable vote system (STV) of PR. The constituencies are larger, so each one elects five or six people. Voters put all the candidates in order of preference, putting 1 against their favourite candidate, 2 against their second favourite, and so on. Candidates with the most votes overall win their seats in parliament.

One issue: one vote

In a referendum you vote on a particular issue, so people really feel that they can have an effect. This might encourage more people to vote because they can pick and choose the policies they agree with. It is, however, very difficult for a government to plan if referenda are held on every topic.

A Banksy graffiti

Are you persuaded?

Eddie Izzard gave just under £10,000 to Labour. Steve Lazarides, who sells work by the graffiti artist Banksy, gave them £120,000. The Tories got £25,000 from Chris Rea, whose hits include The Road to Hell and Driving Home for Christmas. Dave Whelan, the chairman of Wigan Athletic FC, gave £250,000.

What's the message?

Many people say they don't know what it's all about and parties don't seem to be very good at telling them.

Party political broadcasts are watched by a falling number of people. The proportion of the population watching them fell from 70 per cent to 50 per cent between the elections of 1997 and 2005. Perhaps short American-style election adverts might interest more voters.

The internet is developing into an influential tool for political parties. They can provide information and organise online surveys of public opinion. People might want to vote if they could join in debates and had easier access to information.

The Democratic Party used the internet to great effect in the 2008 US election. Many people put Obama's win down to the use of the internet.

Would people vote if:

- **they could vote by post?**
- **they could vote before election day?**
- **they could vote on Sunday?**
- **they could vote online?**
- **they could vote at the supermarket?**

Check your understanding

1. Why might low voter turnout be a bad thing for democracy?
2. What does 'first past the post' mean? How does it affect small parties?
3. Why might proportional representation be a fairer system than 'first past the post'?
4. Comment on the different ways of helping increase participation in elections. Do you think they would be successful? Are there any disadvantages? Give reasons.
5. Plan your own campaign to attract young voters and present it to the class.

... another point of view?

'People should be able to vote at 16.'

Do you agree with this statement? Give reasons for your opinion, showing you have considered another point of view.

Key Terms

electorate: all those registered to vote

first past the post: an electoral system where voters have one vote per constituency and the candidate with the most votes wins

postal vote: when voters make their vote by post, rather than by going to a polling station

proportional representation: an electoral system in which the number of seats a party wins is roughly proportional to its national share of the vote

Not the only way?

Getting you thinking

Azerbaijan, a country on the Caspian Sea – next door to Russia – has been run by the Haydar Aliyev and his son, Ilham, since 1993. Heydar Aliyev ruled Azerbaijan with an iron fist. His record on human rights and media freedom was often criticised in the West.

From a very early age, children in Azerbaijan learn about how Heydar Aliyev brought stability to the country and got the West to invest in the country's oil riches. All this made him very popular. Children in school even recite poems about him.

He died of a heat attack – on television.

Before he died he announced that his son Ilham was his successor. Ilham won the 2003 presidential elections by a huge majority. He was already Prime Minister and vice chairman of the national oil company. Observers were very critical of the campaign, in which they said there had been voter intimidation, violence and media bias. Demonstrations by the opposition were met with police violence. There were many arrests.

Ilham runs a country that has great oil wealth. But there is also widespread poverty, much corruption and mass unemployment.

1 What do you think it means to run a country with an 'iron fist'?

2 Why had Heydar Aliyev become very popular?

3 How democratic is Azerbaijan? Explain your answer.

4 What difficulties do people face when countries do not have democratic processes?

What a way to run a country!

Democracy is quite a new idea for most countries. In the UK it is less than 100 years since everyone has had the vote. Countries all over the world have different ways of organising their government. Some are more democratic than others. Although Azerbaijan (see Getting you thinking) has elections, there is clearly little choice for the population.

There are many countries that have elections but the ruling party takes control and ensures that it wins. Zimbabwe hit the headlines because Mr Mugabe, the president, wanted to stay in power despite everyone being aware that the population wanted the opposition to take over.

You will discover that other countries have different systems for deciding who runs the country.

The political spectrum

In a democracy, power is held by the people under a free electoral system. They have equal access to power and enjoy freedoms and liberties that are recognised by everyone.

As you have seen in recent pages, there are aspects of democracy in the UK that people challenge – from 'first past the post' voting to regional government. In general, however, the UK is accepted as a democratic country.

Dictatorship is at the other end of the scale. A dictator has total power and can make decisions about what happens in the country without consulting anyone else. There is often a group of people who support a dictator because they benefit from being part of the ruling elite.

Questions are often asked about human rights in countries ruled by a dictator. People's political freedoms are limited and opponents are often badly treated to keep them and others quiet.

There are many stages in between democracy and dictatorship. Countries that are moving towards democracy often have a mix of the two systems.

At the local level

In Southampton, New York State, voters have a big say in what goes on in their local community. At election time, they vote for the people who run the town just like we do in the UK, but they also choose the judge, the receiver of taxes, the fire chief and the people to sit on the school board. And they don't only pick people – they make decisions about other things going on in the local community, too, such as whether the new powerlines should be buried underground or on pylons as usual. At election time, there are always some questions like this to be decided.

The people of Southampton voted to bury the powerlines

... in the USA

In local elections in the USA, people select a wider range of local officials than we do in this country. In the UK, councillors are elected and people are appointed to run local services. The law is also quite separate from the political system. In the USA, the town justice is an elected post. This also happens at the national level. The President can appoint judges to the Supreme Court.

Action

Chose three countries outside the EU and western Europe and find out how democratic they are. What effects do their systems have on people living there? Are there any human rights issues in the countries you have chosen?

Check your understanding

1 What is a democracy?
2 What is a dictatorship?
3 Why do some people question the degree of democracy in the UK?
4 What drawbacks are there to a dictatorship?
5 Why do some people work hard to keep a dictator in place?
6 How is local democracy different in the UK and the USA?

... another point of view?

'Countries should be allowed to run whatever political system they want.'
Do you agree with this statement? Give reasons for your opinion, showing you have considered another point of view.

Key Terms

dictatorship: a country's leader makes all the decisions with no reference to the population

Power, politics and the media: the exam

Source A: Influence and opinion

- Most newspapers contain an opinion column arguing the point of view of its editor or, perhaps, its owner.
- Often newspapers will select and present news so that readers are encouraged to share its point of view.
- A reader's letter to a newspaper may be seen by leading politicians looking for good ideas.
- Some radio and television stations and all newspapers carry paid advertisements designed to influence those who see or hear them.
- Although the BBC is supposed to be unbiased, certain BBC programmes are said to be biased against a particular political party.

1. Use Source A and your own knowledge.
   Explain two ways in which public opinion may be influenced by what is printed in the newspapers. *(2 x 2 marks)*

   Papers usually have a point of view so they write their stories in a persuasive way, which influences readers to the same way. The Sun for example, decides which political party to support in an election then persuades its readers to vote for it.

   > You'll only get one mark if you don't use the source and your own knowledge.

   > An example always helps when you are asked to explain.

   Readers' letters often give views which are the same as the views of the paper. Politicians often read the papers carefully to see what people think. They know that Conservatives read the Daily Telegraph and the Sun whereas Labour voters read the Guardian and Mirror.

   > You might also say that the cartoons and pictures in the papers are used to make fun of the party that a paper doesn't support.

2. Use Source A and your own knowledge.
   'Television and radio are much less biased than the newspapers.' Explain two reasons why this claim might be true. *(2 x 2 marks)*

   Television and radio are more closely controlled. The BBC is meant to be unbiased because it is funded by public money and has to keep to the rules laid down for it by the government. Newspapers are owned by individuals and businesses and often follow the views of the owners, but they mustn't tell lies about people because this is libel.

   > You might also point out that people can complain to the Press Complaints Commission if they think that a newspaper is breaking the rules.

Source: Adapted from Edexcel Citizenship Studies

Leave margin blank

Source B: Privacy and the media

David Murray, aged five, yesterday joined the list of names shaping Britain's privacy laws. The son of the Harry Potter author JK Rowling and her husband, Dr Neil Murray, won a court ruling establishing that the law protects the children of celebrities from the publication of unauthorised photographs, unless their parents have exposed them to publicity.

Rowling and her husband said in a statement: 'We wanted our children to grow up, like their friends, free from intrusion into their privacy.'

Source: Adapted from The Guardian, *Thursday 8 May 2008*

Leave margin blank

3. Explain what is meant by 'intrusion into their privacy'. *(2 marks)*

It means that photos of JK Rowling's son were taken without permission when they were having a private time.

> This answer uses the source material to help answer the question. It shows that the student can apply Citizenship knowledge.

4. i. Was this a civil or criminal case? *(1 mark)*

It was civil.

4. ii. Explain the difference between civil and criminal law. *(2 marks)*

Civil law is about disputes between people or groups of people. Criminal law is about things like murder. People are prosecuted by the Crown Prosecution Service.

> A good answer. Students are often uncertain about the difference between the two.

5. JK Rowling's son might have been awarded damages. What does this mean? *(1 mark)*

He would have been given an amount of money, decided by the judge, to make up for the intrusion into his privacy.

6. Which statement is totally based on fact as opposed to being wholly or partly based on opinion. *(1 mark)*

- [ ] A. Celebrities should not complain about being photographed.
- [✓] B. A photograph of JK Rowling's son was printed in a newspaper.
- [ ] C. If celebrities want media attention, they should expect to be photographed on all occasions.
- [ ] D. The law should protect people from the media.

> Understanding the difference between fact and opinion is important in all aspects of Citizenship.

Extended writing

'More people would vote in general elections if 16-year-olds were given the vote.'

Do you agree with this statement?

Give reasons for your opinion, showing that you have considered another point of view.

You could include the following points in your answer and other information of your own.

- Why is it important to increase the number of voters at elections?
- What reasons affect whether people turn out to vote?
- Do 16-year-olds have enough experience and responsibility to vote?
- How important is having the vote in a democratic society?

(12 marks)

Source: Sample exam, Edexcel Citizenship Studies 2009

I think more people would vote in general elections if 16-year-olds were given the vote but some people say that they don't have the experience to make such an important decision.

> A good start. If you don't make it clear that you have considered another point of view, you can't get more than half marks.

The number of people voting in elections is falling so we need to do things that help people to vote. Voting at 16 is one way of doing this.

> The student is using the bullets to build an argument. Remember you need to build the points into your argument – not just answer the questions. The bullets are aimed to help!

If people don't vote, they don't have their say, then they complain about what the government does. If people don't vote, the country isn't very democratic and laws might not be respected.

> The student is making the links between the question and Citizenship knowledge.

People don't bother to vote for all sorts of reasons. Some people say they don't know enough about it and others don't care. Sometimes people feel that it won't make any difference and they have lost respect for politicians. They might be away and don't bother to get a postal vote. Voting at 16 might persuade more people to vote because they know more about politics.

> The student is making it clear that they are using the bullets to help answer the question.

At 16 you can do all sorts of things including joining the army, get married and pay taxes but you can't vote. I don't see why I should have to pay taxes when I can't have my say in an election.

> The student is using examples that support the argument.

It might make more young people responsible when they realise that their voice counts. When you have learnt all about it in school you lose interest by the time you are 18 and can vote. Even some 16-year-olds say they don't know enough but they know lots more than many older people.

> The other point of view is built into the argument. It is explained and an alternative perspective is there too.

People fought very hard for us all to have a vote. The suffragettes went on hunger strike and one even threw herself under the King's horse at the races. We should take our vote seriously whatever age we are. The government makes laws that affect us but we have no say – so it's not very democratic. No one asked us if we wanted to stay at school until we are 17.

> This paragraph has a mix of Citizenship knowledge – about the struggle for the vote and some up-to-date knowledge about laws the government has passed. It really shows a great understanding of the issue.

The voting age must be lowered to 16. I don't want people making rules that affect me when I don't have any say. I can work things out for myself and make up my own mind.

Unit 1: theme 3

The global

3.1 Achieving sustainability   98–103

What is sustainable development?   98   Setting standards for
                                         sustainability?   102
Local solutions to global problems 100

3.2 The economy at work   104–15

What is an economy?   104   When prices rise – or fall   110

Who does what?   106   Making ends meet   112

Success or failure   108   Balancing the budget   114

3.3 People's impact on the community   116–19

Making a difference   116   Working together   118

community

3.4 The UK's role in the world   120–7

What does the European   120   The Commonwealth   124
Union do?
                                        The United Nations   126
Citizens of Europe   122

3.5 Challenges facing the global community   128–41

Can the world be fairer?   128   We all share the same air   136

Globalisation: the challenges   130   Transport crisis?   138

Sweet shops and sweatshops   132   Global crisis – global action. 140

The rights and wrongs of protest 134

3.6 The UN, the EU and human rights   142–7

The UN at work   142   Protecting human rights   146

International justice   144

The global community: the exam   148–51

What is sustainable development?

Getting you thinking

Farmers need to fertilise fields to keep yields up. Fertilisers can damage the environment

1 What land, energy and resources are being used in each of these activities?

2 Look at each image and make a list of the costs to the environment of each activity.

3 What will happen if we continue to increase the number of holidays we take by plane or the miles we drive?

4 Fertilising fields means more can be produced – so food is cheaper. Make a list of the advantages and disadvantages of doing this.

5 Why is it important to think about the effect of our actions on the environment?

6 Why can it be difficult to decide how to limit environmental damage?

Hard choices

Imagine you live in a very poor country, in a small rural village. You need fuel to cook food for your family. You may also need fuel to boil your drinking water to stop your children getting sick. The only way to get this fuel is to cut down the trees near your village. But you know that, if you do this, the precious topsoil will blow away and eventually the desert will swallow up your village.

The villagers have to make the hard choice between solving a problem they have now and not making problems for the future. This kind of choice has to be made by everybody, although the circumstances are different everywhere.

In the UK and other **MEDCs** where there is economic growth, people expect their standard of living to improve. People can buy all sorts of things to make life more comfortable. They usually work shorter hours than people in **LEDCs** and have better access to healthcare and education.

These can all be good things but there are some drawbacks.

Growing food and building homes, roads, schools and hospitals uses land, energy and resources. The demand for products and services can mean pollution increases, and natural resources are used up. In time, these factors could actually decrease the standard of living. So the choice is between having what we want now and making sure future generations don't suffer.

You will find out about sustainable development and consider ways in which it can be achieved.

Sustainable development

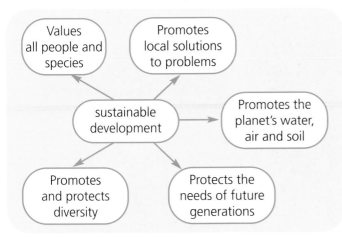

Sustainable development means we can improve the way people live today without harming the prospects for the future. Different resources can be used so that scarce or dangerous materials are no longer needed. New materials can be designed to use less energy. Standards of living can be improved in ways that protect the environment, and harmful products can stop being made.

Sustainable solutions

There are many issues and many solutions in the search for sustainability. You will find more examples from a global perspective on pages 128–141.

Action

Organisations such as Comic Relief, Oxfam, Christian Aid, Action Aid and many more sponsor sustainable development projects. Research the work of one or more of these organisations and identify two to three problems they have addressed, and the solutions they and their local partners employed.

Check your understanding

1 In your own words, explain what is meant by 'sustainable development'.
2 Give one reason why it will be important in future to find sustainable solutions to environmental problems.
3 Why are the following considered to be sustainable developments?
   • digging wells • building schools • planting trees
4 Can wind power be described as a sustainable energy source? Give reasons.
5 Why has commercial fishing in the North Sea been restricted?

Energy

As supplies of coal, oil and natural gas are limited, they will only sustain our needs for so long before we will be forced to find alternative, sustainable sources of energy.

One solution could be wind power. The UK already has many wind farms, mostly in Wales, Scotland and Cornwall. The amount of the world's electricity generated by wind power has grown five times so far this decade. Offshore wind farms could, in theory, produce twice the UK's electricity requirements.

Food

For decades, large UK and European fishing fleets have fished in the North Sea. In recent years it became clear that fish stocks there were so low that there was a real danger the North Sea would be fished out. Over-fishing had not allowed enough time for fish to breed and stocks to recover. Now fishing here is strictly controlled. Stocks are starting to recover and are a sustainable resource for the future.

Resources

Similarly, if you cut down forests for timber and paper faster than nature can replace them, you will end up with no trees. However, trees are a **renewable** resource. Many countries now plant fast-growing trees to replace those chopped down. You now often see goods labelled: 'Made from timber from a sustainable forest'.

... another point of view?

'We should pay higher taxes on energy from non-sustainable sources.'

Do you agree with this statement? Give reasons for your opinion, showing you have considered another point of view.

Key Terms

economic growth: this happens when the country produces more goods and services from year to year

LEDC: a less economically developed country

MEDC: a more economically developed country

renewable: able to be replaced or restored

sustainable development: living now in a way that doesn't damage the needs of future generations

Local solutions to global problems

Getting you thinking

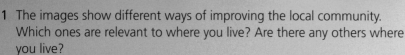

1 The images show different ways of improving the local community. Which ones are relevant to where you live? Are there any others where you live?

2 Why might the list be different in different communities?

3 Do you think the list will change over time?

4 Has your school been involved in improving the environment in any of these ways – or others? Is so, explain how.

Is Agenda 21 the answer?

At the United Nation's 'Earth Summit' in Rio de Janeiro in 1992, member countries agreed to work together to promote sustainable development around the world. **Local Agenda 21** (LA21) sets out how this is to be done at a local level. Although LA21 is a 'global' plan, it stresses the importance of involving local people when planning projects. They should be asked what they want for their local area. Local people often have valuable knowledge and experience, and are more likely to support a project if they feel they 'own' it. All LA21 projects should provide for the needs of the local community as a whole, and not exclude or discriminate against any group or minority.

Since 1992, local councils in the UK have been working with local people on a wide range of projects. These are some of the long-term aims of the LA21 projects.

Chicago, USA

Rooftop gardens in the heart of Chicago will improve the air quality in the city because the plants absorb carbon dioxide and produce oxygen. The gardens will keep the sun's heat off the buildings, making them cooler, and will cut down the energy needed for air conditioning. The gardens also encourage birds to nest in the heart of the city.

You will find out about Local Agenda 21.

Surrey County Council promotes walking buses

Schools are encouraged to organise walking buses for children who live less than a mile away. The walking buses:

- improve the children's health through exercise
- make them more alert in class
- increase their awareness of the local environment
- are a valuable social opportunity
- prepare them for independence as they grow older
- reduce traffic outside schools.

Want to know how much energy your electrical equipment uses?

Woking LA21 group has bought 20 energy meters for measuring the electricity consumption of household appliances. These can be borrowed from the group, who then keep records of the results submitted to show how efficient electrical products are. Some items are much more efficient than others and some are still using power when they seem to be turned off.

Saving energy in Sandanski, Bulgaria

- Energy efficient street lighting – replacement of old, inefficient lamps with new energy efficient ones
- Solar installations for hot water in four small hotels and 30 residential buildings
- Installation of six hydro-electric power plants

Action

Find out if your local council is promoting LA21 projects. For example, are they trying to reduce traffic congestion, pollution and noise? Are they introducing traffic calming schemes or trying to make streets safer for children and older residents?

Check your understanding

1. In your own words, what is the main aim of Local Agenda 21?
2. Which of the LA21 aims do you think is the most important for your local area? Give reasons.
3. Do the LA21 projects above offer sustainable solutions? Explain your answers.

... another point of view?

'Local solutions are likely to be more successful than global solutions.'

Do you agree with this statement? Give reasons for your opinion, showing you have considered another point of view.

Key Terms

Local Agenda 21: a global plan to ask local people how they think their immediate environment could be improved

Setting standards for sustainability?

Getting you thinking

The European Union leaders said

'We will maintain our targets and timetable for tackling climate change, despite objections from some nations.'

Some countries have threatened to block a deal agreed last year for EU-wide cuts in greenhouse gas emissions. Some Eastern and central European countries are unhappy at the burden of cuts they will be expected to bear under the existing climate agreement.

Government's climate change targets for 2050 come into force

By 2050 the UK aims to decide emissions of CO_2 by 60 per cent. The government is to publish carbon budgets annually from 2008, with advice from the Committee on Climate Change. The committee will advise on issues involving domestic emission and potential changes to the 2050 reduction targets.

The independent Climate Change Committee's advice to the government is that the UK should set a 2050 target of cutting greenhouse gas emissions by at least 80 per cent including the emissions from aviation and transport, which were previously excluded.

The US president said

'We will establish strong annual targets that set us on a course to reduce emissions to their 1990 levels by 2020 and reduce them by an additional 80 percent by 2050.'

1 Why do people want to reduce carbon emissions?
2 Which governments are in agreement?
3 Why do you think some disagree?
4 Does everyone think the targets are strong enough?

Policies for sustainability

It is increasingly recognised that we live in an unsustainable way. We are damaging the environment and are unlikely to leave it unharmed for future generations.

Sustainability is about more than the environment. The United Nations, to which most countries of the world belong (see page 127), set millennium targets to improve sustainability. If people are fit, healthy and well educated, they are more likely to look after their environment and are not desperate to scratch a living in damaging ways.

Practices for sustainability

If the UK is to achieve sustainability, all parts of society must work together to manage resources more effectively. The UN therefore offers advice and support for all these groups.

Businesses need to think about ways to become more sustainable.

Prevent extreme poverty and hunger

Achieve universal primary education

Promote gender equality and empower women

Reduce child mortality

UN's Millennium Goals

Improve maternal health

Combat HIV/AIDS, malaria and other diseases

Ensure environmental sustainability

Develop a global partnership for development

You will find out about the changes that will need to take place if the UK is to be sustainable.

Create better products and services

A cool belt made from recycled bicycle inner tube

A USB stick made from recycled newspaper

Use resources more efficiently

Boots:

- introduced a new free-standing display unit which could be moved about as needed and could be reused more flexibly
- introduced plastic bottles with 30 per cent recycled content
- installed baling machines in its warehouses to organise the waste packaging.

These changes not only helped the environment but also saved the business money.

Persuade customers to shop more sustainably

- Businesses show customers how energy efficient their products are by providing them with information
- BSkyB will not promote or sell set top boxes that waste energy

Is it working?

Despite all the efforts governments and other organisations are making to encourage people and businesses to become more aware of the need to behave sustainably, few countries are on schedule to meet the targets. Most will miss the renewable energy target, the rational use of energy, and clean energy for transport.

Action

The UN advises that, in order to achieve the Millennium Goals, people and organisations should:

- campaign and mobilise people through advocacy
- share the best strategies for meeting the goals
- monitor and report progress towards the goals
- support governments in tailoring the goals to local circumstances and challenges.

Explain why they give this advice. You can find out more at http://www. undp.org/mdg/

Check your understanding

1 Why is the UK not sustainable?
2 Why is sustainability about more than the environment?
3 Explain how each of the Millennium Goals helps to make the world more sustainable.
4 How can businesses help to improve sustainability? What advantages can there be for businesses?

... another point of view?

'It's all the government's responsibility. If people and businesses won't be responsible, the government should pass laws to make them behave differently.'

Do you agree with this statement? Give reasons for your opinion, showing you have considered another point of view.

What is an economy?

Getting you thinking

1. How many of these people provide a product or service that we might buy or use?
2. List those products or services that you think are supplied by the council or government.
3. Do any of the people provide goods or services without getting paid?
4. How many are consumers of goods and services?
5. Make as many links as you can between these people.
6. Which of the people or services do you think might need more financial support?

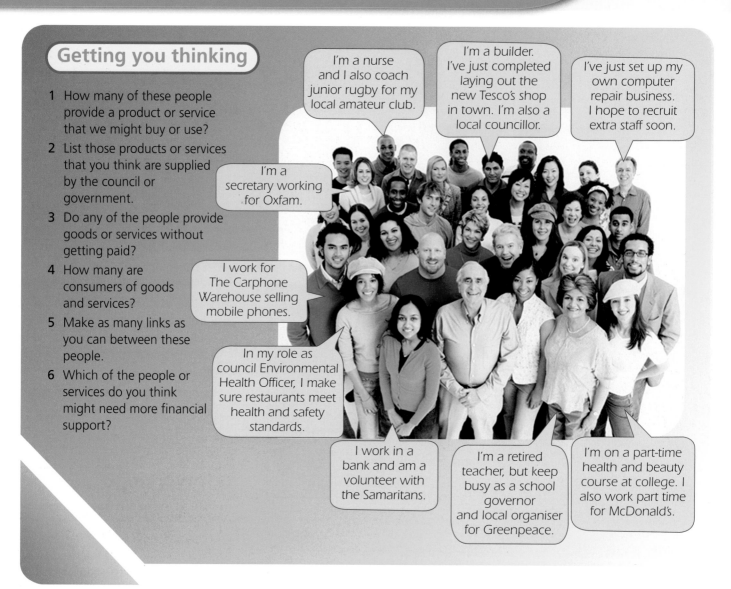

I'm a nurse and I also coach junior rugby for my local amateur club.

I'm a builder. I've just completed laying out the new Tesco's shop in town. I'm also a local councillor.

I've just set up my own computer repair business. I hope to recruit extra staff soon.

I'm a secretary working for Oxfam.

I work for The Carphone Warehouse selling mobile phones.

In my role as council Environmental Health Officer, I make sure restaurants meet health and safety standards.

I work in a bank and am a volunteer with the Samaritans.

I'm a retired teacher, but keep busy as a school governor and local organiser for Greenpeace.

I'm on a part-time health and beauty course at college. I also work part time for McDonald's.

What is an economy?

Everyone in the United Kingdom is part of the **economy** as a consumer, producer or citizen.

We are all consumers: whatever our age, we buy the products of businesses.

Some of us are producers who help make products or provide services. That includes the part-time employee for McDonald's, as well as the secretary working for Oxfam.

The economy is measured by adding up either the value of everything produced or the value of every-thing consumed in one year. Both calculations should come to the same amount. For the UK, in 2007 this figure reached over £1,400 billion. This works out at over £23,000 per person.

Private and public sector

Most of the things we buy are made by businesses in the **private sector**. These businesses are run by individuals or **shareholders**. A shareholder owns part of the company but leaves the organisation to its managers.

The main objective of businesses in the private sector is to make a **profit** for their owners, but the private sector also includes charities that raise money for good causes.

The rest of the economy is owned or run by the government and local councils. This is called the **public sector**. It includes social services, fire and police, education, defence, law, community and sports centres, housing and transport. Some of these services are contracted out to companies that want to make a profit. A key objective for the public sector is to satisfy local residents. If it fails to do so, the political party that controls the council may not be re-elected at the next election.

You will find out what we mean by the economy.

The power of competition

The economy is fired by people wanting to buy things. Businesses will provide these things if there is a profit to be made. If consumers buy less of a product, less will be produced. The resources that were used to make it may be used by another business for another purpose. Many food shops in town centres closed because people use out-of-town supermarkets. The empty shops, the resources, are now used by other businesses, such as mobile phone shops. Food shops are also coming back into town as small convenience stores. Businesses want to make a profit and will look for new opportunities.

What would happen if everyone had to pay for healthcare?

What effect does competition have on business?

Is it fair?

People who don't have enough money to pay for things they need and want aren't able to have them.

If everything was provided by the private sector, many people would suffer. If you can't afford education and are in poor health, it can be difficult to find a job and do the things other people do.

As a result, the government provides these public sector services and other social benefits. Some are free for all, while others are provided according to need. We pay taxes to cover the costs of these and other services.

Action

Do a survey of ten people you know to find out how they contribute to our economy. You could ask whether they produce goods or services. Do they work in the private or public sector? What have been their major purchases over the past year?

... another point of view?

'Taxes are just a burden. They should be as low as possible.'

Do you agree with this statement? Give reasons for your opinion, showing you have considered another point of view.

Check your understanding

1. How can you work out what the economy is worth in a year?
2. What makes up the economy?
3. What is the difference between the private sector and the public sector?
4. Why do we need the public sector?
5. Why do the government and local councils collect taxes?
6. What effect does it have when supermarkets move back into the high street?

Key Terms

economy: this is made up of all the organisations that provide goods and services, and all the individuals and organisations that buy them

private sector: this section of the economy is made up of businesses or organisations that are owned by individuals or by shareholders

profit: the money that you gain when you sell something for more than you paid for it or than it cost to make it

public sector: this is made up of organisations owned or run by the government and local councils

shareholder: someone who owns part of a business by owning shares in a company

Who does what?

Getting you thinking

Larkhill high street

1 How many businesses are shown on the map?

2 Which businesses either support or depend on others?

3 Some businesses are similar, which means they are in competition with each other. Which businesses are these?

4 Estimate how many employees you think this high street has.

5 Which parts of the high street might the council be involved in?

6 How is Larkhill similar to and different from your local high street?

Small businesses

In order to survive, businesses need to make a profit. This means their income from sales must be more than the money they spend on things such as wages, rent and buying stock. These payments are called costs. A business makes a loss if more money is spent running it than it receives from its customers. If a business keeps making losses, it will collapse.

Many businesses need each other. Jill's Newsagents (see map above) needs suppliers to provide the shop with stock. If the suppliers fail to deliver the newspapers on time, Jill will not be able to provide what the customers want, and Jill's Newsagents will lose business. Businesses that produce newspapers depend on newsagents because they sell their stock. The two businesses are interdependent.

Many of Larkhill's businesses are probably run by one person. This is fine for small businesses but bigger businesses, like the bank, are usually companies that are owned by many shareholders.

Interdependency

Many businesses are dependent on each other. Here are a few of the links between Larkhill's businesses:

- The bus company allows customers to travel to Larkhill.

- The local bank allows customers to take out loans and pay in cash from their sales.

- Suppliers of local and national newspapers, magazines and confectionery provide stock.

- The local window-cleaner cleans the shop windows every week.

- Electricity suppliers provide power to all the shops and offices.

You will discover how people and resources are organised to produce goods and services, and that businesses are interdependent.

Specialisation

There are many different jobs involved in making a product. The flow-chart shows how a newspaper reaches the customers.

Each stage needs different types of people to do different jobs: the printers know how to print and the designer is an expert in design. The distributors need drivers and the newsagents have close contact with their customers who want to buy the paper. All the people and businesses involved are **specialised** in the type of work they do.

Journalists, photographers, editors, advertising staff, designers and others put the paper together

The papers are printed on an automated press

They are delivered by van to the newsagent

The newsagent sells the papers to the public

Action

1 Choose a small shopping area or industrial estate near you and make a simple map of the businesses there.
2 Show how one of the businesses uses division of labour and/or specialisation to be more efficient.

Check your understanding

1 Choose a small business in your local area and list as many of its links as you can.
2 Why do you think you have specialist teachers in your secondary school, but a class teacher in your primary school?
3 What different types of non-teaching jobs are there in your school?
4 Why would your school be less well run if your teachers had to carry out all the tasks currently done by non-teachers?
5 How does the division of labour work in a restaurant? How does it help the business to be more efficient?

... another point of view?

'People would be happier if they were responsible for making the whole product rather than just part of it.'

Do you agree with this statement? Give reasons for your opinion, showing you have considered another point of view.

Division of labour

If one person did all the jobs needed to sell newspapers, they would have to write the articles, design the pages, print the paper, take it to a shop and sell it. The newspaper would take far too long to produce and it would be of low quality. It's much quicker and more efficient in terms of cost and quality if each stage is carried out by people who are expert in their field. This is known as **division of labour**. It works in many parts of the economy and means that the country produces more and makes us better off.

Key Terms

division of labour: where employees concentrate on a particular task or job at which they are expert

interdependent: where businesses need each other to survive

specialised: where employees or businesses concentrate on tasks they can do well

Success or failure

Getting you thinking

1 In what ways can the business claim to be successful?

2 How might The Carphone Warehouse be contributing to the economy?

3 Why do you think The Carphone Warehouse takes its customers seriously?

4 What evidence is there to suggest that The Carphone Warehouse could be a good employer?

5 Why is it important to look after staff and customers?

6 What evidence is there that The Carphone Warehouse helps the community?

The Carphone Warehouse started trading in 1989. It now has over 2,400 stores in nine countries, and employs over 21,000 people. Its profit is over £124 million. The Carphone Warehouse also actively supports charity work.

- If we don't look after the customer, someone else will.
- Nothing is gained by winning an argument but losing a customer.
- Always deliver what we promise. If in doubt, under promise and over deliver.
- Always treat customers as we ourselves would like to be treated.
- The reputation of the whole company is in the hands of each individual.

The company helps Get Connected, a helpline for children and young people under 25 who are, for whatever reason, vulnerable to danger. The charity's HQ is based at the company's offices.

We want all our people to enjoy working at The Carphone Warehouse. Parties, family days out and an annual ball are a feature of life here. We have our own Events Club, with everything from paint-balling and go-karting to concert and theatre trips.

Going for growth

At The Carphone Warehouse, success comes from the growing market for mobile phones and from providing good customer service. The mobile phone business is very competitive, so The Carphone Warehouse has to invest in new buildings and equipment so that they keep ahead of competitors. It also needs to employ, train and motivate the staff.

Supporting individuals

Employees are paid and many receive training to develop their skills. Individuals will be able to use, or transfer, skills such as good customer service to a new job.

Supporting communities

Employees will help local businesses by spending money in local shops, pubs and restaurants. Businesses pay taxes from their profits and people pay taxes from their earnings. They also pay tax when they buy things. These taxes provide the government and councils with money that can be used in the community.

Supporting the wider community

A growing business helps to create or support jobs in other businesses. These jobs may be in the local community, but others might be further away. A growing business will do things like:

- communicate more
- use more energy and water
- buy extra equipment such as computers
- buy more materials from suppliers
- buy more services from other businesses.

All these contributions help the country's economy to grow. Successful businesses often create jobs and pay more taxes, so people benefit.

Markets moving on

Businesses and industries come and go. The motor industry is a prime example. In the 1970s almost 2 million cars a year were made in the UK. By the beginning of the 1980s, this had fallen to below 1 million. It has risen again to about

You will understand the consequences of success and failure of businesses on individuals, communities and beyond.

1.5 million – but the industry is very different. Instead of factories full of people, they are now full of machinery and robots. In the Longbridge area of Birmingham, for example, almost all the population worked in the car industry. The factory is long since gone and people have had to retrain and find other jobs.

Markets failing communities

When markets move on, people may lose their jobs. Some of the businesses that supported the declining industry close down. Local shops and traders lose out because people have less money to spend.

Those employees made redundant may have the wrong skills for new types of business. New businesses won't start up in areas where people don't have skills they need, or where other businesses are failing.

The market is said to have failed a community when unemployment is much higher than in other parts of the country.

Action

Find out about:
- a business in your area that helps the community
- businesses that have closed down: can you work out why?
- new businesses that have moved in: can you work out why?

Check your understanding

1. How can employees benefit from working for a business?
2. How might growing businesses create jobs both in the local community and beyond?
3. In what other ways can businesses help the community?
4. How do businesses and their employees provide money for local services?
5. What knock-on effects might there be when a big employer in a local community closes down?
6. How might the government reduce the impact of a big employer closing down?
7. What would happen if more businesses were closing down than expanding in the country?

... another point of view?

'Businesses just want to make a profit.'
Do you agree with this statement? Give reasons for your opinion, showing you have considered another point of view.

Economic decline and growth

It is natural for some businesses to grow and others to decline. The market system brings about a shift of resources towards making things that are most in demand. The economy will grow if the value of the new sales of the expanding businesses is greater than the value lost from declining businesses. If it is the other way round, however, the economy is declining.

Where this happens, the government needs to step in to help. By introducing **retraining** schemes and investing in roads and other communications, it can make areas where lots of people are unemployed more attractive to new businesses.

Key Terms

retraining: learning new skills that can be used in a different job

When prices rise – or fall

Getting you thinking

The changing value of money

£1,000 in 1971 would buy as much as £10,670 in 2008

£1,000 in 1981 would buy as much as £2,950 in 2008

£1,000 in 1991 would buy as much as £1,560 in 2008

1 What happens to the value of money over time?

2 If a small car cost £1,000 in 1971, what might you expect to pay for it today?

3 What do people expect to happen to their pay?

Why do prices change?

Inflation happens when things we buy get more expensive as time passes. Sometimes prices fall, and this is known as **deflation**. Inflation often happens because people want to spend more. Deflation occurs because people spend less. The diagram shows how inflation occurs. In fact it's one big circle:

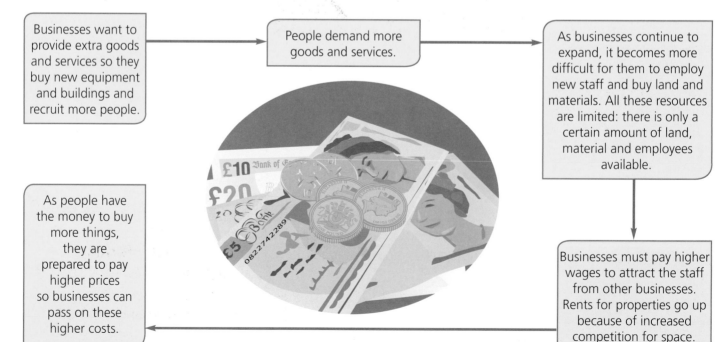

> Businesses want to provide extra goods and services so they buy new equipment and buildings and recruit more people.

> People demand more goods and services.

> As businesses continue to expand, it becomes more difficult for them to employ new staff and buy land and materials. All these resources are limited: there is only a certain amount of land, material and employees available.

> As people have the money to buy more things, they are prepared to pay higher prices so businesses can pass on these higher costs.

> Businesses must pay higher wages to attract the staff from other businesses. Rents for properties go up because of increased competition for space.

You will find out what causes inflation, the problems caused by changing prices and ways prices can be controlled.

Who is affected by changing prices?

When prices rise:

- People with savings lose out because their savings will not buy so much in the future.
- People with incomes that do not grow at the **rate of inflation** will also lose out. Some pensions are not linked to the inflation rate, so their value falls when prices rise.
- UK businesses can also lose out if inflation in other countries is at a lower rate. The price rises make our products and services more expensive to buy.
- Borrowers will gain because the value of their debt will fall.

When prices fall:

- Savers gain because their money goes further.
- Borrowers lose because they have to repay money that is now worth less.

Can it go too far?

A little bit of inflation (about 2 per cent each year) doesn't do any harm. However, if prices rise too fast, businesses start losing money because people stop buying their products. To stay in business, companies cut their costs by making people redundant. This may keep the business going, but unemployment will rise.

When prices fall because people are buying less, the economy shrinks and businesses find it difficult to keep going because they can't sell enough. Eventually businesses close down and unemployment rises.

The government has to work hard to keep the economy on track – often with a little bit of inflation.

If pensions don't increase at the same rate as inflation, pensioners can suffer

What can be done to control inflation?

Prices can be controlled in three ways:

- **Change interest rates**

  Every month, the Bank of England decides whether to change interest rates or keep them the same. If the Bank believes inflation will increase, it raises interest rates. The cost of borrowing will increase so people will buy less.

- **Make sure there are enough staff**

  A shortage of trained people makes wages go up. One way of reducing inflation is to make sure that there are plenty of people with the right skills. The government can provide training courses and help businesses train their staff.

- **Keep business costs down**

  In order to remain competitive, businesses will try to reduce their costs. They need to reduce their costs by keeping their payments for materials, land and staff as low as possible. They may need to reorganise so they are making their products as efficiently as possible. They will want to keep prices down to attract consumers.

Check your understanding

1. In your own words, explain what inflation is.
2. Explain what happens when prices fall.
3. Name two things that can cause inflation. Explain why these things can lead to an increase in prices.
4. How might inflation affect someone who:

   a) is saving money?

   b) has a pension that is not linked to inflation?

   c) has trained in an area of work where there is a skills shortage, such as computer programming?

   d) is working in a business that is losing money and who doesn't have any specialist skills?
5. What can businesses do to help keep inflation rates down?

Action

What is happening to prices at the moment? Is the level of inflation seen to be good for the country? You could look at www.treasury.gov.uk.

Key Terms

deflation: the general fall in prices

inflation: the general rise in prices

rate of inflation: the rate at which prices rise

Making ends meet

Getting you thinking

Borrowing

We took out a £200,000 mortgage. This is three times my partner's and my joint salaries. The value of the house has fallen too. Our daughter has taken out a student loan to go to university. I took out a loan to buy a new car. This summer we went to Florida using our credit cards.

I own four properties and rent the rooms to students. The rent, after taking away costs, gives me an income of £47,000 over the year. I also own shares in several companies and I earned £3,000 from them this year. I earn £50,000 a year from my job. I'm going to take out another mortgage and buy another property.

My work is looking after my three children and making ends meet. I'm a single parent. The £145 I get from benefits doesn't cover my food and bills. I'm already behind in my rent and have had to borrow from the local moneylender. If I don't pay it back, he will take my furniture. I've had to take on evening cleaning work, earning £30 a week, with my sister baby-sitting my children.

1 How much income does each person receive?
2 Rank the people according to how much they earn.
3 Who is finding it most difficult to manage their money?
4 What is borrowing?
5 Who have these people borrowed money from? How do they repay it?
6 What risks is each individual taking?

Spending or saving?

People use the money they earn each month to buy products and services. If they have some money left when they have bought everything they need, they can save.

If they spend more than they earn, they will have to borrow money or use their savings.

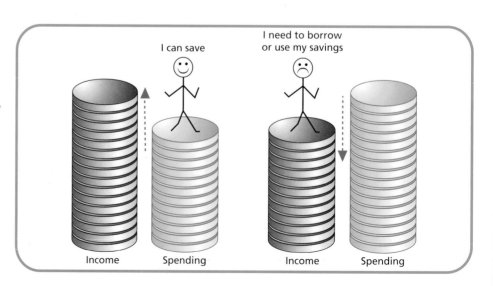

I can save

I need to borrow or use my savings

Income   Spending   Income   Spending

112

You will find out why borrowing money can cause problems and how people can be protected from poverty.

Is borrowing the solution?

If you want to borrow money, you must find someone to lend it. You will pay **interest** on the loan. This is an amount of money paid in addition to the amount borrowed, so everything you buy on credit will cost more in the end. It is only safe to borrow money if you know you can pay it back.

People with low incomes and low skills will find it hard to borrow because it will be difficult for them to repay the loan. They may be below the **poverty line** and at risk of being economically excluded from society. This means that they don't have enough money to pay for the goods and services they need, such as housing, food and heating. Children in these situations can never have a birthday party or go to the cinema, so they really feel left out.

In Britain:

- about 18 per cent of the population is living below the poverty line
- in more than one in six families, nobody works
- 35 per cent of families have no savings
- the bottom 20 per cent earn 8 per cent of all earnings
- the top 20 per cent earn 42 per cent of all earnings.

Fairer shares

The government uses some of the money it raises from taxes to help the poor. It provides benefits, free healthcare and education for all, and subsidised housing. People who earn more pay more taxes. Poorer people receive more help. This is called **redistributing income**.

Providing real opportunities

The government doesn't want people to depend on benefits all the time. It wants them to be able to support themselves and become an active part of the economy. The government trains people in different skills and encourages them to find work.

> Unemployed lose benefits if they refuse training

> Mums back to work when kids turn one

> Reading, writing and computer classes to be compulsory for the unemployed

1 What is the government trying to achieve with these policies?
2 What advantages do these policies have for the economy?
3 What difficulties might they cause for individuals?
4 What do you think government policy should be in this area? Explain your answer.

Action

Discussion point: Do you think it could be a problem for the whole of society if some people are economically excluded?

Check your understanding

1 Why do people borrow?
2 What problems can result from borrowing?
3 What does being economically excluded from society mean?
4 The government receives money from taxes. How does it use it to help the poor?
5 Why does the government run schemes to retrain people in new skills?

... another point of view?

'Redistributing income is so unfair. I work hard for my money: why should I help pay for people who don't work?'

Do you agree with this statement? Give reasons for your opinion, showing you have considered another point of view.

Key Terms

interest: extra payment made to a lender by someone who has borrowed money

poverty line: the income level below which someone cannot afford to live

redistributing income: taking money from wealthier people through taxation, to give it to poorer people through benefits

Balancing the budget

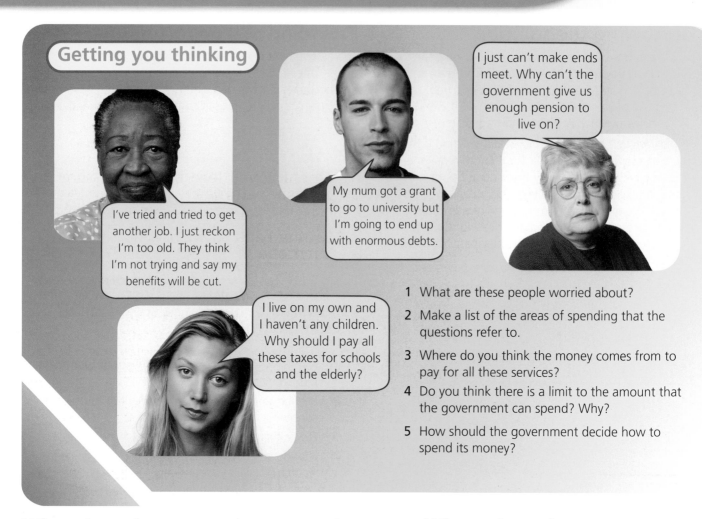

I've tried and tried to get another job. I just reckon I'm too old. They think I'm not trying and say my benefits will be cut.

My mum got a grant to go to university but I'm going to end up with enormous debts.

I just can't make ends meet. Why can't the government give us enough pension to live on?

I live on my own and I haven't any children. Why should I pay all these taxes for schools and the elderly?

1 What are these people worried about?

2 Make a list of the areas of spending that the questions refer to.

3 Where do you think the money comes from to pay for all these services?

4 Do you think there is a limit to the amount that the government can spend? Why?

5 How should the government decide how to spend its money?

What does the government spend?

The government spends its money on a wide range of services. The pie chart below shows the main areas of spending and the proportion spent on each area. The way it is divided up varies a little from year to year but the overall picture stays much the same.

Where does the money come from?

If the government is to provide these services, it needs to raise money to pay for them. The money, or **government revenue**, comes from taxation or borrowing, as the pie chart below shows.

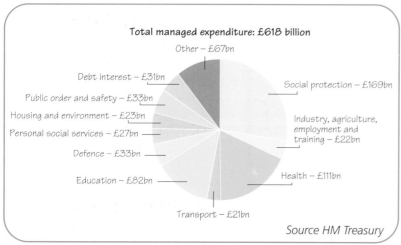

Total managed expenditure: £618 billion

Other – £67bn
Debt interest – £31bn
Public order and safety – £33bn
Housing and environment – £23bn
Personal social services – £27bn
Defence – £33bn
Education – £82bn
Transport – £21bn
Social protection – £169bn
Industry, agriculture, employment and training – £22bn
Health – £111bn

Source HM Treasury

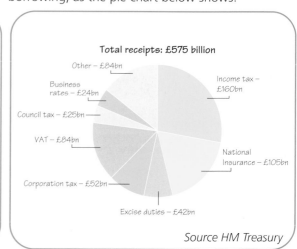

Total receipts: £575 billion

Other – £84bn
Business rates – £24bn
Council tax – £25bn
VAT – £84bn
Corporation tax – £52bn
Excise duties – £42bn
Income tax – £160bn
National Insurance – £105bn

Source HM Treasury

You will find out that the government has to make choices when it spends the money it raises in taxes.

What taxes?

Corporation tax is paid on the profits of all businesses.

National insurance is a tax on income. People often think it pays for pensions and benefits but it just goes into the pot with the other taxes.

Excise duties are charged on a range of items, many of which are not very good for you if you have too much of them. These include alcohol and cigarettes.

Income tax is not paid by people who earn very little, but as your income rises you pay more tax. It is worked out as a percentage of your earnings. People on high incomes pay a higher percentage of their earnings in income tax.

Value added tax (VAT) is paid on almost everything we buy apart from food, children's clothes, books and newspapers. The amount paid is a percentage of the total value of the products.

Other taxes include those on cars and petrol. These allow governments to tax particular items to raise money or to try to reduce the amount we buy. Some taxes are raised in local areas. These include council tax and business rates.

Making ends meet

The decisions on taxes and spending happen each year in the **Budget**. The **Chancellor of the Exchequer** is responsible for deciding where the money comes from and how it is spent. The Chancellor works with government departments to decide what is needed and what must come first. It can be difficult to get the right balance, because often every department will want to spend more.

Just like everyone else, if the government wants to spend more than its income, it has to borrow money. When it borrows, it has to pay interest to the people who lend it the money.

Over the years, there has been a steady increase in the amount that governments spend. At the moment, it amounts to about £10,000 per person, per year. People's voting decisions often depend on what the political parties say they will do about taxes and spending if they win the election.

... another point of view?

'If the NHS wants more money, it should get it.'

Do you agree with this statement? Give reasons for your opinion, showing you have considered another point of view.

Action

The Treasury is the government department responsible for the Budget. Look at its website at www.treasury.gov.uk to find out how the government raises and spends its money. Click on the 'Budget' heading on the site. You will find a summary document that explains the government's spending decisions.

Check your understanding

1 What does the Chancellor of the Exchequer do? Why can this work be difficult?
2 Explain the different types of taxation that the government uses to raise money.
3 What has been happening to the amount of government spending over the years?
4 Why might government spending influence the way people vote?

Key Terms

Budget: the process each year when the Chancellor of the Exchequer explains how the government will raise and spend its money

Chancellor of the Exchequer: the member of the government who is responsible for the country's finances

government revenue: the money raised by the government

Making a difference

Getting you thinking

SMASH stands for Swindon Mentoring And Self Help. It aims to support vulnerable young people who need help achieving their full social, emotional, health and educational potential. The overall aim of the project is to increase their potential for achievement in the future.

The charity depends on **volunteers** who want to give something back to the community. SMASH matches a volunteer to an individual they get on with and who has similar interests. They commit to meeting once a week for a year. It works well because the mentors are not officials or family, so it's often easier to talk.

All sorts of problems

Trouble with the police?

Problems at home?

Problems with their friends?

Problems with confidence or anger management?

Trouble at school?

Maybe you just need someone you can talk to.

1 What sort of organisation is SMASH?

2 Why might young people want help?

3 How are the mentors making a difference to their community?

4 Why is it important to help these young people?

5 Why do you think people become mentors?

6 Why do you think communities benefit from the help of volunteers?

Taking action

The people who set up SMASH were working together to offer a service to their local community. The mentors are taking individual action to help people in their local community. Each young person who is helped by SMASH knows that their mentor is giving up their own time and isn't being paid – so they must really care.

You will discover how individuals and groups can make a difference in their local community.

Why volunteer?

People volunteer for all sorts of reasons, as the chart suggests. Most people get personal satisfaction from seeing the results of their contribution to the community. They really enjoy the activity too. Many feel that it helps them because they develop their skills.

I wanted to improve things, help people	53
Cause was important to me	41
I had time to spare	41
I wanted to meet people	30
Connected with needs, interests of family or friends	29
There was a need in the community	29
Friends/family did it	21
To learn new skills	19
Part of my religious belief	17
To help get on in my career	7
Had received voluntary help myself	4
Already involved in the organisation	2
Connected with my interests, hobbies	2
To give something back	1

Business volunteers

Volunteering can happen in all sorts of ways. Many businesses encourage their staff to get involved. There are benefits for both sides. When a business gives its staff time off work to become involved with voluntary activities, they find that they learn all sorts of new skills because they learn to work with all sorts of different people.

Costain and Katesgrove Primary School

Ours is a very old Victorian school and the playground was showing its age. The walls were last painted years ago and the old wooden equipment was suffering from rot.

Costain came in and brightened it up using long-lasting paint, which the children love. One wall was decorated with the children's handprints. The team who did the work put their handprints on the wall too. The younger children were thrilled that their little playground had finally got some attention.

The fact that Costain can offer its time and fund something that's going to impact young people so positively is fantastic. And the team that came in really engaged with the children – they didn't cut themselves off. This project felt like a partnership from the beginning and we are very keen to keep that going.'

1 How did the school benefit?
2 How did Costain benefit from helping the school?

Action

Find out about volunteering activities that are going on in your local area. Work out who benefits from the activities. Make a presentation to the class or a larger group about how the community works together.

Check your understanding

1 What is volunteering?
2 Who benefits from volunteering?
3 Why do people volunteer?
4 Why do some businesses encourage their staff to volunteer?
5 What impact does volunteering have on communities?

... another point of view?

'I don't want to give up my time to help others.'

Do you agree with this statement? Give reasons for your opinion, showing you have considered another point of view.

The value to the economy

If all the work done by volunteers had to be paid for, it would cost £38.9 billion. This clearly helps communities to help people who need support. Without the volunteers, they might miss out because there might not be enough money to pay for the support.

Money is not the only benefit to the economy. It brings people closer together and helps communities to become more sustainable.

Key Terms

volunteer: someone who works for free for a community

Working together

Getting you thinking

Collective action

A squalid refugee camp in Ghana was home to hundreds of child soldiers and **refugees**, many of whom had fled from Liberia. Mediators beyond Borders, a charity, was training a group of them in practical skills as well as offering help with anger management and counselling.

Pump Aid is a charity that aims to bring clean water and sanitation to Liberia, one of the poorest countries in the world. The trainees from the refugee camp offered the basic skills and the enthusiasm to help. Cynthia and Benjamin, now in their twenties, were two of the first ex-child soldiers to be employed by Pump Aid. They assess the needs of places and install the pumps. In a country where there is 85 per cent unemployment, the security of a job makes life very different.

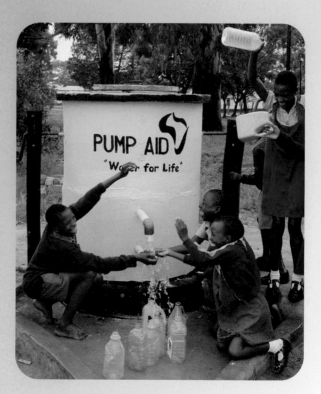

1 Who has helped these young people?

2 How have they been helped?

3 How are they helping others?

4 How are the charities supporting people's human rights?

5 Why do you think that charities can find it easier than government organisations to work in areas like this?

Voluntary organisations

The people behind Pump Aid, Mediators beyond Borders and Amnesty International all have a mission to help other people. By working together on issues like this they can have a greater effect. It takes a lot of organisation to provide services to challenging parts of the world. They all have to raise money to keep the work going. If you look at any of their websites (just Google them), you will find they are looking for donations. They are drawing on public support to have a greater impact.

Some people believe that a country with many voluntary organisations is a healthy country because people are prepared to give up time to help others. On the other hand,

people will give their time to support organisations that interest them – and others may be ignored. It is much easier to find supporters and raise money for dogs, cats and children rather than the elderly. This imbalance may have to be adjusted by the government by providing help for less fashionable causes.

Amnesty uses the power of the individual to put on the pressure. The organisation publicises human rights abuses and asks its members to write to the relevant governments or authorities, in protest. One letter would have little effect but hundreds or thousands might make people listen. These are the sorts of strategies used by many large pressure groups.

You will understand how individuals can work with international organisations to help bring about change in the world.

TORTURE is wrong, unjust and it should never happen to anyone

EVERYONE has the right not to be tortured. Everyone also has the right to be free of the threat of torture. But in the world in which we live, many people are tortured. In fact, in more than 150 countries, torture is used to hurt, frighten and punish people.

This booklet is about torture and what you can do to stop torture. It has been written by an organization called Amnesty International. Please help us to make the world free of torture. **Stop Torture**

1 Why are people tortured?
2 How many countries use torture?
3 Why is it wrong?
4 How do you think you can help Amnesty International to end torture?

Young man missing in the Russian Federation

Ibragim Gazdiev was 29 years old when he 'disappeared'. On 8 August 2007 he was reportedly seized by armed men in camouflage. He has not been seen since and his family believe that he is – or was – held incommunicado.

The authorities deny that they are holding him. Amnesty International fears that Ibragim is in real danger of being tortured or killed in secret or held in incommunicado detention.

Action

1 Is there an Amnesty International local action group in your area? Interview members of the group and find out what they do.
2 Choose an international pressure group and find out how it works. What are its successes? How did they happen? Present your findings to the class.
3 Why is group pressure more effective than individual pressure?

Check your understanding

1 How do voluntary organisations contribute to communities?
2 What is the main focus of Amnesty International's work?
3 How can individuals join in Amnesty International's campaigns?
4 Why do you think people participate in voluntary organisations? Is it all about giving?
5 Why are some issues ignored by the general public? How might this problem be resolved?

... another point of view?

'Voluntary organisations should be unnecessary. Governments should pay for all the services that they provide.'

Do you agree with this statement? Give reasons for your opinion, showing you have considered another point of view.

Key Terms

refugees: people who have been forced to leave their country and must live somewhere else

What does the European Union do?

Getting you thinking

Fish catches in Europe are limited to preserve fish stocks

The European Union (EU) is a trading area. When countries sell things to each other, taxes often have to be paid on products before they are allowed into the other country. The EU removed these taxes between countries within the EU so that they could trade freely with each other.

In order to allow this trade to be as free as possible, rules have been drawn up about a range of things that affect the way businesses work. The rules aim to make competition fairer between countries, so they are all working on 'a level playing field'.

The rules are about:

Protecting employees
Without EU regulations, one country could allow children to work in factories. That country could make things more cheaply because wages would be lower.

Protecting the environment
If one country allowed businesses to pollute the environment, production would be cheaper because they wouldn't have to clean up the mess that was made.

Guaranteeing product standards
If a country is making poor-quality products, they may be dangerous.

Promoting fair competition
Businesses are not allowed to have too much power. For example, if a business controlled prices unfairly, this would hurt the customer.

1 Why do you think the European Union has rules like this?

2 If one country broke the rules, how might this affect other countries in the EU?

3 Why is it necessary to have rules for all European countries about things like fishing?

4 What other things do you think Europe should have rules about?

What is the European Union?

At the end of World War II in 1945, the countries of Europe were anxious that war should not break out again. By joining together more closely, they felt that war would be less likely. Ever since 1958, more countries have become involved and have worked together ever closer in all sorts of areas, including economics, politics, the environment and social issues.

The European Union:

- promotes economic and social progress
- gives the EU a voice on the international scene
- introduces EU citizenship
- develops an area of freedom, security and justice
- maintains and establishes EU regulations.

You will explore the structure of the European Union, what it does and how its power is distributed among its institutions.

How the EU works

All member countries, or **member states**, of the EU elect Members of the European Parliament (MEPs). MEPs have much bigger constituencies than MPs in each country because the European Parliament has to represent all the member countries: 380 million people in total. The European Parliament has 732 members altogether. The UK parliament has 646 MPs compared with 78 MEPs.

The European Parliament is one of the five organisations that run the EU. It is, however, not quite like the UK Parliament, which has the power to make laws. Look at the diagram below to decide where the power lies.

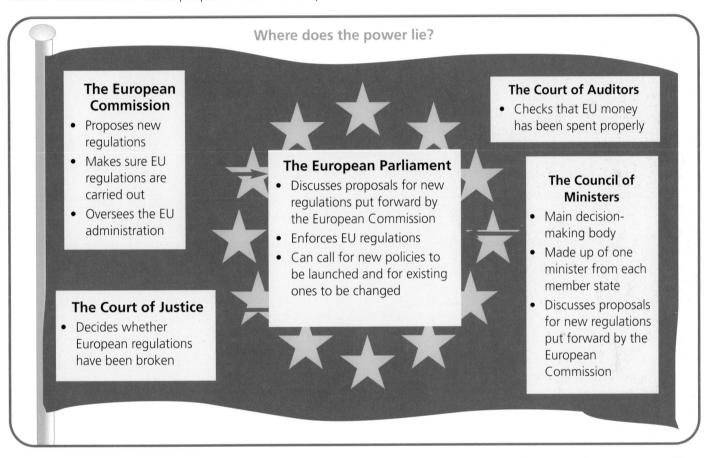

Where does the power lie?

The European Commission
- Proposes new regulations
- Makes sure EU regulations are carried out
- Oversees the EU administration

The Court of Justice
- Decides whether European regulations have been broken

The European Parliament
- Discusses proposals for new regulations put forward by the European Commission
- Enforces EU regulations
- Can call for new policies to be launched and for existing ones to be changed

The Court of Auditors
- Checks that EU money has been spent properly

The Council of Ministers
- Main decision-making body
- Made up of one minister from each member state
- Discusses proposals for new regulations put forward by the European Commission

Action

1 Which European constituency are you in?
2 Who is your MEP?
3 Which political party does your MEP belong to?

Check your understanding

1 What are the organisations that run the EU?
2 Which organisation in the EU holds most power?
3 How is the EU different from the UK in this respect?
4 How democratic is decision-making in the EU compared with the UK?

... another point of view?

'Countries that trade together should all have the same rules for running businesses.'

Do you agree with this statement? Give reasons for your opinion, showing you have considered another point of view.

Key Terms

member state: a country that is a member of the EU

Citizens of Europe

Getting you thinking

A bigger market

Roy Stewart turned his hobby into a business when he developed remote-controlled golf bags. At first he thought he would just sell to the UK market through his internet site. Once on the web, he found that he had started to trade internationally. He now has a growing business in both the UK and Europe. There is lots of competition in the golf market so Roy must keep his costs down and his prices competitive.

When he sells to countries in the European Union there are no taxes to pay. An American company selling to the EU would have to pay taxes on its products.

1 Do you think Roy Stewart thinks the EU is a good or a bad thing?
2 What advantages are there in making products in the UK rather than the USA, for example?
3 Why does Roy have to keep his cost down?
4 What effect does the EU have on the prices customers pay?

Inside or out?

The European Union has a population of around 500 million people – more than the US and Japan put together. This makes one very big market for businesses to sell to. It also means there is lots of competition, so prices should be lower.

The downside is that things bought from countries outside the EU are more expensive. A tax, or **customs duty**, has to be paid on goods from other parts of the world, so these goods would probably cost more for an EU consumer. These factors have meant that the UK buys more products from and sells more products to EU countries than any other part of the world.

What about the Euro?

The **Euro** was set up on 1 January 1999. It is the **single currency** for some members of the EU.

When the Euro was launched, the UK decided not to join because, among other things, the UK economy was not in line with that of other European countries.

The Euro can make things more straightforward.

- People and businesses don't have to change money from one currency to another when they travel to different countries within the European Union. This makes things cheaper, because banks charge for changing money.
- It makes things more certain. The value of currencies change against each other. If you go on holiday to the USA, the number of dollars you can buy with your pounds will change from day to day. If everyone in Europe uses the Euro, a business knows that there will be no change in the price it receives for products sold in other European Union countries.

Not everyone is in favour of the Euro. The main concern is that it reduces a country's control over its own economy. If a lot of people are unemployed, the government might want to use policies that help to create jobs. This might be difficult if these policies did not fit with EU policy.

You will investigate how business and citizenship in the UK are affected by European Union regulations.

Citizens of the European Union

Any citizen of a country within the EU is automatically an EU citizen. This does not interfere with your national rights but adds four special rights to them:

- **Freedom to move and take up residence anywhere in the Union**

  You can get a job anywhere in the EU. It is much harder to get work in other parts of the world.

- **The right to vote and stand in local government and European Parliament elections in the country of residence**

  A British citizen living in another EU member state could stand for election there.

- **The right for EU citizens to be protected by representatives of any member state in countries where an individual's country is not represented**

  Wherever you are in the world, an EU representative can help you out if you are in difficulties.

- **The right of appeal to the European ombudsman**

  If you feel that EU rulings have not been carried out properly, you can appeal to the **European ombudsman** to investigate.

Ken Tatham, an Englishman, became mayor of his village in France

Action

1 Collect as much information about the Euro as possible. Make a display, using the evidence you have collected, about how the Euro is affecting the UK.

2 What does European citizenship mean to people who you know?

3 Would they describe themselves as Europeans? Are there any situations in which they would be more or less likely to call themselves Europeans?

Check your understanding

1 Give two reasons why it can be cheaper to buy goods from within the European Union than from outside it.

2 Why could belonging to the Euro be a problem for individual EU countries?

3 As a British citizen, would you be allowed to work in Spain? Give reasons.

4 If you were travelling outside the European Union and you needed help from officials, who could you go to if you found out there was no British embassy or representative in that area?

... another point of view?

'I am a European.'
Do you agree with this statement? Give reasons for your opinion, showing you have considered another point of view.

Key Terms

customs duty: taxes on products bought from other countries

Euro: the name of the single currency used by a group of countries within the European Union

European ombudsman: a person who investigates complaints against the EU

single currency: this is the Euro, so called as it is used in some of the EU member states

The Commonwealth

Getting you thinking

Human rights is at the heart of the Commonwealth's values. To support the work of member countries' police forces, the Commonwealth has developed a programme of training in human rights. The programme covers all aspects from arresting people to dealing with vulnerable people.

'Most Commonwealth police officers would no doubt see themselves as servants of the public: as protectors, not violators, of human rights.'

Commonwealth grant supports 60 pupils in rural areas

When Abigail was just a child, both her parents died. Her elderly grandmother took her in, but Abigail could not afford to buy the clothes, the books or the stationery she needed to go to school. A £20,000 grant from the Commonwealth Secretariat is supporting 60 young women like Abigail to continue their education at rural schools in Zambia. Poverty makes it difficult for girls in rural Africa to stay in school and gain qualifications, which in turn makes it harder for them to find employment to break out of the cycle of poverty.

'When I start working, I want to help other orphaned children and put them through school. Teaching a girl is a very beautiful thing,' she says.

1 Why do police need to be trained in human rights?
2 What difference does this make to the way a country runs?
3 How has the Commonwealth helped Abigail?
4 How has the Commonwealth helped Zambia by helping Abigail?

The Commonwealth today

The **Commonwealth of Nations**, usually just called the Commonwealth, is an association of countries, most of which were ruled by Britain. However, today's Commonwealth is a world away from the handful of countries that were the first members. From Africa and Asia to the Pacific and the Caribbean, the Commonwealth's 1.7 billion people make up 30 per cent of the world's population.

The modern Commonwealth helps to advance democracy, human rights, sustainable economic and social development within its member countries and beyond. Zimbabwe was thrown out of the Commonwealth in 2003 because it infringed human rights and its elections were not very democratic. All the countries have English as a common working language and similar systems of law, public administration and education. The Queen, like her predecessors, is head of the Commonwealth. It has built on its shared history to become a vibrant and growing association of states.

How does it do its work?

The Commonwealth has all sorts of ways of helping people and encouraging them to work together. Read about two examples on the page opposite.

You will find out how the Commonwealth has changed from its origins, and the type of work it does today.

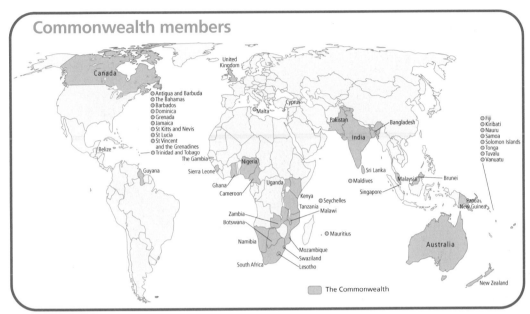

Commonwealth members

- Canada
- United Kingdom
- Cyprus
- Malta
- Antigua and Barbuda
- The Bahamas
- Barbados
- Dominica
- Grenada
- Jamaica
- St Kitts and Nevis
- St Lucia
- St Vincent and the Grenadines
- Trinidad and Tobago
- The Gambia
- Belize
- Guyana
- Sierra Leone
- Ghana
- Cameroon
- Nigeria
- Uganda
- Kenya
- Tanzania
- Malawi
- Zambia
- Botswana
- Namibia
- Mozambique
- Swaziland
- Lesotho
- South Africa
- Pakistan
- India
- Bangladesh
- Sri Lanka
- Maldives
- Seychelles
- Mauritius
- Malaysia
- Singapore
- Brunei
- Fiji
- Kiribati
- Nauru
- Samoa
- Solomon Islands
- Tonga
- Tuvalu
- Vanuatu
- Papua New Guinea
- Australia
- New Zealand

The Commonwealth

The Commonwealth Fund for Technical Cooperation (CFTC)

The CFTC promotes economic and social development, and helps to overcome poverty in member countries. The skills of member countries are used to help others. Advisors go to other countries to help in agriculture, enterprise, trade, legal issues, etc.

The Commonwealth Youth Credit Initiative (CYCI)

The CYCI is a small enterprise scheme for young people, providing 'micro-credit', training and enterprise development, which can bring economic self-sufficiency to the poorest young people. The CYCI uses the following methods:

- use of young people to support each other, and to encourage saving and the paying back of loans
- low interest rates
- low training costs
- ongoing training and monitoring of enterprises.

The Commonwealth's mission

A platform for building global agreement
It holds conferences that bring all the countries together to discuss major issues. This helps everyone to work together better.

A source of practical help for sustainable development
The Commonwealth helps people to work so they can look after themselves, and has programmes that aim to look after the environment.

A force for making democracy work
The Commonwealth helps its members to develop working democracy. It sends observers to check that elections are carried out properly.

Theme 3: The global community

3.4: The UK's role in the world

... another point of view?
'The Commonwealth is the same as it has always been.'
Do you agree with this statement? Give reasons for your opinion, showing you have considered another point of view.

Action

1 Have any countries joined the Commonwealth recently?
2 What are the conditions for joining the Commonwealth?
3 Why do countries want to be members of the Commonwealth?
4 Find an example of a recent Commonwealth sustainable development programme and present your findings to the class.

Check your understanding

1 What are the origins of the Commonwealth?
2 How has it changed over the years?
3 What is its mission today?
4 Describe some ways in which it achieves its mission.

Key Terms

Commonwealth of Nations: a voluntary group of independent countries

micro-credit: making small loans to individuals to help them help themselves

The United Nations

Getting you thinking

UNICEF

In Sri Lanka thousands of families have fled from the civil war. Vithuskya and her friends at least have a school to go to. UNICEF has provided a school-in-a-box with basic materials such as notebooks, pens and pencils.

'I had no luggage with me, just the clothes I was wearing. I was happy to get these supplies, especially the notebooks. I put them in a plastic bag when I am at home, so that they don't get wet when it rains heavily and rain leaks into the shelter.'

For the displaced children, going to school every day is more important than ever. It gives them a sense of normality. They can play with their friends, learn and be out of their shelters for part of the day.

1 How has UNICEF helped individual students like Vithuskya?
2 How has this project helped the community?
3 Why does the UN spend money on projects like this?

The aims of the United Nations

Nearly every nation in the world belongs to the **United Nations**. Its membership totals 192 countries. When states join, they agree to accept the UN charter. The aims of the charter are:

- to maintain international peace and security
- to develop friendly relations among nations
- to cooperate in solving international problems and in promoting respect for human rights
- to be a centre for harmonising the actions of nations.

The UN is not a world government and it does not make laws. It does, however, help to resolve international conflict and makes policies on matters affecting us all. At the UN, all the member states have a voice and can vote in this process.

The organisation of the UN

The UN's General Assembly is made up of representatives of all the member countries. Each country has one vote. The Assembly makes recommendations, which are approved by the Security Council and put into action by the Secretary General. You will find out more about the legal aspects of the UN later on (see pages 146–7).

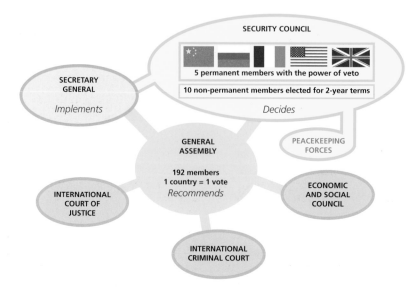

You will explore the work of the United Nations and consider its role in the world.

The Agencies

The UN has agencies that deal with the whole range of human and economic development, including the environment, population, food and agriculture, health and tourism. They carry out the activities agreed by the General Assembly and the Security Council. Here are just a few of them.

UNDP	United Nations Development Programme
UNIFEM	United Nations Development Fund for Women
UNHCR	Office of the United Nations High Commissioner for Refugees
UNICEF	United Nations Children's Fund
UNESCO	United Nations Educational, Scientific and Cultural Organisation
WB	World Bank
IMF	International Monetary Fund

Peacekeeping: the work of the UN Security Council

The Security Council is made up of five permanent members, including the United Kingdom, and 15 non-permanent members who are elected for two years at a time. As the world changes, the number of permanent members may change. The Security Council:

- can investigate any international dispute
- can recommend ways of reaching a settlement
- is responsible for peacekeeping forces.

You will find out more on page 144.

Action

1 Check how countries are progressing to achieve the Millennium Goals.
2 Which agencies are likely to be useful in achieving the goals? Explain how.
3 Make a presentation to others explaining the Goals and how the UN is helping to achieve them.

Check your understanding

1 What is the UN?
2 Who are the members?
3 Explain the structure and responsibilities of the main organisations of the UN.
4 Why did the UN set up the Millennium Goals?
5 Which agencies will help countries to achieve them?

... another point of view?

'There are too many challenges for the UN to be any use.'
Do you agree with this statement? Give reasons for your opinion, showing you have considered another point of view.

UN's Millennium Goals

In the year 2000, world leaders agreed that development in the poorer parts of the world was moving too slowly. They all agreed to promote eight Millennium Goals, which aim to encourage and support further development. The target year for change is 2015. Some regions are being more successful than others. China, for example, is going well, but much of sub-Saharan Africa is not making a great deal of progress,

Develop a global partnership for development
– Address the needs of countries in order to achieve economic growth through trade and development

Prevent extreme poverty and hunger
– Reduce hunger and poverty by a half

Achieve universal primary education
– Primary education for all girls and boys

Promote gender equality and empower women
– Access to secondary education for all women

Reduce child mortality
– Reduce by two-thirds the number of children who die before they are five

Ensure environmental sustainability
– Integrate sustainability into government policies

Combat HIV/AIDS, malaria and other diseases
– Halt the growth and reverse the incidence of diseases

Improve maternal health
– Reduce by three-quarters the number of mothers who die during birth

Can the world be fairer?

UK and Niger – what's the difference?

1 What evidence is there to suggest that the UK is better off than Niger?

2 Do you think the cost of buying basic needs is the same?

3 What data might suggest the gap between the two countries is increasing?

4 Why does this data suggest that Niger will have difficulty catching up with more economically developed countries?

	Niger	UK
How much the economy is worth per citizen	$244	$36 509
How fast the economy grew	−0.5%	2.5%
Doctors per 100,000 people	2	230
How long people live	54.5 years	79 years
Number of children dying before the age of five for every 1,000 people	256	7
Internet users per 1,000 people	2	473
Adults who can read	28.7%	100%
Children enrolled in secondary school	8%	99%
International aid	Receives aid	Gives aid
Free education, healthcare and state pensions	No	Yes

Source: Human Development Report 2007/8

LEDCs and MEDCs

The world falls into two groups:

- the more economically developed countries (MEDCs), such as the UK
- the less economically developed countries (LEDCs), such as Niger and The Gambia.

This is a crude way of splitting the world into rich and poor countries. It masks different rates of economic growth, and some countries do not fit into one group or another.

People living in Niger. How does their standard of living compare with yours?

Debt: a cause of poverty?

41 poor countries, 33 of them in Africa, owed about £150 billion in foreign debt. The poorest countries of sub-Saharan Africa were paying £20 million of their debt to the West, while their economies declined, infant mortality rose and life expectancy fell.

To repay these debts, poor countries were forced to divert money away from healthcare, education and other vital services. Many children didn't get the chance to go to school, mothers didn't have prenatal care, and HIV-infected persons didn't get the treatment they need.

The beginnings of international debt

In the 1970s, the world's richest nations lent huge sums of money to poorer countries. This money was sometimes lent to undemocratic, corrupt governments. Much of it was spent on weapons, or wasted. It wasn't used to develop the country or help people living in poverty.

Many indebted countries, like Niger, are unable to escape the poverty trap because their economies have been growing at a slower rate than that of other countries. They are often dependent on selling one or two primary products, such as oil, bananas, uranium, copper or coffee. The prices they get for these products have fallen. This means they need to borrow more to maintain the same level of imports. This causes greater debt.

You will find out just how unequal the world is – and why it is difficult for poor countries to develop.

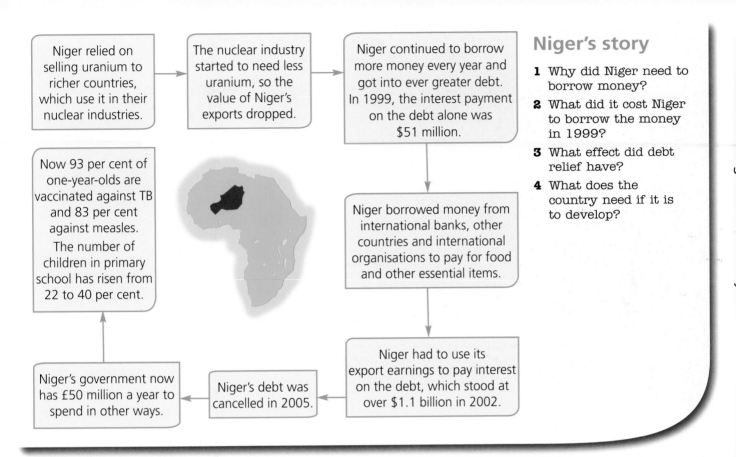

Niger relied on selling uranium to richer countries, which use it in their nuclear industries.

The nuclear industry started to need less uranium, so the value of Niger's exports dropped.

Niger continued to borrow more money every year and got into ever greater debt. In 1999, the interest payment on the debt alone was $51 million.

Niger borrowed money from international banks, other countries and international organisations to pay for food and other essential items.

Niger had to use its export earnings to pay interest on the debt, which stood at over $1.1 billion in 2002.

Niger's debt was cancelled in 2005.

Niger's government now has £50 million a year to spend in other ways.

Now 93 per cent of one-year-olds are vaccinated against TB and 83 per cent against measles. The number of children in primary school has risen from 22 to 40 per cent.

Niger's story

1 Why did Niger need to borrow money?
2 What did it cost Niger to borrow the money in 1999?
3 What effect did debt relief have?
4 What does the country need if it is to develop?

Action

What is happening to world debt? Look up: www.oneworld.net, www.oxfam.org, www.dfid.gov.uk, and www.worldbank.org (and go to the schools section).

Check your understanding

1 What are LEDCs and MEDCs?
2 Why can't indebted countries spend much money on vital services such as health and education?
3 How did some governments damage their country's chances?
4 Give two reasons why it is difficult for the economies of LEDCs to grow.
5 Why would indebted countries be in a better situation if their debts were cancelled?
6 What progress is being made on debt cancellation?

... another point of view?

'Debt should only be cancelled in countries where people's human rights are respected.'
Do you agree with this statement? Give reasons for your opinion, showing you have considered another point of view.

The UN says

'Debt relief has been or will be provided to 33 out of 41 eligible countries, cancelling more than 90 per cent of their external debt. In 2006, 52 developing countries were still spending more on debt service than on public health. Ten spent more on debt service than on education.'

Ban Ki-moon, Secretary General of the United Nations

Globalisation: the challenges

Getting you thinking

In an average week, we eat food and use products from many countries. In this way you will be linked to people all over the world. We depend on them to grow food and make many other products. They depend on us to buy them. The decisions we make can affect other people's lives.

1 List some advantages and disadvantages of being able to buy products that are made all over the world.

2 How does this affect your wellbeing?

3 What economic, social and environmental issues are the results of this trade?

4 Do you think this interdependence means the world has become a 'smaller' place?

A shrinking world

Modern technology, combined with improved communication and transportation, has made it easier to trade around the world. Our nations are interdependent. It is not really the countries themselves that trade, but the businesses and consumers within those countries. The importance of trade is likely to increase with advances in technology. Already the internet allows us to buy from anywhere in the world.

Added together, local economies, right down to the smallest local high streets, help make up a nation's economy. Added together, national economies make up the world economy.

The globalisation game

Globalisation has many players. Consumers, employees, large companies and nations all take part. There are winners and losers.

Consumer power

Consumers have power because they can buy from someone else if they don't like the price or quality. Businesses often try to produce as cheaply as possible in order to attract customers. People can choose whether to pay the lowest prices or spend a bit more and buy things that have been produced more fairly.

Producer power

Producers have power because many businesses are very large. They can:

- force down the price they pay for resources, because suppliers are frightened of losing their biggest customer
- keep wages down, because workers have few alternative jobs to go to
- fix prices higher if there is no competition
- fail to look after the environment if there are no laws to protect it.

Who is more powerful: big businesses or nations?

Economy of Republic of Ireland	$201.8 billion
Microsoft's sales	$60 billion
Economy of Niger	$3.4 billion

Source: Human Development Report 2007/8; www.microsoft.com

Some companies' sales are bigger than many countries' economies. A country is stuck in one place (it can't move), whereas a multinational company can produce wherever costs are lowest. Products, such as trainers, are often made in countries where labour is cheap. Businesses buy services, from accounting to IT, from countries around the world where labour is cheap. Many countries, however, welcome multinational businesses because they provide employment and skills. This helps the economy to grow.

You will find out about the challenges created by globalisation.

Global branding

Some people are worried that global brands such as McDonald's, Coca Cola, Pepsi, Nike and Gap erode the traditional culture of communities.

Action

1 Visit the Accessorize website at www.monsoon.co.uk/page/ethicaltrading and find out about its trading code.

2 Look up a newspaper page on the internet and search for articles about Nike, Coca Cola or McDonald's. Then visit the company's website. Try also to find websites that publish views against the company. Present your findings to the class.

Check your understanding

1 In what ways might people think that producers have too much power?

2 In what situation might a supplier agree to sell goods to a buyer for a lower price?

3 If there is high unemployment in an area, why can companies pay lower wages?

4 Why do multinational companies produce their goods and services in different countries?

5 Explain why people might be worried about global brands.

... another point of view?

'Global companies should not be allowed to employ people in LEDCs.' Do you agree with this statement? Give reasons for your opinion, showing you have considered another point of view.

Can business be good?

More and more businesses are looking closely at their impact on the communities they serve. The Body Shop, The Co-op Bank and Fairtrade organisations monitor their actions. Businesses are very aware of the damage that bad publicity can do. They run schemes to monitor their activities around the world. It is often difficult to carry this out and meet the standards set. One supplier to a high street fashion shop has 5,000 home workers. The company tries to monitor what's going on, but it's hard to be perfect.

Key Terms

globalisation: the increasing interdependence of the world

131

Sweet shops and sweatshops

Getting you thinking

Drissa was sold to a plantation owner, taken to a remote plantation and forced to work from dawn until dusk with no pay. The work was exhausting but if Drissa showed signs of tiredness he was beaten. When Drissa was caught trying to escape, he was tied up and beaten until he couldn't walk. At night, along with 17 other young men, he was locked in a small room with only a tin can as a toilet.

Fair Trade is the only guarantee that products, such as chocolate, are 'slave free' and have not been made using forced labour. All Fair Trade products have to meet strict conditions, including ensuring that no forced or illegal child labour has been used. Fair Trade goods also give producers a fair price for their produce, thus helping to challenge the unfair trading systems that keep people in poverty.

Source: Anti-slavery International

The US government wants chocolate manufactures in the USA to label chocolate as 'Slave Free' if it has been made from cocoa that does not involve the exploitation of workers. The chocolate manufacturers have made a voluntary agreement – but they don't seem to have taken it very seriously.

The average UK consumer spends about £72 a year on chocolate. The total world market is worth £4 billion a year.

1 Why do cocoa producers use slave labour?

2 How does Fair Trade help?

3 Why did US chocolate manufacturers not want a law to be passed?

4 Do customers have a responsibility?

5 When you buy your next bar of chocolate, will you think about how it has been produced?

Making trade fairer

Trade is a very important way for any country to earn money and create jobs. People and countries have traded for thousands of years, but in today's global economy information, goods and money can be moved around the world at an incredible speed. Companies aim to make the best product at the cheapest price.

The World Trade Organization (WTO) is responsible for negotiating international trade agreements. Most rich countries want a **free trade** system in which the prices of goods are determined by the amount that people want to buy and sell. But many people believe such a system favours richer countries such as the USA and Japan and want the WTO to be reformed. They argue that world trade must be managed so the poorest countries benefit more. In other words, they want world trade to become Fair Trade.

Fair Trade is trade that is good for the producer; a system that ensures more of the price consumers pay goes to the producer. Fair Trade staff would be paid a fair wage, have good working conditions and be allowed to form trade unions to defend their rights.

Fair Trade campaigns such as the Clean Clothes Campaign (CCC) have drawn attention to the working conditions of workers all around the world.

You will discover how inequalities resulting from free trade can be reduced.

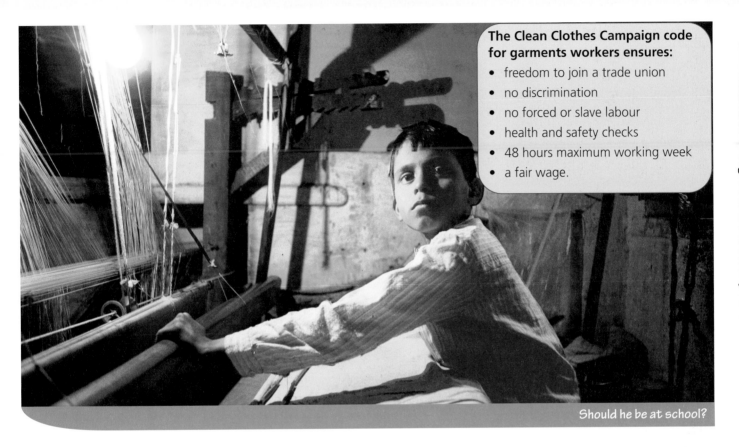

The Clean Clothes Campaign code for garments workers ensures:

- freedom to join a trade union
- no discrimination
- no forced or slave labour
- health and safety checks
- 48 hours maximum working week
- a fair wage.

Should he be at school?

Action

1 Use the internet to research UK companies trying to promote Fair Trade.
2 Obtain details of company 'codes' like the CCC code above. Use these to create a leaflet or poster explaining the issues about Fair Trade and its aims for helping workers in LEDCs.
3 You could run an assembly to explain Fair Trade to the rest of your school.

Check your understanding

1 In your own words, say what the World Trade Organization (WTO) does.
2 Why do some people want to reform the WTO?
3 How would Fair Trade help workers in LEDCs?
4 What human rights do groups such as the Clean Clothes Campaign help to protect?

... another point of view?

'People in the UK should boycott companies that sell "dirty" clothes and trainers.'
Do you agree with this statement? Give reasons for your opinion, showing you have considered another point of view.

To buy or not to buy

The Clean Clothes Campaign does not think consumers should boycott goods that are not 'clean', because it believes **boycotts** will put employees out of work. When the US government talked about bringing in a law to stop anything made by children under 15 from being imported in the USA, many child employees in Bangladesh were thrown out of work and their families often went hungry as a result.

Key Terms

boycott: to refuse to use or have anything to do with something

Fair Trade: a way of buying and selling products that aims to pay the producer a fair price

free trade: trade between countries which is not restricted by things like high taxes on imports

The rights and wrongs of protest

Getting you thinking

Germany was trying to recover from the worst violence for six years yesterday after thousands of masked anti-globalisation protesters went on the rampage, pelting police with firebombs and stones and torching cars in clashes that injured over 900 people.

Police said that 433 officers were injured, 33 of them seriously, in the violence that erupted after a peaceful anti-globalisation demonstration. They wanted their voices to be heard at the summit of G8 leaders who meet to discuss global problems.

'Free trade is like putting the rabbit and the tiger in the same cage, the rabbit being the poor countries,' claims a protestor.

1   What message do you think the protestors wanted the world leaders to hear?
2   Why does the protester compare the rich and poor countries to tigers and rabbits?
3   Why do you think some people object to the actions of the protestors?
4   Use the ideas of human rights and legal rights to work out what you think about direct action of this sort.

Protest

Anti-globalisation protests are a regular feature on the news. The protests are greatest when international organisations such as the International Monetary Fund (IMF) and World Trade Organization (WTO) meet to discuss free trade, poverty and wealth. The protestors are drawn from various pressure groups. This increases the number of protestors, but it means their protests lack a clear aim. Some protestors are concerned with global warming, others with poverty, and still others worry about the impact of multinationals.

One such pressure group is the WDM (World Development Movement), which wants to change world trade rules. It is calling for strong international rules that put people's needs before free trade. It claims that money needed for clean water, health and education in poor countries is still being handed over to rich countries in debt repayments.

Receiving the right message

Your own views on an issue will be determined by what you hear. For some, this will come from discussions with like-minded people. For most, the source will be the TV news or their favourite newspaper.

Whichever way, there is a danger that the information is biased. Biased information will favour one side or another, so it is always useful to hear both sides of the argument.

When the issue is global it can be more difficult to get your opinion across, because you have to influence powerful nations or world institutions. Again, pressure groups have a role to play in influencing opinion and providing an alternative view.

The work of international organisations

There are three major international trade organisations:

- **The World Trade Organization** helps shape rules about trade so that it makes selling to other countries easier.
- **The World Bank** provides loans to poorer countries for projects to help reduce poverty.
- **The International Monetary Fund** promotes international financial cooperation and economic growth of international trade.

You will investigate whether direct action can be justified.

Who says what?

The anti-globalisation movement says:
- International organisations such as the IMF and World Bank cause poverty because they encourage free trade. This can damage LEDCs because they have to compete in world markets.
- The movement itself represents the poor, who have no voice themselves.

The international trade organisations say:
- Globalisation and free trade are good for the poor. More international trade brings more jobs to poorer countries. Therefore it brings greater prosperity to the world and reduces poverty.
- Protest groups are undemocratic because they haven't been elected and so they cannot claim to represent the people.
- Protest groups are, in effect, preventing global efforts to tackle poverty.

Too loud a message?

Pressure groups can lobby governments throughout the world and try to persuade them of their point of view. The groups can promote their case through publicity, including their internet sites, and they can protest in other ways.

Some recent protests have involved outbreaks of violence and damage to buildings. McDonald's is seen as a symbol of multinationals and is an easy target.

Anti-globalisation pressure groups are usually protesting about other people's human rights but may limit others' rights in the process. Such actions are breaking the law. That gets media attention, but the protesters may lose the sympathy of the public.

Protestors close Stansted airport. Fifty flights are cancelled. Whose rights?

Action

Look at the following websites for more information about globalisation. Set up a debate or prepare a presentation on the arguments for and against increased globalisation.

www.oneworld.net	www.worldbank.org
www.wto.org	www.oxfam.org.uk
www.dfid.gov.uk	www.imf.org

Check your understanding

1 Why have different pressure groups joined together at certain world trade demonstrations? Make a list of the advantages and disadvantages of them doing so.

2 What other methods might pressure groups use to get their message across?

3 Why might pressure groups show bias when putting their case across?

4 Should pressure groups break the law while protesting? Justify your answer.

5 Should pressure groups infringe people's human rights while protesting about the human rights of others?

6 Might businesses and governments show bias too?

... another point of view?

'The European Union imposes much higher import taxes on chocolate than cocoa beans. It should continue to do so.'

Do you agree with this statement? Give reasons for your opinion, showing you have considered another point of view.

We all share the same air

Getting you thinking — Pollution doesn't need a passport

Via satellite, we can actually see the clouds of pollution.
- It drifts from the US to the Europe.
- It drifts from Asia to the US.

The Western world has been moving factories to Asia for decades – and the pollution has moved with them. At least 13 major cities in Asia and other regions, including Beijing and New Delhi, get less sunlight because of the pollution. China sees tens of thousands of pollution-related deaths each year.

1 Where does pollution come from?

2 Why is China so polluted?

3 What effect does the pollution have?

4 Why are so many things made in China?

Climate change and global warming

Climate change is a complex subject that is not fully understood. Our climate is changing, but scientists disagree about why it is happening and what the long-term effects of these global changes will be.

Many influential scientists believe the burning of **fossil fuels** is responsible for **global warming**. The concentration of the main greenhouse gas, carbon dioxide (CO_2), in the atmosphere is now at its highest in 400,000 years, and global warming is taking place faster than expected. Temperatures are rising more quickly than at any time in the past 1,000 years.

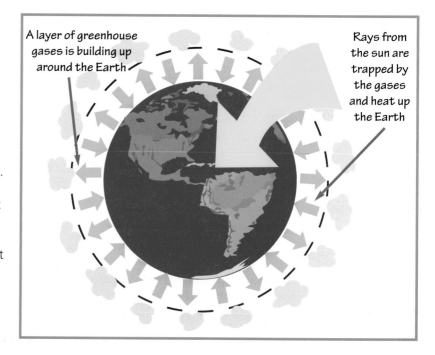

A layer of greenhouse gases is building up around the Earth

Rays from the sun are trapped by the gases and heat up the Earth

You will investigate the challenges the world faces because pollution and global warming are not contained within national boundaries.

What are the effects?

Climate changes can have both positive and negative effects. Higher levels of CO_2 in the atmosphere may improve crop yields, but they could also lead to water shortages.

There are regional winners and losers from global warming. On balance, the LEDCs suffer more than the MEDCs. There are already water shortages in countries such as Rwanda, Somalia and Kenya, and these are likely to get worse, bringing widespread crop failure and famine.

Rise in sea levels

As over half the world's population lives on low-lying coastal plains and estuaries, millions of people could become environmental refugees.

Hurricanes, flooding and droughts

The possibility of more extreme weather threatens the livelihood of many of the poorest people in the world.

Richer nations, which produce the vast majority of greenhouse gases, will be affected by changes in weather patterns too. Violent storms and heavy rains hit some areas and drought affects others.

Disease

Warmer and wetter conditions in other areas will increase waterborne infections like malaria, diarrhoea and dysentery. Higher temperatures will mean a rise in the number of pests, weeds and diseases.

It might be necessary to increase pesticide and weedkiller use, which could lead to polluted rivers and lakes.

Hurricane Katrina strikes in Florida

Flooding in Bangladesh

Action

1 Research the sources, both manufactured and natural, of greenhouse gas emissions. Use this information to suggest ways that emissions could be reduced in future.
2 Research which areas of the UK would be affected by rising sea levels. Which industries would be threatened by floods? How would local economies be affected? What, if anything, can government and/or local councils do to prepare for this?

Check your understanding

1 In your own words, explain what greenhouse gases are.
2 List some of the likely effects of global warming.
3 Why do you think the world's leading climate scientists now argue that all nations must cooperate to reduce emissions of these gases?

... another point of view?

'Global warming's great. It means we have long hot summers.' Do you agree with this statement? Give reasons for your opinion, showing you have considered another point of view.

Cutting carbon: the Kyoto Protocol and beyond

In 1998, world leaders met in Kyoto, Japan, to discuss how to reduce global emissions of greenhouse gases. They agreed to reduce emissions by an average of 5 per cent below 1990 levels by the year 2008. Since then, all EU countries have agreed to cut emissions by 20 per cent by 2020. The UK has set its target at 60 per cent by 2050.

Key Terms

fossil fuel: a naturally occurring fuel, such as coal or natural gas

global warming: the rise in the average surface temperature of the Earth

Transport crisis?

High-speed trains reduce journey times

If you are travelling a distance between 400 and 800 km, high-speed rail is quickest – faster than flying.

Evidence from other countries suggests that high-speed rail links would reduce the demand for domestic air services.

High-speed rail links would link the rest of the country to Europe.

1 What effect would high-speed rail links have on journey times?

2 What effect would they have on domestic flights?

3 What effect might they have on road traffic?

4 How would high-speed rail links help the environment?

Effect of high-speed rail links on journey times

London–Birmingham 1 hr 20 min to 45 min
London–Manchester 2 hr 20 min to 1hr 30 min
London–Leeds 2 hr 15 min to 1 hr 20 min
London–Edinburgh 4 hr 30 min to 2 hr 45 min

The real cost of motoring

A car gives you the freedom to go where you like, when you like. But what is the real cost of motoring?

Over 200 new cars are sold every hour in the UK, and though newer cars have 'greener' engines, they still emit greenhouse gases. Road traffic is now a major cause of air pollution. Traffic fumes not only pollute our cities, they affect rural areas too.

Government figures predict that road traffic will increase by 75 per cent in the next 30 years. As congestion nears grid-lock in many towns and cities, the average UK motorist spends a total of five days a year just sitting in traffic jams. Many people say they would use public transport if it were cheaper, cleaner and safer.

Possible solutions

Road pricing

This involves road users paying to use the roads. Cars can be fitted with electronic number plates that give signals to special computers. The computer works out when the car was on a particular road and the driver is charged. In Singapore, this system has reduced rush-hour traffic, pollution and damage to roads. In London, people pay the congestion charge to drive their cars into the central area. One problem is that the population doesn't like the system very much. In London the extension to the zone was removed and in Manchester every borough in the city voted heavily against the introduction of a similar scheme.

A drawback is that richer people can afford the charges, so poorer people could be disadvantaged.

You will investigate the challenges created by traffic, and consider some sustainable solutions.

Improving public transport

Better public transport might encourage people to stop using their cars so much. Possible plans are to:

- improve bus reliability
- decrease bus journey times
- develop tram systems
- reduce car traffic.

This could be done by:

- creating bus lanes on important routes and making sure cars don't use them
- giving priority at traffic lights to buses, pedestrians and cyclists
- stopping cars from parking on busy routes.

No to congestion zone

The people of Greater Manchester voted against plans to introduce a congestion charge in the region.

Nearly two million people were asked to decide on a peak-time road charge to open up a £2.8bn transport investment.

A majority of voters in all ten boroughs (79 per cent) voted against the plans, and only 21 per cent voted in favour of them. The overall turnout was about 53.2 per cent.

Ze vélorution – a French solution

Le vélo – or 'the bicycle' – is the Parisian solution to city centre congestion. Rental bikes – 20,000 of them – are parked round the city. For 1€ you can use the bikes for the day, for 5€ they're yours for a week and for just 29€ you can use the bikes as often as you like all year. The first half hour is free – and that's what most people do. Every bike is rented out ten times a day. A total of 100,000 people have already signed up for a year's subscription. There was a fear that people would use them to ride down the hills but never back up – but the bikes do seem to find their way back to the top!

Action

1 Research alternative forms of transport that might be used in towns and cities, such as electric-powered cars. Do they offer sustainable alternatives to petrol/diesel-driven vehicles?
2 How does road traffic affect the lives of people in your local area? What could be done to improve the situation?

Check your understanding

1 In what ways should public transport be improved to encourage more people to use it?
2 What are the advantages of the possible solutions to the car crisis? Are there disadvantages?

... another point of view?

'Building more roads is the only solution to the UK's traffic problems.'

Do you agree with this statement? Give reasons for your opinion, showing you have considered another point of view.

Key Terms

road pricing: a scheme that charges road users according to how much they use a road

Global crisis – global action

Getting you thinking

HIV/AIDS: a global problem

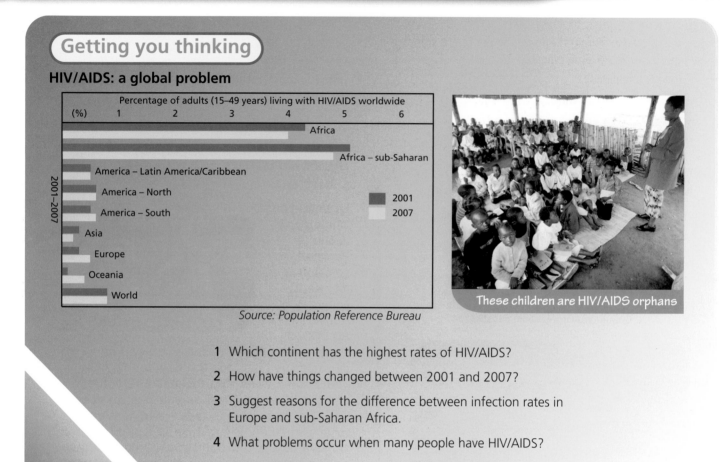

Percentage of adults (15–49 years) living with HIV/AIDS worldwide

(%) 1 2 3 4 5 6

- Africa
- Africa – sub-Saharan
- America – Latin America/Caribbean
- America – North
- America – South
- Asia
- Europe
- Oceania
- World

2001–2007

■ 2001
□ 2007

Source: Population Reference Bureau

These children are HIV/AIDS orphans

1 Which continent has the highest rates of HIV/AIDS?

2 How have things changed between 2001 and 2007?

3 Suggest reasons for the difference between infection rates in Europe and sub-Saharan Africa.

4 What problems occur when many people have HIV/AIDS?

Dying of ignorance

In the year 2000, the number of 10- to 19-year-olds on the planet reached one billion. Most of these young people live in LEDCs.

Half of all new **HIV** infection occurs in young people. Because of a lack of even basic health education, many young people in LEDCs don't know about the risks or how to protect themselves. Poor countries can't afford to set up clinics, provide HIV testing or distribute free condoms.

UNICEF, an agency of the UN, estimates that one-half of today's 15-year-olds in Botswana and South Africa will die from **AIDS**.

UNAIDS

The United Nations works with many other organisations worldwide to fight the spread of HIV/AIDS. UNAIDS runs a global programme with the help of 30 other UN organisations, such as the World Health Organization (WHO) and UNICEF.

UNAIDS' role is to help governments to help themselves, and not to impose a 'UN solution' on a local problem.

Wake up to HIV/AIDS – a UNICEF project

Kindlimuka, which means 'wake up', is Mozambique's first self-help group for people living with HIV/AIDS. UNICEF supports the group.

Over 20 million people in Mozambique are HIV positive, with some 600 new infections every day. Of the new sufferers, 45 per cent are under the age of 25. Most do not know they are infected.

Kindlimuka works with local schoolchildren. The director, Adriano Matsinhe, says, 'Because I look healthy, the children think I'm paid to say I'm HIV-positive.'

Matsinhe is one of the few people in Mozambique who has openly admitted he is HIV-positive on television. The stigma of HIV/AIDS is one of the greatest challenges sufferers have to face, and Kindlimuka has been a breakthrough. It's a real community service. Many families now visit the centre.

You will explore the impact of HIV/AIDS and the work the United Nations does to combat this epidemic.

Projects supported by UNAIDS

UNAIDS teamed up with MTV to promote HIV/AIDS awareness to its one billion viewers around the world.

UNAIDS worked with the Ministry of Health in Brazil on a project which targeted 100,000 'at risk' teenagers and 80,000 injecting drug users.

UNAIDS sponsored the TV soap *I Need to Know*, which goes out on 20 television stations across Nigeria. The programme tries to persuade viewers that 'silence can be deadly', and encourages young people to speak out about taboo topics such as HIV/AIDS.

UNAIDS works with local agencies in southern Africa on a project aimed at preventing HIV/AIDS infection, particularly in adolescent girls.

UNAIDS collaborates with local churches in Chikankata, Zambia, helping to care for 1500 'AIDS orphans' from local villages.

1 Why did UNAIDS team up with MTV?
2 Why did the Brazilian government target teenagers and injecting drug users? What other groups might have been targeted?
3 Give reasons why UNAIDS used a TV soap to get health messages across in Nigeria.
4 Why does UNAIDS think it is important to support local programmes?

Action

1 Using organisations such as the Terence Higgins Trust, research rates of HIV infection in the UK and the support available to those infected.
2 Compare UK rates and support with information for another region of the world.
3 HIV/AIDS will have long-term economic effects in LEDCs such as Mozambique. In groups, discuss how the epidemic might affect the following in a poor country:
- family earnings
- food supplies
- education levels
- health services.

Check your understanding

1 Why are so many young people in LEDCs 'dying of ignorance'?
2 HIV/AIDS is a global problem, but why is it a more urgent problem in Africa than in Europe?
3 Why do you think the Mozambique project is called 'wake up'?
4 In your own words, what is the main challenge faced by AIDS workers such as Adriano Matsinhe?

... another point of view?

'Raising awareness of HIV/AIDS is the most important thing to do when dealing with the disease.'

Do you agree with this statement? Give reasons for your opinion, showing you have considered another point of view.

Key Terms

AIDS: acquired immune deficiency syndrome, a disease that destroys people's natural defences against diseases

HIV: human immunodeficiency virus, a virus that reduces people's resistance to illness and can cause AIDS

The UN at work

Getting you thinking

When civil war broke out in Liberia, 340,000 people fled in fear. Once peace was established, the **United Nations refugee** agency began to bring them home.

The United Nations High Commission for Refugees also worked with communities to rehabilitate and construct schools, water and sanitation systems, shelter, bridges and roads, which were all severely damaged during the 14-year conflict.

A Dutch soldier helps the returning refugees

1 Why do you think people left Liberia?

2 Why do you think refugees needed help to return home?

3 How did the UN help Liberian communities?

4 Why do you think people respect the soldiers from the UN?

Taking action

Keeping the peace throughout the world is one of the aims of the United Nations. When war breaks out and people are suffering, the UN's Security Council discusses what to do. There is a long list of issues and resolutions, as they call the decisions, every year.

The civil war in Liberia, in Getting you thinking, led to a resolution to help.

'The Security Council decides to establish the United Nations Mission in Liberia for a period of 12 months. It will consist of up to 15,000 United Nations military personnel, including up to 250 military observers and 160 staff officers, and up to 1,115 civilian police officers, including units to assist in the maintenance of law and order.'

Their role was peacekeeping and providing humanitarian aid:

'They will contribute towards international efforts to protect and promote human rights in Liberia, with particular attention to vulnerable groups including refugees, returning refugees and internally displaced persons, women, children, and demobilised child soldiers.'

The Members of the Security Council

There are five permanent members of the Security Council and ten elected members who serve for two years. All representatives must be in New York, where the Security Council is based, all the time to deal with emergencies.

The permanent members

France	China
UK	Russia
USA	

The elected members

Africa	3 members
Asia	2 members
Western Europe and 'Others'	2 members
Eastern Europe	1 member
Latin America and the Caribbean	2 members

You will investigate the ways the United Nations carries out its peacekeeping and humanitarian work.

Humanitarian action and human rights

People throughout the world are deprived of their human rights when war breaks out. As in Liberia, UN troops, who come from member countries, are sent in to help solve the problems.

Refugees

For more than five decades, the United Nations High Commission on Refugees has been helping the world's uprooted peoples.

The agency's first task was to help an estimated one million people after World War II. During the 1950s, the refugee crisis spread to Africa, Asia and then back to Europe. It had become a global problem.

During its lifetime, the agency has assisted an estimated 50 million refugees to restart their lives.

Child soldiers

Child soldiers in Africa are often looked after by the UN and educated in order to fit into society again. Often their families can't be found. This is just one of many projects to help people in difficulties.

> 'The soldiers gave me training. They gave me a gun. I took drugs. I killed civilians. Lots. It was just war, what I did then. I only took orders. I knew it was bad. It was not my wish.'

A former child soldier being helped at a rehabilitation centre

Action

1. Research a current UN peacekeeping operation. Why are people fighting? How is the UN helping? Is it 'maintaining international peace and security'?
2. Find a recent example of work done by the UN High Commission on Refugees. Why had the refugees left home? How has the High Commission helped?

Check your understanding

1. What kind of work does the UN do?
2. Is the UN a government? Explain your answer.
3. Describe the Security Council's responsibilities.
4. Why is the UK important in the Security Council?
5. Why do you think the UN needs to intervene in the conflicts mentioned?
6. Why might the UN be able to help refugees more effectively than individual countries?
7. Which human rights are the child soldiers being denied?

... another point of view?

'Countries should not be allowed to be members of the UN if their populations' human rights are not respected.'

Do you agree with this statement? Give reasons for your opinion, showing you have considered another point of view.

143

International justice

Humanitarian horror

Hundreds of fighters, including children under the age of 15, attacked Bogoro – a village in the Democratic Republic of Congo. They were armed with semi-automatic weapons, rocket-propelled grenades and knives. The soldiers circled the village and converged towards the centre, killing at least 200 civilians and imprisoning survivors in a room filled with corpses. Some residents of the village were killed when their houses were set on fire and others were hacked to death with machetes.

Two suspects, Germain Katanga and Mathieu Ngudjolo Chui, have been surrendered to the International Criminal Court by the Congolese authorities. Both men are charged with six counts of war crimes and three counts of crimes against humanity, relating to the attack on the village of Bogoro.

1 Which human rights did the fighters deprive people of?

2 Why do you think the Congolese authorities handed the men over to the court?

International Criminal Court

The International Criminal Court was set up in 2002. It is entirely independent but was born out of the United Nations, which can refer issues to the court.

Over 100 countries have signed up and more are committed to joining. However, some important countries have refused to join because they are critical of the court. These include USA, China, Russia and India.

The court only deals with the most serious crimes, including **genocide**, crimes against humanity and war crimes.

The court is a 'last resort', as it will not deal with cases that countries are dealing with themselves. It will, however, take on cases if a country is holding a trial but is really protecting the offenders.

If the court is going to be understood by the people in the countries affected by its activities, it must communicate with the local people. In the Congo, for example, it has used TV docudramas and interactive radio programmes in local languages as well as holding discussions with ethnic communities.

You will find out how people who commit humanitarian crimes are dealt with.

What law?

For a court to make rulings, it needs laws on which to base its decisions. The **Geneva Convention** sets out the rules for how people should be treated in war. Most countries have signed up to it. There have been some additional rules since the Convention was set up in 1949. These include rules related to the use of biological and chemical weapons and anti-personnel mines.

The Geneva Convention

1 People who are not involved in hostilities must be protected and treated humanely.

2 It is forbidden to kill or injure an enemy who surrenders.

3 The wounded and sick shall be collected and cared for by the people which has them in its power.

4 Captured combatants and civilians are entitled to respect for their lives, dignity, personal rights and convictions. They shall have the right to correspond with their families and to receive relief.

5 No one shall be held responsible for an act he has not committed. No one shall be subjected to physical or mental torture, corporal punishment or cruel or degrading treatment.

6 It is prohibited to employ weapons or methods of warfare of a nature to cause unnecessary losses or excessive suffering.

7 The civilian population must not be attacked. Attacks shall be directed solely against military objectives.

Not to be confused with ...

The International Court of Justice, which is a UN organisation. Its objective is to settle disputes between member countries. It was asked to rule on the West Bank Barrier, which Israel claimed it had built to protect the country from terrorism. The opposition to it claimed that Israel was taking land that wasn't theirs and preventing Palestinians from moving freely in the area – including going to work. The International Court of Justice ruled that the wall was illegal. Israel rejected the ruling and the wall is still there.

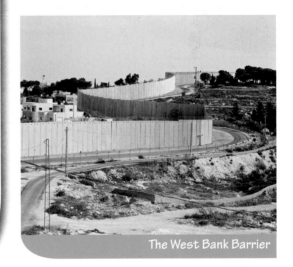

The West Bank Barrier

Action

1 What conflicts are going on in the world today?
2 Find out how people's human rights are affected.
3 Has the UN's Security Council expressed a view?
4 Has anyone been referred to the International Criminal Court?
5 Find out about the trials that are going on.

Check your understanding

1 How was the International Criminal Court set up?
2 What issues does it deal with?
3 Which countries have refused to join?
4 How does it try to explain its activities to local people?
5 What rules does the Geneva Convention set out?
6 What does the International Court of Justice do?

... another point of view?

'Countries should be left to sort out their own humanitarian criminals.'

Do you agree with this statement? Give reasons for your opinion, showing you have considered another point of view.

Key Terms

Geneva Convention: an internationally accepted set of rules on the treatment of people in war

genocide: mass murder of a racial, national or religious group

Protecting human rights

Getting you thinking

'S' was arrested and charged with attempted robbery. He was only 11 at the time. He was acquitted of the charge.

Mr Marper was charged with harassment of his partner. The case was formally discontinued, as he and his partner had become reconciled.

Both 'S' and Mr Marper had their fingerprints and DNA samples taken.

Despite the fact that they were not found guilty of any offence, their fingerprints and DNA samples were kept by the British authorities. The information had been stored on the basis of a law that says it could be kept with no time limit. They asked for it to be removed but their request was turned down.

They decided to take the case to the European Court of Human Rights.

Outcome: The Court decided that keeping the fingerprints, cellular samples and DNA profiles of people who are suspected but not convicted of offences:

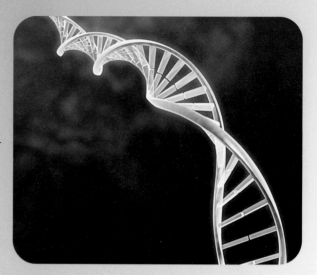

- did not strike a fair balance between the competing public and private interests
- failed to respect private life
- could not be regarded as necessary in a democratic society.

1 Why does the British government want to keep fingerprints and DNA samples?

2 Why did 'S' and Mr Marper want them removed?

3 Why did the Court say that the UK government was in the wrong?

4 What effect might this have on UK law?

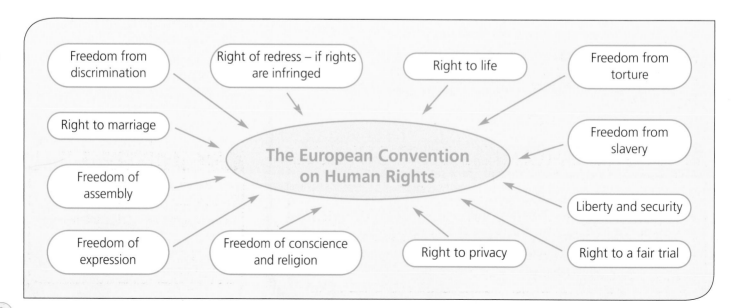

Freedom from discrimination

Right of redress – if rights are infringed

Right to life

Freedom from torture

Right to marriage

The European Convention on Human Rights

Freedom from slavery

Freedom of assembly

Freedom of expression

Freedom of conscience and religion

Right to privacy

Liberty and security

Right to a fair trial

You will find out about how people can challenge those who try to restrict their human rights.

The European Court of Human Rights

The European Court of Human Rights was set up by the Council of Europe.

The Council of Europe aims to protect human rights, democracy and the rule of law. All 47 member-countries have signed up to the European Convention of Human Rights, which forms the basis for the Court's judgements. It is quite different from the European Union, which has economic objectives.

The Court was set up to enforce the European Convention on Human Rights, which had been drawn up by the Council of Europe. The Court can award damages but does not have the power to award other punishments. Ultimately, a country could be expelled from the Council if it did not accept the rulings. The EU also watches carefully to see what the member states are up to.

Not to be confused with ...

The European Court of Justice deals with situations when EU laws, rather than human rights, are involved.

Sharon Coleman, a mum with a disabled five-year-old, took her employer to the European Court of Justice because she wasn't allowed flexible working on the same basis as other people with children. The court ruled that she should be entitled to it. The change means carers could make a discrimination complaint if their colleagues are allowed to work flexibly but they are not.

Implications for UK law

Once a ruling has been given by the Court, governments are expected to change the law so as to take it into account.

The UK government argued that it needed to keep the information in order to fight crime. Others didn't agree:

- Human Rights Lawyer – 'The government should now start destroying the DNA records of those people who are currently on the DNA database and who are innocent of any crime.'

- Liberty, the Human Rights pressure group – 'This is one of the most strongly worded judgements that Liberty has ever seen from the Court of Human Rights. That court has used human rights principles and common sense to deliver the privacy protection of innocent people that the British government has shamefully failed to deliver.'

- Scotland already destroys DNA samples taken during criminal investigations from people who are not charged or who are later acquitted of the alleged offences.

Action

Find out how UK law changed in light of the ruling on DNA and fingerprint records.

Have any other rulings affected UK law?

Check your understanding

1 Which organisation set up the European Court of Human Rights?
2 What is the basis for its judgements?
3 Why do you think the EU is interested in the actions of its members?
4 What do governments have to do if the court finds against them?
5 What is the ultimate sanction?
6 What is the European Court of Justice?

... another point of view?

'A country should be free to decide its own laws.'

Do you agree with this statement? Give reasons for your opinion, showing you have considered another point of view.

The global community: the exam

Urgent action demanded over climate change

- Rapid climate change is becoming increasingly obvious. The Arctic sea ice has melted more than ever before. Fierce hurricanes have done much damage and Spain has suffered droughts like never before.
- Part of the cause could be global warming resulting from rising CO_2 emissions in Europe, including the UK.
- There is clearly an urgent need to develop new technologies.

Leave margin blank

1. What harmful activity is shown in the photograph above? *(1 mark)*

   <u>Pollution from factories</u>

2. Why are so many people worried about the high level of carbon dioxide emissions?

   (1 mark)

   ☐ A. Because the effects of climate change, such as melting ice caps and hurricanes, are creating more carbon dioxide.

   ☐ B. Because carbon dioxide comes from burning fossil fuels which are rapidly running out throughout the world.

   ☑ C. Because carbon dioxide is a greenhouse gas, which leads to global warming.

   ☐ D. Because increased carbon dioxide makes the air harder to breathe.

European Union leaders reached a deal on measures to fight global warming

The 27 member-countries have agreed to cut carbon emissions by 20 per cent by 2020, compared with 1990 levels.

But critics said the package did not go far enough because it gave concessions to both

- heavy industries like coal and steel

and

- Eastern European countries worried that pollution cuts will harm their economies.

Leave margin blank

3. Briefly explain what the European Union is. *(2 marks)*

> The European Union is a group of countries whose governments work together to change the way people live and do business in Europe.

There are a number of ways of answering this question. This sums up the two main objectives of people's lives and business.

4. Which of the following countries is a member of the European Union? *(1 mark)*
   - ☐ A. Norway
   - ☑ B. Greece
   - ☐ C. Albania
   - ☐ D. Switzerland

5. Briefly explain why one country on its own cannot solve the problems associated with global warming. *(2 marks)*

> Pollution doesn't stay in one place. Winds carry it to other countries. It all ends up in the atmosphere so all countries need to join in if we are going to make a difference.

Understanding that countries are linked together in all sorts of ways is important to Citizenship.

6. Explain why Eastern European countries are afraid that cutting pollution will harm their economies. *(2 marks)*

> Cutting pollution costs money because it means installing equipment to remove it from the gases given off. If making things costs more money then people won't be able to buy so much.
> It will make them poorer.

The student brings together an understanding of the environment with its links to the economy.

149

Extended writing

'No country in the whole world can stop or control the spread of globalisation.'
Do you agree with this statement?
Give reasons for your opinion, showing that you have considered another point of view.
You could include the following points in your answer and other information of your own.

- What is globalisation and can it be controlled?

- Who benefits from globalisation – the poor, the rich or everyone?

- How can a country or international organisations like the EU, UN or the Commonwealth influence globalisation?

- What actions would ensure that globalisation helps people rather than harming them?

(12 marks)

Adapted from Edexcel 2008

Leave margin blank

Globalisation means that all countries are becoming more interdependent. We buy things that are made all over the world. It can mean that people are paid low wages because businesses are always looking for the cheapest way of making things. It cannot be controlled by one country by itself but countries can make laws which help.

> A good introduction. The student has defined globalisation then expressed a point of view and put another perspective. This means that they can get more than half marks.

In some ways we all benefit from globalisation.

> The bullet points are being used to build the argument. It is important to build them in and not just answer the questions without thinking about the big question at the top.

Poor people in LEDCs have jobs – even if wages are low compared to here. They may not be so low there because it costs less to live in LEDCs. There need to be controls to make sure people aren't exploited. In Europe and the West we can buy things more cheaply and so we can have more. If we could only buy things made in Europe or the USA, everything would be much more expensive.

> The student shows a good understanding of some of the issues of globalisation and understands that there are trade-offs for all of us.

International organisations can help to make sure that things are fair. The United Nations Universal Declaration of Human Rights lays down people's rights and freedoms. Although not all countries make sure that it is kept, it provides guidelines for them. Organisations like the Commonwealth, the World Bank and the International Monetary Fund help countries to develop and this means people's lives improve.

> This shows that the student knows about the way in which countries are linked together through the international organisations.

Free trade helps countries because they can sell their products round the world. The EU and USA have tariffs or taxes on things they import, which can make it hard for countries to sell things like sugar and coffee.

Fair Trade also helps but this is not about governments but about the decisions individuals make about what they want to buy and sell. It might cost a bit more to buy a Fair Trade chocolate but at least you know that the people who grow the cocoa beans are getting a fair price for their products. When we buy things we need to think about whether we are being ethical. Cheap clothes are likely to have been made in a sweat shop in an LEDC.

> This shows the difference between Fair Trade and free trade. Many students muddle these up.

We can't stop globalisation so we have to try to make it work for as many people as possible. While international organisations can help, individuals must also make decisions about what they buy.

> A good conclusion. It shows that people have a responsibility as well as governments and organisations.

Unit 2:

Participating

Your activity: what's the choice?   154

Making the choice   156

Planning the activity   158

in society

Developing your skills: advocacy and representation   **160**

Participation in action   **162**

The impact of your action   **164**

Your activity: what's the choice?

1 What issues do you think the young people in the picture might be discussing?
2 Think about your community – what needs changing?
3 What do you care about?
4 How do you think you can make a difference?

Young people in Devizes discuss community issues

Questions to ask

Citizenship is all about joining in and having an effect. Participating in society gives you the chance to have a go. There are lots of ways of participating as you will have found out already.

There are lots of questions to ask before you decide on the issue you want to address.

When you've worked out what the issue is, there are two questions to ask:

1   How does it fit into Citizenship?

Whatever issue you choose must fit into one of the categories that make up Citizenship. There are nine in total (see the list opposite) so there are lots of opportunities. If you want to refresh you memory, just flick through Unit 1 and you'll be sure to find an issue you'd like to get involved with.

You may find that your choice links two or more sections of the list – which is great because Citizenship is all about joined-up thinking. If, for example you are concerned about sustainable development, you might want to engage the local council or the media to get your message over.

- What would you like to change?
- Do rules need to be changed?
- What's going on in your local area?
- What needs doing?
- **What's the issue?**
- Who needs helping?
- What's unfair?
- Are there voices that need to be heard?
- Do you need to spread the word?

How does it fit into Citizenship?

1 Political, legal and human rights and freedoms in a range of contexts, from local to global
2 Civil, criminal law and the justice system – police, youth offending teams, courts, lawyers, prisons and probation
3 Democratic and electoral processes and the operation of parliamentary democracy
4 The development of, and struggle for, different kinds of rights and freedoms (in the UK and abroad).
5 The media
6 Policies and practices for sustainable development
7 The economy in relation to citizenship and the relationship between employers and employees
8 Origins and implications of diversity and the changing nature of society in the UK
9 The European Union, the Commonwealth and the UN

How are we going to make a difference?

- Presenting a case to others about a concern
- Conducting a consultation, vote or election
- Organising a meeting, event or forum to raise awareness and debate issues
- Representing the views of others at a meeting or event
- Creating, reviewing or revisiting an organisation's policy
- Contributing to local community policies
- Lobbying and communicating views publicly via a website or display
- Setting up an action group or network
- Training others in democratic skills such as advocacy, campaigning or leadership

2 How are we going to make a difference?

There are all sorts of ways of making a difference. It's all about making your voice heard – or helping others to do so. School might be the right place to start.

- If you want other students to care about your particular issue, you might want to put on an event to help them understand.
- There may be others who care about an issue too. Get them together and form a pressure group.
- If you don't like the school rules, you might want to set about changing them.
- Perhaps Year 7s would enjoy an event that trains them to use the systems of democracy in school.

Perhaps there are issues outside school – is the skate park under threat, should there be more street lights near the school or should local traffic be calmed?

- A website that informed people of the issue could also take their votes.
- A consultation in the local area could provide evidence for your actions.
- A debate would allow people to put their side of the argument.

A voice in the community. Young people in Stoke on Trent voting for their representatives

Care about Fair Trade? Run your own co-operative

Making the choice

A Citizenship activity is an important part of your course. You need to collect evidence and keep a record of what happened at every stage as it is very important that you show what you and everyone else did. You will also need to work out how well it went. You may already be involved in suitable activities but, if not, you'll need to choose what to do. There are many possibilities for you to consider.

What's the issue?

- Is there an open space that could be turned into a garden or other sort of community or school resource?
- Can you work with other young people to discuss community issues such as graffiti, vandalism or services that you would like to see in your area?
- Do you have a school council? If not, could you set one up?
- Could you organise a school event, perhaps to raise money to promote and support a good cause?
- Could you find out about employment rights and responsibilities?
- Could you question the spending priorities of the local council?
- Does your school have a radio station? If not, could you start one up to promote involvement in local issues?
- Could you run a mock election or trial, or hold a meeting for an international organisation?

- Could you organise a petition, opinion poll or display about something you care about, such as an environmental issue?
- Could you run a mini-enterprise related to a Citizenship issue – perhaps a Fair Trade co-operative?

Your activity could be based on any of these ideas or many others. Remember that being involved in something that really interests you always makes the task easier. For example, does the environment concern you? Are you worried about crime in your area? Or do you want more facilities for young people in the area?

If you are making things or providing a service, such as providing ethically produced refreshments at the school fair, you might be able to turn it into a mini-enterprise. This would mean deciding on the costs of all the things you need and thinking about the prices you can charge. You would need to do some research into this. How will you market your product? How much profit do you aim to make? How will you use the profits to benefit your school or community?

The right choice

The one really important thing to remember is that your activity must fit into the Citizenship Studies specification. You might want to run an event to raise money for charity such as a cake sale, or a five-a-side football match, but you must know why you are doing it and understand the benefits that result from it. Your reasoning must appear on your activity response form. The emphasis should always be on working with others and on participation.

Working in a team

The Citizenship activity asks you to work as part of a team. The team may be made up of your school friends or it may be a group outside school. It is important to think about the contribution each person makes to the activity. Make sure that everyone has a role in the activity; it makes it much easier to identify each person's contribution if you can explain their responsibilities.

What's the evidence?

While you were choosing your issue you probably looked at information about it. Did you collect leaflets or newspaper articles? If so, include them and explain why. Were there leaflets or information about it on the web? If you used web-based information, make sure it is relevant! Whatever your source, make sure that it is to the point. Markers don't want to wade through masses of material that isn't to the point. There are no marks for weight!

You need to be able show to the examiner that you thought about your choice and came to a conclusion. You don't have to write lots – just answer the question and add the evidence of what you did.

If you shared out roles, produce some evidence of how you went about it. Perhaps your teacher would sign a witness statement.

How does it link to Citizenship?

Which part of Unit 1 does your issue fit into:

- rights and responsibilities?
- power, politics and the media?
- the global community?

Look carefully at the themes and work out exactly where it fits.

Write four sentences that explain the connections.

1 Make a list of the contributions you think people will have to make in order to plan and carry out this activity.
2 Why do you think it is a good activity for Citizenship Studies?
3 Which part of the course does it relate to? See page 155.

A group of young people work on a community environment project

Take action

Sit down with a blank sheet of paper and think about the Citizenship activity you want to do.

1 Start by writing down all your ideas.
2 List all the advantages and disadvantages of each idea.
3 Put them in order from best to worst.
4 Is the one at the top the one you really want to carry out? If so, go ahead. If not, have another look at the list.

Check point

Before you make a final decision, check with your teacher that your activity is suitable for the course requirements.

On the response form you will need to describe and analyse the contribution you and the others in your group made to the Citizenship activity, so it's a good idea to think about this right from the start of your activity.

Planning the activity

The steps to success

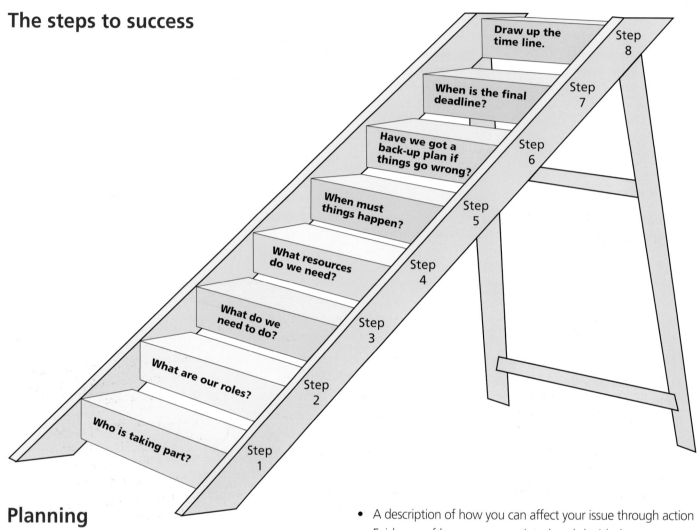

Step 1 — Who is taking part?
Step 2 — What are our roles?
Step 3 — What do we need to do?
Step 4 — What resources do we need?
Step 5 — When must things happen?
Step 6 — Have we got a back-up plan if things go wrong?
Step 7 — When is the final deadline?
Step 8 — Draw up the time line.

Planning

Planning means setting out what must be done and making sure that everyone knows their responsibilities. By following the steps above, you will be on the right track. You will need to gather evidence and be able to explain the links to Citizenship, so you need to build this into your plan. The following pages will help you with the stages of organising your action and gathering the evidence you need.

What will you need to collect?

- Evidence to show why your issue is important locally and nationally
- An explanation of how it links to Citizenship
- Evidence that you have communicated with two people in positions of power or influence and found out what they thought
- An explanation of why people hold different points of view on your issue

- A description of how you can affect your issue through action
- Evidence of how you negotiated and decided on your action
- Evidence of your action
- Evidence of your contribution
- An assessment of the contribution of your action, locally and nationally
- Thoughts on whether you action has affected your views

What will you need to do?

Brainstorm all the things that need to be done.
- Can you easily divide these things into groups?
- Who has the skills needed for each activity?
- Should people work in pairs or on their own?

When you have made these decisions, draw up a list to explain exactly what everyone has to do.

Make sure you keep the list safe. You will need it to check whether everything has been done and to put in your records.

Planning the timeline

Look carefully at your plan and draw up a timeline, putting the name of the person responsible beside every point.

This will enable you to check whether everything is on track. It will also give everyone target dates for getting things done.

Remember that gathering information can take time, so make it a priority.

Example: Planning a Fair Trade event in school

October 1

- Choose activity. Keep a record of how you decided.
- Draw up plan. Set deadlines for each stage.
- Work out who you need to consult – the head teacher? a Fair Trade organisation? Are they in a position of power or influence?
- Work out links with Citizenship.
- Set date for event.

October 7

- Find evidence of why all products are not Fair Trade.
- Work out what you will need for the event and set about organising it – presentations, leaflets, posters, a Fair Trade stall?
- Work out how your action will affect the issue – keep a record.

October 21

- Review materials and resources – are they convincing? Do you need anything else?
- If running a Fair Trade stall, have you got the products, marketing material, a float so you can give change?
- Make sure you have a record of letters etc.

October 28

- Start marketing event – posters, school newsletter, school website?
- Keep copies of the evidence.

November 14

- The event!
- Keep a record of what happened – photographs of your involvement, of the posters, the presentations, people's comments – has the event changed their minds? – record/video them?

November 21

- Review what happened.
- Have you got enough evidence?
- Do you need to find out more about whether you influenced people?
- Work out how your action has affected the issue locally and nationally.
- Work out whether it has affected your views.

Developing your skills: advocacy and representation

Who can you persuade?

Students from Deptford Green School were fed up because of the mess made by pigeons nesting under a bridge that they walked under on the way to school. They organised a visit to Metronet, the organisation responsible for the bridge. It was agreed that work would be carried out on the bridge during the summer holidays to prevent the pigeons roosting. Result!

1 Why do you think the students picked this issue?
2 How did they set about solving the problem?
3 Why do you think Metronet agreed to carry out the work?

Unit 2: Participating in society

What are advocacy and representation?

- Advocacy – arguing for a particular cause
- Representation – speaking on a particular issue

Many young people are very good at this. When they believe in a cause or an issue, they argue and defend it until they have convinced the listener! You just have to put these skills to work in a Citizenship context.

When the students went to see Metronet they were being advocates for their case and representing their issue.

Who do you want to talk to?

You need to find out the views of two people who are in a position of power or influence. They might support your point of view or be against it. You will need to be able to explain why they have different points of view, so think carefully about the questions you want to ask. It's good to practise this skill because you are always expected to put another point of view in the exam.

If you wanted:

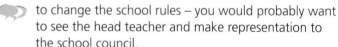

- to change the school rules – you would probably want to see the head teacher and make representation to the school council.
- the school to run a Fair Trade shop – you would need to persuade the senior leaders and again the school council.
- to change something in the community – you might want to talk to your local councillor and perhaps an organisation that holds a different point of view.
- the school to support one charity rather than another – you might want to talk to the charity and people who have a different favourite charity.
- the bus timetable changed – you might want to talk to the bus company and the local council.

160

Why do people hold different points of view?

As you discovered in Unit 1, we all have several identities. This means that we have different opinions about different things. Do you always agree with your friends and family? Start thinking about why you disagree. You will soon realise why there are issues that are difficult to deal with.

If you wanted to support the development of a skate park – can you imagine why others might object?

If you wanted to support a particular charity – work out your reasons and think of reasons why your friends might want to support a different charity.

It is useful to think about other people's views before you discuss an issue with them. Keep a record of what is said.

What's the evidence?

You will need to keep a record of your conversations with people. You could record them and include them with your response form.

If you write letters, include them – and the response. If you send emails, print them out and add them to your work.

Your teacher may provide a witness statement, but you need evidence of what was said.

Check point

If you want to talk to the head teacher, make an appointment. If there are several of you who want to talk about the same thing, work together because everyone is very busy.

If you want to talk to the council, try the local councillor first. They will tell you where to go if they can't deal with it themselves.

If you need to talk to other organisations, email works well because it is quick. Make sure you keep your email and the replies.

Take action

Once you have decided on your activity, you will need to decide who to talk to.

Think of people who are easy to get hold of. If you are concerned that some countries still use child labour, don't attempt to talk to the country's president! You might try to get a view from Oxfam or a business that has been accused of using child labour.

Participation in action

1. How are these students showing their citizenship skills?
2. How are they making a difference – locally and nationally?
3. What do you think they had to do to plan this activity?
4. What sort of evidence do you think they collected?
5. How does their activity relate to the content of the course?

How can you affect your issue through action?

The number of young people who vote is declining. The students in the picture are helping children at the local primary school to understand how voting and democracy work. Not only are they helping these young people, but they are also hoping to stop the fall in the number who vote. An early start is always helpful!

Once you have set up your activity, you need to be able to explain how it will make a difference.

Gather evidence of your action and how you made a contribution

There are all sorts of ways in which you can submit your supporting evidence. It doesn't have to be in writing. You need to submit at least three pieces of evidence showing that you participated in the activity. On some occasions a witness statement will show that you made a contribution. The task response form tells you exactly what you need to produce. Here are some suggestions as to how you could record your activity:

- PowerPoint slides
- videos
- CD-Roms
- letters
- photographs
- banners
- web pages
- audio or written records of presentation work
- questionnaires
- agendas or minutes of meetings.

Different types of evidence

A video that showed the extent of your activity would be fine. An audio recording of a meeting or a presentation about carrying out your activity would also give a clear picture of how you were working.

If you use a PowerPoint or some other presentation software to explain or persuade people of your point of view, that will make a good piece of evidence.

If you create a website to let people know you plans or to persuade them about your issue, this will be helpful evidence as it shows just what you were trying to do and how you went about it.

If you investigate what people want or think, you may use a questionnaire. This, together with the results, would make a good piece of evidence as it would show the way you worked and what you found out.

You might write a document to explain, persuade or justify what you are planning. This would also be a useful piece of supporting evidence, as it would give people a good picture of the activity.

Agendas or minutes of meetings will show what you and others did.

Gathering the information as you go along will help you to put it all together. It's very easy to forget exactly what happened and when!

Take action

Work out how you are going to affect the issue through the action you are taking. The local aspects may be easy. You may need to refer to the content of Unit 1 to decide how you are making the bigger impact. Think about the effect you've had on the people involved – and how you might have changed their attitudes or behaviour.

Work out how you are going to gather the evidence and then make sure you keep it safe!

Check point

Get organised! The evidence is important so build it into every part of your action.

You should describe how each piece of evidence helped you do the activity. For example, an agenda of a meeting helped you plan a particular stage of your activity, or a questionnaire helped you get information about your activity. It is also important that you show how the evidence you have gathered can be used to support arguments and make judgements.

The impact of your action

How has your action contributed to your issue?

A Citizenship activity always aims to make a difference. You might have organised a fund-raising event but you need to know why you were doing it and the impact it had.

Your answers to the questions above will depend on the sort of activity you took part in. For example:

- If your group was involved in helping younger children to learn about democracy, did you feel they enjoyed it and did your activity really help them learn? You might have given them a quiz at the end. Include the results to show what they learnt. Work out how it will affect their views on voting in future.

- If you ran a Fair Trade day, did you influence other students' views? Was there a demand to sell Fair Trade products in school? If your fellow students are now persuading their families to buy Fair Trade products, you are having an effect both nationally and internationally because people growing cocoa beans or coffee or making clothes will have a better standard of living.

- If your group was trying to persuade the local council to provide more sports facilities or to light a subway to make it safer, what was the result? Don't worry if the council didn't accept your idea immediately. If you have got a councillor to support your idea, they will probably bring it up again in the next financial year. Ask them to do so. These things can take time!

Has your action affected your views?

I'm even more committed!

When you came up with the idea for your issue, you probably thought it was worthwhile. You will have done some research to be able to show why your issue is important, both locally and nationally. The evidence you produced may have increased your conviction that things need to be done.

I've changed my mind!

Citizenship is all about points of view.

If you wanted the council to enclose a basketball court or set up a skate park, you might have listened to the arguments about how the council spends its money. Perhaps other people have pointed out that spending money to meet your plans would mean spending less on old people or reducing the hours the library is open.

Did you decide which was more important?

Recording it all

You can write up your activity in stages. There is quite a lot to think about so this is probably the best way. Your teacher will let you know how the writing up should be planned. The most important things are:

- knowing how your action fitted into Citizenship
- that you have collected the evidence for each stage and know what the evidence shows
- that you have worked out the impact you made both locally and nationally.

Once these issues are clear, the writing up should be straightforward. Remember that the coursework is worth 60 per cent of the whole GCSE so you can get lots of marks for doing things rather than just taking an exam.

Unit 3:

Citizenship

Option A: Environmental change and sustainable development 168–85

Making ethical decisions	170	Do targets work?	178
Global warming – the perspectives	172	Sustainability: local or national?	180
		The same rules for all?	182
What can you do?	174	Trade or aid?	184
Not in my backyard?	176		

Environmental change and sustainable development: the exam 186–9

Option B: Changing communities: social and cultural identities 190–207

Making ethical decisions	192	Can we stay?	196
Why come to Britain?	194	Coming and going	198

in context

A melting pot?   200   Attitudes to immigration   204

Are we really equal?   202   Working together   206

Changing communities: social and cultural identities: the exam   **208–11**

Option C: Influencing and changing decisions in society and government   **212–33**

Making ethical decisions   214   What's the point of prison?   224

Influencing change   216   Criminal or civil?   226

Political change   218   What's happening to freedom?   228

Changing democracy   220   Who's listening?   230

Crime: fact or fiction?   222   Can we control the economy?   232

Influencing and changing decisions in society and government: the exam   **234–9**

Option A: Environmental change and sustainable development

The media is full of environmental issues. In Unit 1 you learnt a lot about the environment and now you have a chance to investigate other people's views on the subject. You can then work out the views that you agree with and those you don't and come to your own conclusions.

Topics to investigate

These questions will help you to think about environmental issues. In the exam you will be given a range of points of view on an environmental topic and you will be able to use all the skills and knowledge you have developed in your Citizenship Studies course to answer the questions.

- What are the ethical aspects of environmental change and sustainable development?

Getting going

The question to ask yourself is 'What's going on?'. Whatever media you use, you will find lots of useful material. Just Googling a topic will give you masses of information – but how do you know whether it is accurate? How do you know whether the people who run the website have their own mission? There are lots of questions to ask.

'If built, these units would be the first new coal build in the UK for over 20 years and could set a new benchmark for a cleaner coal-fired generation in the UK.'

E.ON

'The new coal plant that would emit as much carbon dioxide as the world's 24 lowest emitting countries combined. Worse, it could keep pumping out emissions for another 50 years. And it will only be 45 per cent efficient, in an age when power stations can reach 95 per cent efficiency.'

Greenpeace

'We are committed to the development of technology to reduce emissions and we intend to be one of the first countries to demonstrate the technology for a coal-fired station on a commercial scale. Coal is and will remain a vital part of the global energy mix, and this will be the case for many years to come.'

The energy minister

1 What questions would you want to ask?
2 Where would your go to find the answers?
3 Are there alternatives to coal?
4 How do you weigh up the alternatives?

- Is global warming the result of human activity and is there anything humanity can do about it?
- Can individuals make a difference?
- Do individuals and communities genuinely agree with national and global responses to problems of global warming and climate change?
- Is it worth setting targets for reducing emissions in the future and what are the most realistic ways of achieving them?
- What are the local and national agendas, debates and goals and how can local and national governments approach the problem?
- Is it fair to impose the same solutions on LEDCs as on MEDCs?
- Is trade rather than aid a better way of supporting a country so it can develop or become more sustainable more quickly?

Whose perspectives?

Individual
- How can individuals make a difference?
- How can individuals protect people's rights?

Ethical
- What is fair and unfair?
- How can rights compete and conflict?
- How can hard decisions be made?

Community
- How can communities take action?
- How can organisations and governments protect people's rights?

National
- What impact does the media have on national policies?
- What is the significance of identities and diversity?

Global
- How are LEDCs and MEDCs affected?
- Trade or aid?
- How do different kinds of rights and responsibilities affect individuals and communities?
- What challenges face the global community? Conflict? Inequality? Sustainability?

Social
- How do individual and community values affect the issue?

Political
- How do local, national and global green policies affect issues?
- What impact do democracy and justice have in different countries?

Making ethical decisions

Would you buy this dress for £12?

How often have you heard people say 'I don't know how they do it for the money'? The truth is that we do know how they do it. The dress is made in China or another part of the world where labour is cheap and there are few controls over working conditions. Even when there are laws to protect workers, they are often ignored.

1 How are clothes made so cheaply in countries like China?

2 Do you buy clothes because they are cheap?

3 Do you think about why they are cheap?

4 Would you still buy them if you knew about the lives of the people who make the clothes?

5 Are there any arguments for continuing to buy very cheap clothes?

What does 'ethical' mean?

Different people use different words to define 'ethical', but the general view is that it means 'relating to a set of values including compassion, fairness, honesty, respect, and responsibility'.

Making an ethical decision means taking all these aspects into account. In order to do this there are some questions to be asked.

- Which action results in the most good and least harm?

- Which action respects the rights of everyone involved?

- Which action treats people fairly?

- Which action contributes most to the quality of life of the people affected?

These questions can be asked of any issue or dispute in order to come to a decision about what to do.

You will find out about ethical aspects of environmental change and sustainable development.

Who's the winner?

Tesco decided to sell its chickens at £1.99 each. They said it was to help shoppers on a budget. There were loud complaints from people who are interested in animal welfare because they argued that this would encourage people to buy cheap chickens bred in battery farms. The farmers' lobby wasn't happy either because this would lead to Tesco wanting even cheaper chickens, so farmers' incomes would fall.

1 Use the ethical decision-making questions to help you to decide whether Tesco was right to sell cheap chickens.

Is everyone's decision the same?

Even when using the ethical decision-making questions, not everyone's answers are the same. It all depends on our personal values and the weight we give to different questions. People have different approaches to quality of life, for example. For some people, living without a car would make life impossible because of a lack of public transport. Others would value eating organic food because they think it makes them healthier – while others can only afford the cheapest food if they are to feed their family.

Do food miles matter?

We won't buy Ghanaian pineapples because of their enormous food miles – but the Ghanaian farmer has a tiny **carbon footprint**.

Tomatoes from England don't travel very far but lots of energy is used to heat the greenhouses they grow in. In Spain, they grow under the sun.

Beans from Kenya travel a long way, but do they provide jobs for people who might otherwise be unemployed?

Producing a ton of lamb in Britain produces 3 tons of CO_2 compared with half a ton in New Zealand because we use more electricity and fertiliser here. The shipping of the lamb to the UK uses 273 lb of CO_2.

1 Use ethical decision-making to decide whether it is better to buy food that doesn't travel far.

2 What else would you need to know before you made a decision?

Check your understanding

1 What does 'ethical' mean?
2 Use the questions for making an ethical decision to decide what you should do when considering whether to buy cheap clothes.
3 Why do people's answers to ethical issues differ?

... another point of view?

'Every decision we make should be ethical.'

Do you agree with this statement? Give reasons for your opinion, showing you have considered another point of view.

Key Terms

ethical: relating to a set of values including compassion, fairness, honesty, respect and responsibility

carbon footprint: your carbon footprint is the sum of all the emissions of carbon dioxide caused by your activities in a given time period

Global warming – the perspectives

Getting you thinking

Are we causing global warming?

Yes!
Most scientists believe that climate change is caused by the increasing amount of carbon dioxide that people pump into the atmosphere. Temperatures have risen as our output of CO_2 has risen.

No!
Temperatures haven't been rising for the last ten years but we haven't stopped pumping CO_2 into the atmosphere – so are we really causing global warming? There have been periods when England was tropical and dinosaurs roamed the land. At other times, ice covered the country – forming the scenery of much of the north of England.

What do people think?

45% placed global warming behind race and immigration, the NHS and crime in terms of national concerns. Locally, they were more concerned about traffic, litter, graffiti, parks, noise and dogs fouling the pavement.

38% thought it would have an impact.

51% thought it would have little or no effect.

90% thought it would have a significant impact on future generations.

41% thought it was partly caused by both natural and human activity.

56% thought experts were still divided over whether human activity is contributing to global warming.

46% thought a solution could be found to the problems caused by climate change.

37% admitted they were doing nothing about climate change.

70% agreed that the government should take the lead in combating climate change even if it means using the law to change people's behaviour. They are looking to business to take greater action on climate change.

Source: Ipsos Mori

1 What are the effects of global warming? Check Unit 1 page 136.
2 Explain the two points of view about global warming.
3 Are people in general as worried as many scientists are?
4 What issues do people think are more important than climate change? Why do you think they hold these views?
5 Who, in many people's view, should deal with the problem? Why do you think they hold these views?
6 What can be done to persuade people to take it seriously?

You will investigate whether global warming results from human activity and, if so, what people are doing about it.

Is global warming really happening?

Factories pollute the atmosphere

It was tropical when the dinosaurs lived here

What's the cause of global warming?

Most scientists believe that global warning is happening and is the result of human activity. They put it down to three main causes:

- increasing amount of greenhouse gases in the atmosphere
- global changes to land surface, such as deforestation
- increasing concentrations of aerosols in the atmosphere.

Some scientists argue that the cause is less clear. They suggest that it is hard to research the links because governments and environmentalists believe that global warming is happening and is caused by human activity. This makes it difficult to get money for research if they are trying to show that there is no link.

Their main argument is that changes in the sun have a greater effect than human activity. Climate has changed over millions of years and we are just in another cycle. In the past, there have been ice ages and tropical forests in the UK.

People's actions

Many people seem to accept that change is taking place and believe that human activity is the cause but they don't all appear to be prepared to make a personal effort to reduce the effect. Despite this, many people believe that the government must legislate to reduce the impact on the environment.

Whatever your views on global warming, it seems sensible to try to leave the planet as we found it, so that it may be sustainable for future generations. Political parties take different views on how this can be achieved. Should we find ways of encouraging people to recycle, for example, or of punishing them for not doing so?

Action

1 Carry out an opinion poll of fellow students to discover their attitudes to global warming.
2 Collect evidence about global warming. Look carefully at the sources and work out how much you trust the evidence.

Check your understanding

1 What is global warming?
2 What changes are taking place as a result of global warming?
3 What do most scientists think is the cause of global warming?
4 Why do some scientists disagree?
5 Why will the government have to legislate if global warming is to be controlled?
6 Do you think the government should encourage people to act to protect the environment or punish them for not doing so?

... another point of view?

'As scientists don't agree on global warming, I shouldn't have to do anything to reduce my carbon footprint.'

Do you agree with this statement? Give reasons for your opinion, showing you have considered another point of view.

What can you do?

Getting you thinking

Every one of us, whatever age we are, can do something to help slow down and reverse some of the damage to the environment. We cannot leave the problem-solving entirely to the experts – we all have a responsibility for our environment. We must learn to live in a sustainable way, i.e. learn to use our natural resources which include air, fresh water, forests, wildlife, farmland and seas without damaging them. As populations expand and lifestyles change, we must keep the world in good condition so that future generations will have the same natural resources that we have.

Source: Young People's Trust for the Environment

Making sustainable consumption 'cool'

Since it has become increasingly clear that target audiences are turned off by the judgmental tone of traditional messages about the environment, the United Nations Environmental Programme has joined with social scientists in a new bid to make saving the planet 'cool'.

With a little help

Community Champions introduce community groups, clubs and organisations to easy environmental actions they can take. They help the group decide on an action plan. And they help them get it underway. The government's Environment Agency has appointed 1,000 Community Champions across the country.

Working together

The Spacemakers project involved young people, who were aged 13 when the project started, in designing a public space within their own community in the Hartcliffe and Withywood area of Bristol. Working together on this environmental project helped to create a sense of ownership and develop feelings of community.

1. What can individuals do to look after the environment?
2. Why do you think young people are turned off by judgemental messages?
3. How would you make environmental messages 'cool'?
4. Why might Community Champions help people to look after the environment more effectively?
5. What effect did working together on an environmental project have on young people in Bristol?
6. Why can people working together often be more effective than individually? (See Unit 1, pages 116-9 for some help.)

You will investigate whether individuals can make a difference.

What can individuals do?

We can all work to reduce our carbon footprint. First of all, we need to know what it is. The average household in the UK produces 13,999 kg of carbon every year. The average Indian household produces only 1,300 kg. To meet the government targets for 2050, we would need to reduce our household footprint to 5,200 kg. Quite a difference! There are many footprint calculators on the web so check up on yours.

Reducing your footprint

Check how you might reduce your footprint. The diagram shows a variety of ways in which you can help cut emissions.

Working together

There are many things we can do to help protect the environment. The UK has discovered, however, that young people don't really think it's cool. Sometimes it is hard to stand out from the crowd, so perhaps some people don't do all they might as a result.

It often takes a little more time and effort to take the environment into account when we make plans and sometimes, when we are working alone, we just can't be bothered!

When we work with other people there is much more incentive to make the effort. We encourage each other and often have fun in the process. The young people in Bristol clearly benefited both themselves and the community when they worked together on the park.

In order to help us to work together, the government has set up a system of Community Champions to help groups plan and organise their activities,

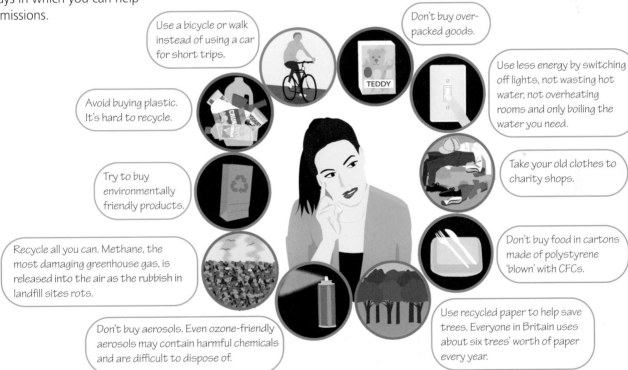

Use a bicycle or walk instead of using a car for short trips.

Don't buy over-packed goods.

Avoid buying plastic. It's hard to recycle.

Use less energy by switching off lights, not wasting hot water, not overheating rooms and only boiling the water you need.

Try to buy environmentally friendly products.

Take your old clothes to charity shops.

Recycle all you can. Methane, the most damaging greenhouse gas, is released into the air as the rubbish in landfill sites rots.

Don't buy food in cartons made of polystyrene 'blown' with CFCs.

Don't buy aerosols. Even ozone-friendly aerosols may contain harmful chemicals and are difficult to dispose of.

Use recycled paper to help save trees. Everyone in Britain uses about six trees' worth of paper every year.

Option A: Environmental change and sustainable development

Check your understanding

1 Why is it important for individuals to try to reduce their carbon footprint?
2 How can they go about it?
3 Why can it be difficult to work alone?
4 Are there any examples of community activities in your area?
5 How can the government encourage people to look after the environment?

... another point of view?

'I don't want to stand out from the crowd so I'm not going to bother to reduce my carbon footprint.'
Do you agree with this statement? Give reasons for your opinion, showing you have considered another point of view.

Not in my backyard?

Getting you thinking

The congestion charge

In 2003, congestion charging was introduced to London. The objective was to reduce congestion and pollution in the city centre. Not everyone thought it was a good idea.

Freedom for Drivers, a pro cars pressure group, says

The London Congestion Zone has:

- not reduced pollution
- not reduced congestion
- not raised much revenue for transport improvements
- caused extreme congestion on the edges of the zone.

£8 per day
Mon - Fri
7 am - 6 pm
½ mile ahead

Protesters in Dorset say

The scheme had already devalued my house by £75,000–100,000. No one's particularly against wind turbines, it's just where they're being located next to houses. My house has a beautiful backdrop, that's what I paid for and now everything I've worked for is being taken from me.

1 Why are people objecting to each of these activities?
2 What are their motives?
3 What is the effect of them getting their way?
4 Do you think each of the measures helps the environment? Do a little research on each topic to help your answer.
5 How would you decide whether such schemes should go ahead?

Residents say no to two-weekly collections

Basingstoke and Deane councillors gave in to pressure when a poll revealed that 93 per cent of residents were against proposals to collect recyclable material and household waste in alternate weeks.

It was hoped the move would have improved the borough's recycling rate, particularly in Basingstoke, where the recycling rate is very low.

You will consider whether individuals and communities genuinely agree with national and global responses to problems of global warming and climate change.

It's fine – but not here

When asked, most people say we should look after the environment, but when decisions affect them personally, they are not nearly so keen.

The examples in 'Getting you thinking' show how it happens. You may not think wind farms are beautiful if they reduce the value of your house. People who have always had their household waste collected every week can see lots of disadvantages to its only being picked up every two weeks. Such people are often referred to as NIMBYs – not in my backyard.

There are many stakeholders in environmental decisions and everyone's point of view needs to be taken into account. The decision-makers then have to decide which points of view have the greatest weight.

Trade offs

If the UK is to meet its targets, there will have to be some sacrifices. Many people have already adjusted some of their habits. There was a time when we all used plastic carrier bags when we went to the supermarket, but now more and more people take their own. Some supermarkets charge for bags now but, even where they don't, many customers have decided it is worth making the effort to avoid using them.

Sometimes it costs more or takes more time to look after the environment. Sometimes it is important to look ahead. It may cost more in the first instance to install insulation or buy low-energy light bulbs, but in the long run you save money and the environment benefits.

Individuals have to decide whether they think it is worth-while. There are occasions when we need encouragement. It is often easy to put all the rubbish in the bin rather than sorting it. There is a debate about whether we should be helped to recycle or fined for not doing so.

Who makes the decisions?

Many decisions about environmental issues are made democratically by local, central or European governments. The EU sets targets, which the UK government builds into its laws or plans.

Environmental issues often first come to light at the local level when people start to protest. The local council then has to decide whether wind turbines or a congestion charge offers more benefit for the community. If so, it will outweigh the individuals' objections.

Ethics is involved in the decisions. It is important to weigh up everyone's point of view in order to come to a conclusion. Because people hold different values, even an ethical decision-making process will bring people to different conclusions.

Check your understanding

1 What is a NIMBY?
2 Why do people become NIMBYs?
3 What trade offs are there in making decisions about being green?
4 Should we be given more help to be green? Explain your answer.
5 What is the government trying to achieve with its environmental policy?
6 How does the government have to come to a conclusion about decisions involving the environment?
7 Who are the stakeholders in the Dorset wind farm issue?
8 Use the ethical decision-making questions on page 170 to help you decide whether a wind farm should go ahead in Dorset.

... another point of view?

'People are always wrong to protest against decisions to help the environment.'

Do you agree with this statement? Give reasons for your opinion, showing you have considered another point of view.

Do targets work?

Getting you thinking

The UK's performance

Carbon dioxide emissions by source (UK): 1990–2006

million tonnes

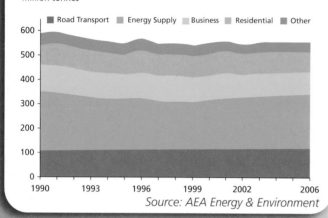

Legend: ■ Road Transport ■ Energy Supply ■ Business ■ Residential ■ Other

Source: AEA Energy & Environment

EU will meet 2012 targets

Many countries will not meet the greenhouse gas reduction target for 2012 unless they fulfil the new policies which have been brought in by the EU. The UK government has been criticised for its failure to take the issue seriously. The aim was to reduce the amount to 8 per cent less than the 1990 figure.

The new EU target: 2020

The EU's climate change package spells out how the EU aims to cut greenhouse gas emissions by 20 per cent by 2020 and increase the use of renewable energy to 20 per cent of the total.

This will be done by:

- renewable energy production
- capture and geological storage of carbon dioxide
- reduction of CO_2 from cars
- revision of the European emissions trading scheme – in which countries are set limits but can buy and sell their allowance if they need more or haven't used it all.

Source: EU

Not ambitious enough

The Finnish representative at the EU believes that the proposals put forward by the Commission are not ambitious enough. She told us they 'fall short of what is needed in order to keep global warming below the 2°C'.

She would like industrialised countries to aim for targets of 80 per cent reductions by the middle of the century. This is higher than the 25–40 per cent cuts scientists believe are necessary to contain temperature rises at 2°C.

Is it all too late?

Professor Lovelock created the Gaia theory that the Earth behaves as a single organism. He now believes that even the gloomiest predictions of the climate change scientists underestimate the problem because they do not go into the consequences of the current pollution in the atmosphere which will last for centuries.

Professor Lovelock believes that six to eight billion humans will be faced with ever diminishing supplies of food and water in an increasingly intolerable climate and wildlife and whole ecosystems will become extinct.

1 What changes have taken place in the UK's emissions of greenhouse gas since 1990?
2 Why are new measures required if countries are to meet their targets?
3 What is the level of reduction in greenhouse gas in the targets for 2020?
4 How will these be achieved?
5 How does emissions trading help?
6 Why does the Finnish representative think it's not enough?
7 What would happen if everyone accepted Professor Lovelock's point of view?

You will investigate whether it is worth setting environmental targets and whether people can be persuaded to play their part.

Reducing emissions

There is general acceptance of the need to reduce the output of greenhouse gases. The Kyoto Protocol established targets for 2012 and the EU has set more ambitious ones for 2020.

The targets are not popular with everyone. The USA, for example, has not signed up to the agreement. Reducing the output of gas can be expensive for businesses and therefore makes products more expensive. If countries don't all follow the same rules, this can make it harder to sell the products of countries that obey the rules.

Enforcing the rules?

There is a variety of ways of getting people to achieve the targets.

- **Persuasion**
  We are encouraged to take shopping bags to the supermarket instead of using plastic bags – although many still offer them to customers. We are provided with bins to recycle all sorts of things – but many people still just throw all their rubbish away. Snooping eyes in wheelie bins have been shown not to work and have been ridiculed in the media.

- **Taxation**
  People can be more easily encouraged to look after the environment if they have to pay for damaging it. Cars that produce high levels of CO_2 pay more road tax, for example. Businesses are targeted by the Climate Change Levy, which uses taxes to persuade businesses to reduce their energy consumption or use energy from renewable sources. There are also taxes on the amount of waste businesses send to landfill sites.

  Taxation can be controversial because some people claim that it is just a method used by the government to raise more revenue. Over £35 billion a year is raised from green taxes. If all countries do not have the same rules, taxation makes some countries less competitive.

Option A: Environmental change and sustainable development

Action

Find out how other countries control emissions. Are their strategies effective?

Check your understanding

1 Why do we have targets to reduce emissions?
2 Why are some countries less willing to sign up than others?
3 Will the targets solve the problem?
4 Why does persuasion not always work?
5 What are the advantages and disadvantages of using taxation?

… another point of view?

'Taxation and laws should be used to control our emissions.'
Do you agree with this statement? Give reasons for your opinion, showing you have considered another point of view.

Sustainability: local or national?

Getting you thinking

Back-2-Bikes

A charitable project originally set up as part of the Bicyle Recycling Project by Stafford Borough Council's Local Agenda 21 programme, Back-2-Bikes helps people find their way back into work, especially if they have been facing difficulties in their lives.

The project accepts unwanted bicycles from the public and local organisations. After refurbishment and safety checks have been carried out, they are sold to offset the project's costs. B-2-B also repairs customers' bikes and sells quality used parts for people who wish to carry out their own repairs.

Stansted airport saves 1,600 tonnes of CO_2

By careful management of heating and ventilation, Stansted airport has made great reductions in its output of CO_2. It is continuing to work on strategies for further cuts. These include solar powered lights on airport roads, a biomass boiler which burns renewable woodchip fuel and the installation of more efficient air conditioning. Not only does the reduction in the consumption of CO_2 help the environment, but in the long run it saves money too.

Bath students compete to save energy

A competition between student residences led to great savings in energy use. In the first year of the competition, energy use fell by 10 per cent. Students used catchy marketing strategies to tempt other students to turn off the lights and not use standby facilities on the televisions. There were prizes for winning residences.

... and in Zimbabwe

Mutare is Zimbabwe's fourth largest city. Despite the turmoil in the country, a group of young people are working together to help the environment – and themselves. They make enough money from collecting paper to give each of the group's members an income greater than the minimum wage. What's more, employing a very sensible strategy, this group first puts aside around 10 per cent of their income to cover the maintenance and repair of pushcarts.

1 What groups are involved in these environmental improvement groups?

2 How does each one help to increase sustainability?

3 Are there other incentives for people to try to make their environments more sustainable?

4 Are the motives of young people in Zimbabwe the same as those in the UK?

5 What is Local Agenda 21? Check with Unit 1, page 100.

6 What are groups doing in your area to make the world more sustainable?

You will find out about the local and national agendas, debates and goals and how local and national governments can approach the problem.

What are the targets?

The UK plans to reduce carbon dioxide emissions by at least 60 per cent by 2050 and by at least 26 per cent by 2020, on the basis of levels in 1990.

The target will be reviewed to decide whether it should be even stronger. Questions are also being asked about the implications of including other greenhouse gases and emissions, from international aviation and shipping, in the target.

Emission reductions purchased overseas may be counted towards the UK's targets, consistent with the UK's international obligations. This ensures emission reductions can be achieved in the most cost effective way, recognising the potential for investing in low-carbon technologies abroad as well as action within the UK to reduce the UK's overall carbon footprint.

Business are given a limit to the amount of pollution they can produce. They will have to buy permits to cover each tonne of CO_2 they emit above the cap. They can buy permits from other businesses whose emissions are below their cap. Permits cost about £10 per tonne.

Local authorities are responsible for issuing permits for businesses to pollute the environment. The permit must contain ways in which the business must aim to reduce pollution.

Local sustainability

Agenda 21 is a 'world-wide action plan' that was agreed to by the United Nations at the Earth Summit in Rio de Janeiro in 1992. It aimed to bring communities together to work towards sustainable development. Local authorities were expected to play a big part in achieving the objectives by creating development plans and involving the local community. These have now been running for a long time and have developed into broader Sustainable Community Strategies. These meet the government's broader objectives of helping communities to work together to help themselves.

Developing a sustainable community. At the Gatehouse Centre in Bristol you can do learn new skills for employment, look after your children and even grow food

A sustainable community is likely to:

- be safe and inclusive
- be well planned, built and run
- offer equality and opportunity for all.

It is therefore sustainable in a number of ways – not just environmentally. If a community is to be sustainable, people need jobs and opportunities too. Sustainable communities are all different as communities are all different and one size can't fit all.

Option A: Environmental change and sustainable development

Check your understanding

1 What is Agenda 21?
2 When did it begin and why?
3 How does it affect central and local government's environmental practice?
4 What sort of activities contribute to Local Agenda 21?
5 How has Local Agenda 21 changed?
6 How do the activities in Getting you thinking contribute to the development of sustainable communities?
7 How is the pollution produced by businesses measured and controlled?

... another point of view?

'Actions on sustainability should always be led by central government.'
Do you agree with this statement? Give reasons for your opinion, showing you have considered another point of view.

Key Terms

sustainable communities: places where social, economic and environmental activities form a community where people thrive both at home and at work

The same rules for all?

Getting you thinking

Methane mining in India

Villagers in India brought the public hearing to a halt when they walked out. The plan to extract methane would damage their environment by polluting waterways, harming agriculture and reducing biodiversity. The plans that had been submitted made no reference to the roads, pipelines and other building that would take place on the site. The route that elephants use across the site was not even mentioned.

A chemical plant in China

Xiamen is widely known for its natural beauty and was recently ranked one of China's cleanest and most livable cities. Demonstrators are protesting against the construction of a chemical plant that has government approval. The sign they are holding says 'Protect the Health of Future Generations'. They complain about the products which the plant will emit and about the fact that, even though the construction is not yet finished, they can already smell industrial odours.

Chopping down China's trees

China has been using vast amounts of timber as its economy has developed. The government has imposed a 5 per cent tax on disposable wooden chopsticks in order to protect China's vanishing forests.

China throws away 55 billion pairs of chopsticks every year and exports a further 15 billion pairs.

The demand for chopsticks sends millions of poplar, birch and bamboo trees to the sawmill each year and employs about 60,000 workers.

The chopstick tax is part of a broader package of consumption taxes aimed at protecting the environment and narrowing China's income gap.

Setting targets

LEDCs have argued that they should not be subjected to the same rules as the industrialised world. Preventing pollution is expensive and can push up the price of the products they make. The plan that seems to be most acceptable sets pollution targets for specific industries such as cement, steel or aluminum. If the 37 industrial countries miss their goals, they are fined – but this is not the case for the LEDCs.

The plan fits well with Beijing's intention of increasing the efficiency of its key industries, which produce the bulk of its carbon emissions.

1 Why do LEDCs not want to have to obey the same rules as industrialised countries?

2 What effect will the chopstick tax have on China?

3 What do the protesters want in both China and India?

4 Why is it difficult for LEDCs to meet everyone's objectives?

5 Look at page 102 in Unit 1 and think of ways in which countries can develop sustainably.

You will explore whether it is fair to impose the same environmental rules on LEDCs as on MEDCs.

In whose interests?

In Unit 1 you will have found out about environmental targets (page 102). There is much debate about how we should control pollution in countries across the world. An instant answer is to set rules for all, but not everyone agrees.

We have got used to buying cheap products from LEDCs. Why are they cheap?

- **Labour**
  People are prepared to work for much lower pay than we would be prepared to accept in MEDCs. This leads to inequality, but the cost of living in LEDCs is generally lower, so the money earned buys more.

- **Environmental regulations**
  In countries where environmental rules are stronger, the costs of production are higher because factories have to install special equipment to ensure that harmful emissions do not escape into the atmosphere.

We like buying cheap products – but should we think again? If we do, we might reduce job opportunities for people who may be desperate for work. It is clearly not a simple question.

The timescale

The industrialised world developed and grew rich in times when no one worried about the environment. The smogs were infamous – just as they are in Beijing today.

Reducing pollution increases a business's cost of production so the end product will be more expensive and therefore less will be sold. Many LEDCs argue that they should not have to conform to the same rules until their industry is more advanced.

On the other hand, the businesses are challenged by the people, as 'Getting you thinking' shows. Many people die from respiratory diseases – just as they did in England during the Industrial Revolution in the 18th century.

A solution?

One suggestion to solve the problem is to set limited targets for some industries and not fine the country. This seems to be an acceptable start. In countries where democracy is strong enough, the population may bring pressure on the government to reduce pollution.

Check your understanding

1 Draw a spider diagram showing the issues that affect decisions on controlling pollution in LEDCs. Put the case for control on the right and the case against it on the left.
2 Why can things be made more cheaply in LEDCs?
3 Should we think more carefully before buying cheap products that have been made in LEDCs?
4 Why does democracy need to be strong for the population to put pressure on the government?
5 Use the ethical decision-making strategy from page 170 to help you to decide what should be done.

... another point of view?

'Pollution doesn't matter as long as a country can develop and create jobs for its people.'

Do you agree with this statement? Give reasons for your opinion, showing you have considered another point of view.

Trade or aid?

Getting you thinking

Aid to the starving

Five million Afghans face serious food shortages as winter comes, but donors have put forward less than a fifth of the money needed to cope, Oxfam warned.

Time is running out to avert a humanitarian crisis, said Oxfam as it urged governments to respond to the emergency humanitarian appeal.

Aid for trade

If a country is to increase its overseas trade, it needs efficient ports and roads, trained customs officials with the right equipment and entrepreneurs who know an opportunity when they see one. Without these, no country will be able to produce the quantity and quality of goods at the right price for world markets. Many LEDCs need help to achieve this.

Why does trade help an economy to grow?

When one country sells products to another, it receives payments, which help the economy to grow because people are employed and paid to make the things that are sold. These people then have more to spend so the economy grows more.

As countries grow richer:

- children get a better education and therefore grow up to take more responsible jobs
- healthcare often improves, so children can go to school more frequently and adults can go to work regularly.

Both these factors make it easier for a country to become more competitive. Better education means that people work more efficiently and may come up with brighter ideas. Better health means that they have less time off work, so increase efficiency further. An efficient business thinks carefully about the products it makes, to ensure that they are things that people want to buy.

How can aid help?

People usually want aid that helps them to help themselves. Giving food and shelter in emergencies is clearly necessary, but if people are to become self sufficient, the aid needs to be more targeted. The fishermen in Chad are a good example. Working out just what will help is important, as the experiments in Kenya showed.

You will investigate whether trade rather than aid is a better way of supporting a country so it can develop or become more sustainable more quickly.

Aid helps you to help yourself

'If you don't have a canoe,' says Michel Adjibang, 'you'll always be poor.' Nets are essential too, along with the smoking ovens which preserve the fish for taking it to market. Walta is a community-based organisation in Chad whose name means 'to take responsibility for yourself'. With the help of **aid** from the UK, a new canoe-building technique has been developed using locally available planks, which are easier to use and kinder on the environment. Trainers have shown local carpenters how to build the canoes,

and a micro-credit scheme helps fishermen buy canoes and nets. 'With what I earn from fishing, I invest a part of it in farming,' says one fisherman. 'I even get to hire extra hands sometimes. Today my children are in school, and it is what I earn from fishing that even helps me to care for myself'.

What sort of aid?

Experiments in Kenya found that providing poor students with free uniforms or a simple porridge breakfast increased school attendance. But giving them drugs to treat the intestinal worms that infect more than a quarter of the world's population was more cost effective. It cost only $3.50 for each extra year of schooling achieved. Healthier children are more likely to go to school.

When countries trade with other countries, the population usually gets richer. To do this, they need skilled people at all levels, so it is important to get them all to school.

1. In what situations is aid essential to help people survive?
2. How does aid help the fisherman of Chad? What effects does this aid have on the wider community? How does it help the economy of Chad to grow?
3. What is trade? Check on page 134 in Unit 1.
4. What do countries need if their trade is to grow?
5. Why do they often need help to achieve trade growth?
6. Why is it important to target aid carefully?
7. Some people argue that aid is a waste of time. Explain why.

Working together

Both trade and aid have their places. Trade will help countries to grow and therefore lift people out of poverty. Aid can help to develop the skills and competitiveness that people need in order to work and make the products – or provide services – that people in other countries want. Trade and aid can help to ensure that development is sustainable because businesses grow on the basis of having markets to sell their products.

Check your understanding

1. When is aid essential?
2. Why does trade help to reduce poverty?
3. How can countries be helped to trade?
4. How can trade help development?
5. How do trade and aid help development to be sustainable?

... another point of view?

'Aid is more important than trade.'

Do you agree with this statement? Give reasons for your opinion, showing you have considered another point of view.

Key Terms

aid: help given by one country to another

Environmental change and sustainable development:

Source A

Britain announces wind energy plans

The Government outlined plans to develop 15 offshore wind farms off Britain's coast. They will be in three areas and are expected to produce 7 per cent of the UK's energy needs. This will reduce the country's use of fossil fuel and the amount of greenhouse gas produced.

The energy minister said 'This is the biggest expansion of renewable energy and shows that we are serious about moving towards a cleaner, greener future. The Government is committed to cut pollution.'

Environmental pressure groups have welcomed the plans, as they show that Britain is taking the Kyoto targets seriously.

The British Wind Energy Association represents businesses that sell wind farm equipment. A representative said 'This is a win, win for our industry, our environment and our economy as these 15 projects should create thousands of new jobs and provide clean power for one in six UK homes.'

Source B

Protestors fight wind farm in Somerset

'The scheme had already devalued my house by £75,000–£100,000. No one's particularly against wind turbines, it's just where they're being located next to houses. My house has a beautiful backdrop, that's what I paid for and now everything I've worked for is being taken from me.'

1. The main aim of a pressure group is to: *(1 mark)*
- ☑ A. influence government policy.
- ☐ B. achieve victory in elections.
- ☐ C. reduce active citizenship.
- ☐ D. control local councils.

2. The following is an example of renewable energy: *(1 mark)*
- ☐ A. Coal
- ☑ B. Tidal power
- ☐ C. Oil
- ☐ D. Gas

3. An opinion is different from a fact because: *(1 mark)*
- ☑ A. there will always be someone who disagrees with an opinion.
- ☐ B. opinions are always supported by reliable evidence.
- ☐ C. opinions usually relate only to religion and politics while facts might apply to many other things.
- ☐ D. if in doubt, opinions can be tested or verified.

4. Explain briefly what is meant by Kyoto targets in Source A *(2 marks)*

Kyoto targets were set by countries at a world summit in Kyoto. They set targets for cutting greenhouse gases in order to prevent global warming.

> This is a good answer because it explains how the targets came about and what they were trying to achieve.

5. Briefly explain two reasons, taken from Source A, why the new proposals to build wind farms should be welcomed.

Reason 1 *(2 marks)*

It will cut the use of fossil fuels and therefore reduce the amount of greenhouse gases that are being produced.

Reason 2 *(2 marks)*

It shows the rest of the world that Britain is taking the Kyoto targets seriously and that the government is committed to making Britain greener.

> Remember that a 2-mark question needs an answer that gives an explanation of each point.

6. Using Source B and your own knowledge, explain why people are protesting about a wind farm being built near where they live. *(2 marks)*

The protestors are objecting to their local area being spoilt by wind farms. They are also worried about the effect the wind farms will have on the value of their houses.

7. Explain why the British Wind Energy Association supports the Government proposals. *(2 marks)*

It is a pressure group which represents businesses which sell wind farm equipment. If the government promotes wind farms, the businesses will sell more equipment.

> Remember that you need to look at people's motives.

8. Do you agree that all countries must work together to achieve environmental sustainability? Give reasons for your opinion showing you have considered another point of view. *(8 marks)*

Leave margin blank

If we are going to be sustainable, all countries need to join in because it can't just be done by one on its own but it may be difficult to get all countries to work together because they are all in different stages of development.

> The two points of view are there in the first paragraph.

Countries like China argue that they will be held back if they have to stick to the targets for Europe. India and Africa will also find it difficult.

Some countries also need to set an example. In 2008, the British government set tough targets for the country. These are more demanding than many other countries.

As businesses need to be competitive, they often don't want strict targets. They can make production cost more because they have to install equipment to clean up their waste products. If businesses are going to go green, it takes laws. If it is going to be fair to businesses in different countries, they all need to have the same laws.

> The student is giving the point of view of different groups who have an interest in controlling pollution with an explanation of how they can be managed.

Pollution permits are used to limit the amount of pollution so businesses have to pay if they go above the limits.

> This shows that the student has an understanding of recent changes in the law.

We need to work together but at the moment the system cannot be perfect.

Extended writing

'Less Economically Developed Countries (LEDCs) need trade not aid.'
Do you agree with this view?
Give reasons for your opinion showing you have considered another point of view. You must support you argument with examples wherever possible.
You could consider the following points and other information of your own.

- Why do some countries need aid and what do they do with it?
- What are the disadvantages to a country which receives aid?
- Is trade or aid more likely to help a country develop and grow more prosperous?
- Is providing aid or trade of more benefit to European countries such as the UK?

(15 marks)

When there is a flood or a drought, countries often need aid just to help people survive. So there are times when aid is necessary.

Aid can also offer help for a country to develop. Education often receives help from a variety of sources. By educating children to a higher level, a country can start to do more complicated things. As people move out of farming and into industry, they can produce things that are more valuable and can be sold to other countries. In this case, aid helps trade to develop.

> This is very good because it explains the link between aid and trade and demonstrates clearly that the student understands the issue.

The question is really saying that aid gets used up and doesn't help in the long run. Trade means that a country can buy the things it needs to develop and sell the products it makes to other countries and earn money to help it develop.

A country which receives aid such as food and clothes can become dependent on the help. This means they don't learn to be self sufficient. A pump for water can make a difference over a long time. People are healthier because the water is less likely to be polluted – so they can go to school and work.

> The student is following the bullet points and is continuing to develop the argument.

When a country is suffering from extremes – like bad weather – it needs short-term help but after that it needs aid to help it to set up the industries which mean that it can sell things to other countries. India, for example, has lots of well educated people who now work in call centres for western businesses. This could not be done by people who only have primary education.

In the end a country must aim to trade but it probably needs aid to help it to trade.

> The argument on the benefits of trade and aid is still here and shows how both can be needed by countries at different stages.

Countries in Europe, for example, will benefit when countries develop because people living there get richer and want to buy more from other countries. The demand for the products from Europe and the USA will tend to go up. Once countries have developed these industries it can mean that businesses set up factories there. Many call centres for example have been closed down in Europe because it is cheaper to run them from India.

> This last comment shows that the student is thinking about what happens next. There are lots of trade offs in global issues and it takes careful thought to work out the winners and losers from any situation.

Option B: Changing communities: social and cultural identities

Communities are constantly changing as people move and develop. In Unit 1 you learnt a lot about communities and people's identities and now you have a chance to investigate other people's views on the subject. You can then work out the views that you agree with and those you don't and come to your own conclusions.

Topics to investigate
These questions will help you to think about the community issues. In the exam you will be given a range of points of view on a community topic and you will be able to use all the skills and knowledge you have developed in your Citizenship Studies course to answer the questions.

- What are the ethical aspects of social and cultural identity, including immigration?
- Why do economic migrants and asylum seekers apply to settle in the UK?

Getting going
The question to ask yourself is 'What's going on?'. Whatever media you use, you will find lots of useful material. Just Googling a topic will give you masses of information – but how do you know whether it is accurate? How do you know whether the people who run the website have their own mission? There are lots of questions to ask.

They would say that, wouldn't they?

The school
Abare Girls' School in Wales has a 'no jewellery' rule and only allows students to wear watches and ear studs. Sakira Watkins-Singh refused to take off her bangle because she said it was a religious symbol of Sikhism and she therefore had to wear it. She was suspended.

With the support of the human rights group Liberty, she took the school to the high court.

The judge said
'In this case there is very clear evidence it was not a piece of jewellery but to Sarika it was, and remains, one of the defining symbols of being a Sikh. The school is guilty of indirect discrimination under race relations and equality laws.'

Liberty, the human rights pressure group, said
'This common sense judgment makes clear you must have a very good reason before interfering with someone's religious freedom. Our great British traditions of religious tolerance and race equality have been rightly upheld today.'

The National Secular Society, which campaigns for religion to be kept out of public life, said
'The undesirable element of this case is that it mixes up the issues of race, ethnicity and religion. Sikhism and Judaism are defined as races as well as religions. Religion and race are not the same thing. You cannot change your race, but you can certainly change your religion.'

1 Why did each organisation hold its point of view?
2 What other questions would you want to ask?
3 Where could you look for the answers?
4 How do you weigh up the different points of view?

- How have political developments here and in Europe changed the flow of those who migrate to and from our country?
- Why do overseas citizens decide to live and work in the UK and why do Britons choose to settle overseas?
- Is the UK a genuinely multicultural society?
- How diverse is the UK in terms of national, regional, ethnic and religious cultures, groups and communities?
- Has discrimination on the grounds of age, race, gender or sexual orientation ended?
- Why do groups of people react in different ways to new arrivals from other countries?
- Why do problems of community cohesion exist and how can they be resolved?

Whose perspectives?

Individual
- How can individuals and groups establish identities and deal with diversity?
- What are the different perceptions of being a citizen in the UK?
- What images does the media offer?

Social
- Why are community cohesion and tolerance important?
- Should there be a balance between rights and responsibilities?

Ethical
- Why is respect important?
- Is it right to limit people's freedom?

Community
- What unifies and divides communities?
- Why are communities complex and changing?
- What encourages community cohesion and brings about change in communities?

Global
- Why do people migrate?
- What are the effects of diversity?
- How are groups in the UK, the rest of Europe and the wider world connected?
- What is the UK's role in the world (with Europe, the EU, the Commonwealth and the UN)?
- What challenges face the global community (including international disagreements and conflict, and debates about inequalities, sustainability and use of the world's resources)?

National
- What is the effect of national migration policies?
- What is the impact of the media?
- Is the media accurate?
- What connections exist between diverse national, regional, ethnic and religious cultures, groups and communities in the UK?
- How have rights and freedoms been achieved in the UK?

Political
- What policies and actions address inequalities?
- In a range of contexts, from local to global, what political, legal and human rights and freedoms are there?
- How is information (including that from the media and from pressure and interest groups) used in public debate and policy formation?
- What is the impact of democracy and justice in the UK and other countries?

Making ethical decisions

A new girl called Sarah arrived at school. Ellen was jealous because she took over her best friend, Aesha, so she set about making her life difficult. She got the rest of the girls to gang up on her, spread nasty rumours, tried to trip her up and insulted her. They even made a little book called 'Ten Things We Hate About Sarah', which said she was fat, stupid, ugly, a know-it-all and a show-off.

After a while, Sarah stopped coming to school.

1 Should Sarah have become best friends with Aesha?

2 Should Ellen have reacted as she did?

3 Why do you think the rest of the girls joined in?

4 What would you have done? Explain why.

5 How might the problem have been solved?

What does 'ethical' mean?

Different people use different words to define 'ethical' but the general view is that it means 'relating to a set of values including compassion, fairness, honesty, respect, and responsibility'.

Making an ethical decision means taking all these aspects into account. This can be done by asking the following questions:

- Which action results in the most good and least harm?
- Which action respects the rights of everyone involved?
- Which action treats people fairly?
- Which action contributes most to the quality of life of the people affected?

These questions can be used when trying to make a decision about any issue or dispute.

Who's the winner?

Deportation from Britain

Ama Sumani, whose visa had expired, was deported from Britain despite being in desperate need of kidney dialysis.

British officials claimed to have checked that treatment would be available in Ghana before they sent her back, but she could not afford the high hospital fees she faced on arrival so she is unable to get this essential care.

The hospital there asked for £3,060 to cover just three months of treatment. British officials said they would pay for three months but the hospital would not start the treatment because she would be unable to pay beyond that time.

She died two months later.

1 Use the ethical decision-making questions to help you to decide whether Ama Sumani should have been deported.

You will find out about the ethical aspects of social and cultural identity, including the issue of immigration.

Does equal pay matter?

Bridget Bodman was financial controller for a large engineering firm. When she left, she was replaced by a man who received a salary of £8,000 more than she had been paid and a car allowance of £8,640.

Bridget took the company to court and won. She said: 'I'm glad I fought the case, although it was very stressful. At first, when I realised there was this pay divide, I went through a lot of doubts – was I not good enough at my job, maybe there was a genuine reason. But then I realised that it wasn't right and that I had to make a stand. Hopefully it will set a good precedent for other women, although I find it amazing that in 2008 this kind of discrimination is still happening, and on such a wide scale.'

> Women in Britain earn 17 per cent less than men for full-time work and considerably less than women in other European countries. For part-time work, the difference between men and women rises to 36 per cent. In the course of their working life, women earn, on average, £330,000 less than men.

1 Use ethical decision-making to decide whether women should be paid less than men.

2 What else would you need to know before you made a decision?

Is everyone's decision the same?

Even when using the ethical decision-making questions, not everyone's answers are the same. It all depends on our personal values and the weight we give to different questions. People may have different approaches to their community. If they have lived there for many years, they may feel threatened by change. Some people feel that immigration threatens their jobs despite the fact that it is often the case that immigrants take the jobs that no one else wants to do. Prejudice is often built on misunderstanding, but this does not prevent people from holding such views.

Check your understanding

1 What does 'ethical' mean?

2 Use the questions for making an ethical decision to decide what you should do if someone in your class is being bullied.

3 Why do people's answers to ethical issues differ?

... another point of view?

'Every decision we make should be ethical.'

Do you agree with this statement? Give reasons for your opinion, showing you have considered another point of view.

Key Terms

ethical: relating to a set of values including compassion, fairness, honesty, respect, and responsibility

Why come to Britain?

Getting you thinking

Earning a living

'I have been working in London for two years and it is hard work. I came from a village near Krakow in Poland to London with the hope of earning money but it has been less easy that I thought. I now work two jobs, one as a kitchen porter and the other as a cleaner early in the morning. This gives me enough money to live and to save but it also means constantly working. I don't want to do this forever – I am tired all the time. I'm planning to go home next year.'

Should he be sent home?

Mehdi Kazemi
Pegah Emambakhsh

Don't Send LGBT Asylum Seekers to their DEATH
uฑรน

Medhi Kazemi, 19, came to London to study English in 2005. He applied for asylum after discovering that his former boyfriend had been hanged in Iran because he was gay.

Fleeing

'My mum woke me one morning and said we had to go. Life in Somalia had become intolerable. Half my family had been killed in the war and we feared being rounded up and sent to a camp. We trekked across Kenya and stayed there while we raised the money to buy plane tickets to England. It was strange at first but I've settled down now and school is good – much better than in Somalia – but I do miss my friends. Life is very different now.'

Unaccompanied children arriving in the UK

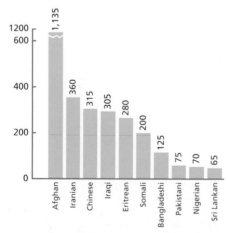

Country	Number
Afghan	1,135
Iranian	360
Chinese	315
Iraqi	305
Eritrean	280
Somali	200
Bangladeshi	125
Pakistani	75
Nigerian	70
Sri Lankan	65

Children as young as three have been found in ports and airports. It is hard to send children home when the authorities don't know where they come from.

1 Use page 10 in Unit 1 to explain what is meant by immigration.
2 Why do these people want to leave home and move to another country?
3 What is the difference between the motives of the Polish person and those of the others?
4 Some don't want to return. Why not?
5 What reasons could a parent have for leaving a child at a port or airport?

You will investigate why economic migrants and asylum seekers apply to settle in the UK.

What is an asylum seeker?

In Unit 1 you looked at immigration and emigration (page 10). Asylum seekers have a particular reason for wanting to come to the UK. They are usually refugees who have fled from their home country because of war or because of persecution by the state or other groups or individuals. They will have applied for asylum but will not have received an answer from the government of the country where they are now living.

To qualify for refugee status in the UK, an asylum seeker must prove that he or she has been persecuted because of their race, religion, nationality, membership of a social group or political opinion, as laid out in the UN Convention on Refugees. This was drawn up in 1951, and 145 countries are now signed up. The key point of the convention is that refugees should not be returned to a country where they fear persecution.

Most asylum seekers flee to neighbouring LEDCs. Those who reach the UK and other western countries often have language or cultural links with the country.

The UK has a reputation as a safe and democratic country and is a popular destination despite the Netherlands and France offering better healthcare and benefits to asylum seekers. Asylum rules in the UK have become increasingly tough, and the number of applicants has fallen to a quarter of what it was in 2002.

What is an economic migrant?

Economic migrants are people who leave their country of origin in order to improve their quality of life. Some pretend to be asylum seekers in order to be able to stay in their chosen country. Others are legal migrants because they come from an EU country that has an agreement with the country they are moving to. These agreements mean that people can move freely in order to work.

Why do they come to the UK?

Migrant workers often send money to help their families at home. About 10 per cent of the world's population benefits from this money. In total, this money is three times as much as the money given in aid by rich countries, so it plays an important role in helping LEDCs to grow.

Many people from European countries are young and come to the UK because the wages are higher than what they could earn in their home country. They often come to the UK for a few years and go home again, having saved money to improve their lives on their return. These movements of people depend on the state of the economy. People are attracted if there are plenty of jobs and wages are high. If there is a downturn and unemployment rises, they go home or decide not to come in the first place.

Others come to study or to join family members.

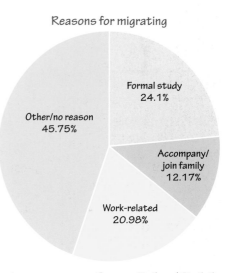

Reasons for migrating

Formal study 24.1%
Other/no reason 45.75%
Accompany/join family 12.17%
Work-related 20.98%

Source: National Statistics

Check your understanding

1 What is a refugee?
2 What is an asylum seeker?
3 What is an economic migrant?
4 Explain the motives of each group.
5 Research the issues in one or two of the countries from where the lone children come.

... another point of view?

'We should accept everyone who wants to come to live in the UK, whatever their motives.'

Do you agree with this statement? Give reasons for your opinion, showing you have considered another point of view.

Key Terms

economic migrant: someone who leaves his or her country to seek a more prosperous way of life

Can we stay?

Getting you thinking

Applications for asylum in the UK

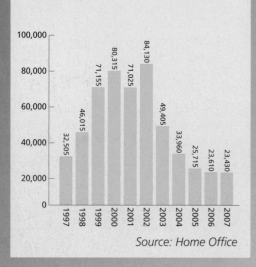

100,000

80,000

60,000

40,000

20,000

0

1997	32,505
1998	46,015
1999	71,155
2000	80,315
2001	71,025
2002	84,130
2003	49,405
2004	33,960
2005	25,715
2006	23,610
2007	23,430

Source: Home Office

People refused asylum or permission to stay in the UK

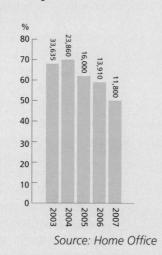

%

80

70

60

50

40

30

20

10

0

2003	33,635
2004	23,860
2005	16,000
2006	13,910
2007	11,800

Source: Home Office

The UK Border and Immigration Minister said

'Our new points system aims to meet the needs of British business while ensuring that only those we want and no more can come here to work. This strict list means 30 per cent fewer jobs are available to migrants via the shortage occupation route. Those that do come will need to work hard, play by the rules and speak English.'

Watching Europe's borders

Plans are in place for a satellite surveillance system to clamp down on illegal immigration. The 'spy in the sky' would keep a watch on remote borders of European countries, looking for suspicious movements by boat or vehicle. Non-EU foreigners visiting the travel zone would have to provide biometric details, such as fingerprints, to record their points of entry and exit and the length of allowed stay.

The fingerprints would be kept in a database, which border guards could access to ensure visa and visa-free travellers do not overstay. The aim is to launch the system by 2015.

This would not affect many EU visitors, as they have the right to work in other European countries.

1 What has happened to the number of people applying for asylum?

2 What has happened to the percentage of people who have been refused permission to stay in the UK?

3 Why do you think the number of people applying for asylum has changed?

4 Why do you think the UK has tightened the rules about people coming to work here?

5 What rights do many EU residents have in other EU countries?

6 What sort of migrants does the EU surveillance system aim to keep out?

You will explore how political developments here and in Europe have changed the flow of those who migrate to and from our country.

What's changed?

The number of asylum seekers and economic migrants coming to the UK has fallen for a number of reasons:

- **The growth of the European Union**
  By 2009 the EU had 25 member countries, so the movement of people has steadily increased. As the countries of Eastern Europe joined, young people in particular decided to explore other countries. Many came and found jobs in the UK and other countries. They often come for a while and then go home again. People from countries that have joined recently have to register when they come to work. Those from Bulgaria and Romania need permission.

- **Rules for the rest of the world**
  A points-based scheme has been set up to work out whether an individual can work in the UK. If you are highly skilled, a successful entrepreneur with money to invest, or have been to a UK university, you may be accepted.

- **Stricter rules on asylum**
  While the UK still supports the UN's definition of a refugee as someone who is unable to return to their country for fear of persecution, it has been much stricter about deciding who meets the criteria. Fewer people are therefore arriving in hope of being accepted.

Countries throughout Europe have been changing the rules in the same way, so it has become more difficult for people to come to live here.

A detention centre for asylum seekers

Action

1 Find out more about the EU residents who are free to come to the UK and those who have to register.
2 Check what is happening in the EU about immigration rules.

Check your understanding

1 What is the trend in the number of asylum seekers?
2 Explain the three reasons why the number of immigrants has fallen.
3 Why have countries tightened the rules concerning asylum seekers?
4 What is the main advantage of immigration? Can you think of others?

... another point of view?

'If we accept anyone who says they will be persecuted if they go home, some people will cheat because they want to live here – so we need to be very tough.'

Do you agree with this statement? Give reasons for your opinion, showing you have considered another point of view.

Various points of view

Some governments have responded to the media's negative stories about immigrants and toughened the law. Immigration has its positive sides too, but these are not often mentioned in the press.

Most European countries have ageing populations, so an increase in the number of young people can help the economy because they work, earn money and pay taxes. They generally need less healthcare than the old and probably go home before they need a pension. They therefore put money into the economy rather than taking it out.

Coming and going

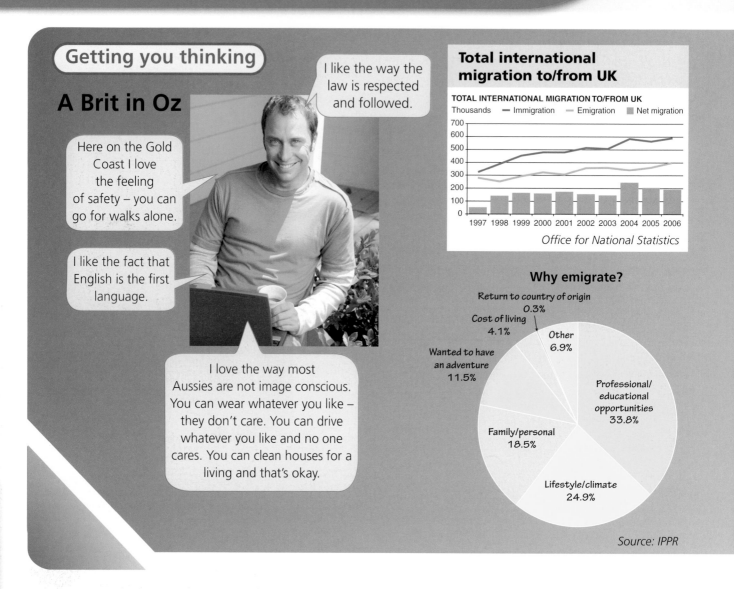

Getting you thinking

A Brit in Oz

I like the way the law is respected and followed.

Here on the Gold Coast I love the feeling of safety – you can go for walks alone.

I like the fact that English is the first language.

I love the way most Aussies are not image conscious. You can wear whatever you like – they don't care. You can drive whatever you like and no one cares. You can clean houses for a living and that's okay.

Total international migration to/from UK

TOTAL INTERNATIONAL MIGRATION TO/FROM UK
Thousands — Immigration — Emigration ■ Net migration

Office for National Statistics

Why emigrate?

Return to country of origin 0.3%
Cost of living 4.1%
Other 6.9%
Wanted to have an adventure 11.5%
Professional/ educational opportunities 33.8%
Family/personal 18.5%
Lifestyle/climate 24.9%

Source: IPPR

Motives for moving

Most people want to move to another country to improve their way of live. This may be because of job opportunities, education, lifestyle or because of family and friends. Many people move in and out of the country in any one year, as you discovered in Unit 1 (page 10).

Language is one of the factors that make Britain attractive to people from the rest of the world. English is the first language many students learn in school, and they are used to seeing films in English with subtitles in their own language. Other European countries may be less attractive because fewer people are familiar with French, German or Italian. Many Britons who want to live abroad go to English-speaking countries such as Australia, Canada and the USA.

The economy also influences people's decisions. Most people need to find a job when they move. A growing economy means more jobs are available. People from Eastern Europe came to England when the economy was healthy and went home again as jobs became harder to come by. The cost of living can be important, as can the property prices. Houses are cheaper in rural France and Australia than in the UK – but you also have to consider the amount you are likely to earn.

The state of the economy can also affect how much a country wants immigrants. A booming economy means that employers can find it difficult to fill jobs and therefore want to tempt people from overseas. When the economy is less strong, however, the government may want to limit people coming in to those with skills that the country needs. These conditions might encourage people to think about moving abroad too.

You will investigate why overseas citizens decide to live and work in the UK and why Britons choose to settle overseas.

Why be a student in the UK?

- **Diversity:** There is a wide mix of cultures in the UK. There are foreign communities from most parts of the world.
- **Tolerance:** British people are usually tolerant to foreigners, and respect the freedom to have different opinions and beliefs.
- **Freedom:** People usually feel free to express their own opinions and wear what they want. Don't expect people to agree with you all of the time.
- **Humour:** British people have a strong sense of humour, but it can be hard for foreigners to understand when someone is joking.
- **Cautiousness:** People often avoid talking to strangers until they have been introduced, partly to avoid any possible embarrassment.
- **Creativity:** Individual ideas are encouraged. Arts and music are creative.

Source: ukstudentlife.com

- **Modesty:** People are quite modest. They do not like to complain directly: life is peaceful, but poor service is not challenged.

1 What is happening to the number of people leaving and coming to the UK?
2 What effect does this have on the total population?
3 What is meant by emigration? Use Unit 1, page 10 to help you.
4 What are the main reasons for leaving the UK?

5 What factors do you think are most important for people who are thinking of coming to live in Britain?
6 What factors do you think people who come to live in Britain might find difficult to deal with?
7 Are there any contradictions in the reasons for leaving and those for coming here?

The way of life in a particular country is an important factor for many who are thinking about moving. People who live in busy cities often long to live in the country, by the sea or in the sun. Young people who are looking for adventure may want the buzz of a big city like London.

Check your understanding

1 What are the trends in movements of people in and out of Britain?
2 What are the main reasons for people moving from one country to another?
3 How can the state of the economy affect people's decisions?

Action

What would persuade you to move to another country? How would you make your decision?

... another point of view?

'You should be loyal to your country – and stay there – whatever happens.'

Do you agree with this statement? Give reasons for your opinion, showing you have considered another point of view.

A melting pot?

The religious mix

The religious mix in the UK (%)		
	1996	2006
Christian	52.8	47.5
Non-Christian		
Islam/Muslim	1.8	3.3
Hindu	0.6	1.4
Jewish	0.3	0.5
Sikh	0.2	0.2
Buddhist	0.5	0.2
Other non-Christian	0.4	0.4
No religion	42.6	45.9
Refusal/not answered/didn't know	0.8	0.6

Office for National Statistics

Happy here?

When asked, 59 per cent of Muslims said they felt they have as much, if not more, in common with non-Muslims in the UK as with Muslims abroad. Most Muslims (84 per cent) said they believe they have been treated fairly in this society.

Source: Policy Excange

Active integration

'Immigrants change us, mostly for the better. They don't just bring their labour with them. They create more choice for everyone – of food, of music, of literature – all aspects of the benefits of two-way integration. They compete hard, they lift our standards.

Most immigrants change too. We expect those who come to Britain to play by the rules and to do their best to share in the responsibilities of living together as well as enjoying the rights – for example by learning English so that they can participate fully in the workplace and in the life of the community. And if people want the rules to be different they campaign to change them by the democratic means we have available.

But an integrated society isn't only the sum of what individuals do. It's also what governments and civil society do too. So that means we all – immigrant and home grown – have the right to expect that we will be treated fairly, not exploited and that our dignity is respected.'

Trevor Phillips, Equality and Human Rights Commission

1 What proportion of the population is made up of ethnic minorities? Check with Unit 1, page 9.

2 What are the two main religious categories?

3 What changes have taken place in people's religious beliefs?

4 How do the majority of Muslims feel about living in the UK?

5 How does Trevor Phillips think immigrants change us and change themselves?

6 Why does he think it is important to learn English?

You will find out how diverse the UK is in terms of national, regional, ethnic and religious cultures, groups and communities, and whether it is a genuinely multicultural society.

Differences and similarities

People in the UK have much in common, as you discovered in Unit 1 (pages 6–15). Our varied identities overlap all the time. People from all sorts of backgrounds support the same football team, for example. More than 70 per cent of us watch television, spend time with friends and listen to music.

In some ways, however, there are more differences between the people living in this country than is the case in other countries. In Portugal, Greece and Poland, for example, more than 80 per cent of the population believe in God. In the UK, the figure is less than 60 per cent.

As more people from different countries have come to live in Britain, there have been strong movements to develop a multicultural society to ensure that people can live together while maintaining their individual identities. This has worked reasonably well. There have been some disturbances in cities where ethnic groups are living but many communities exist happily together.

Living apart together?

The term 'melting pot' has been used to describe New York, where immigrants arrived and became Americans. Recently, in the UK, questions have been asked about the objectives of government policy on our communities.

Multicultural can have two meanings:

- relating to, consisting of, or participating in the cultures of different countries, ethnic groups, or religions

- supporting integration: advocating or encouraging the integration of people of different countries, ethnic groups, and religions into all areas of society.

Source: Encarta

The UK is going to have an increasingly diverse population as more people come and go, but there is a growing view that people should work harder to integrate so they can participate in society and their local community. To become a UK citizen, people must learn some English and take a test that shows that they have some understanding of the country's history, how democracy works and the features of everyday life.

Some people feel that this means that ethnic groups will lose their identities. Others feel that it will help them to be more successful members of UK society.

Check your understanding

1 What proportion of the UK population are ethnic minorities?
2 What proportion of the UK population believes in non-Christian religions?
3 What does multicultural mean?
4 What is the effect of multiculturalism?
5 What are the advantages and disadvantages of integration?

... another point of view?

'Integration means the end of ethnic identity.'
Do you agree with this statement? Give reasons for your opinion, showing you have considered another point of view.

Are we really equal?

Getting you thinking

Nineteen year old wins age discrimination case

Administrative assistant Leanne Wilkinson claimed she had been unfairly dismissed from her job at Springwell Engineering in Newcastle, having been told she was too young for the job and they needed an older person with more experience.

The employment tribunal ruled in her favour, finding that evidence relied on by the company did not show Wilkinson lacked in performance, and judged she had been discriminated against on the grounds of age.

He was bullied

My son was bullied at primary school and secondary school. The bullying was all about him being gay, although he never came out in school. As a result, he is now on medication, possibly for the rest of his life. The only thing he (and those who bullied him) learned in school about gay people was they were gassed in the Holocaust. Surely, as a nation, we can do better than this? What's wrong with children knowing that sometimes people of the same sex fall in love with one another? What's wrong with explaining to children that this is OK, that they are committing no crime, and that it isn't a reason to call them names or bully them until they are ill?

Telegraph comments,
19 September 2008

Race discrimination claim costs boutique chain £5,000

A sales assistant who claimed she was fired from a fashion boutique owned by Sadie Frost because of the colour of her skin was awarded more than £5,000 compensation.

What's happened to women's pay?

The gap between women and men's pay is shrinking but:

Full-time pay for men	£14.98
Full-time pay for women	£12.40
Full-time gender pay gap	17.2%

Part-time pay for men	£13.10
Part-time pay for women	£9.65
Part-time gender pay gap	35.6%

There are few women in the highest paid groups and many in low paid groups.

Over the course of her working life, the gender pay gap would lose an average woman working full time a grand total of £3,300.

What colour? What gender?

Mrs M, an assistant accountant, claimed that she was unfairly dismissed because of being a woman of Indian origin. During her five months of employment she was told by a colleague that the three company directors, who were also of Indian origin, did not approve of Asian women working for the company.

1 How have each of these people been discriminated against?
2 What laws have been broken?
3 How has the wage gap between men and women changed?
4 What do the figures on women's wages hide?

You will investigate whether discrimination on the grounds of age, race, gender or sexual orientation has ended.

What does the law say?

Laws are in place to protect people from all sorts of discrimination – age, race, gender and sexual orientation, as you discovered in Unit 1 (pages 22–25). More and more aspects of difference have been included in the legislation over the years, as we have become aware of the effect of discrimination on different groups of people. Despite the fact that laws are in place, people still discriminate, as court records show.

Laws to protect people	
Equal Pay Act	1970
Sex Discrimination Act	1975
Race Relations Act	1976
Disability Discrimination Act	1995
The Employment Equality (Sexual Orientation) Regulations	2003
Employment Equality (Religion or Belief) Regulations	2003
Employment Equality (Age) Regulations	2006

When cases come to court, there can be arguments that someone is too old to do the job or one person has less experience than another. It is not always easy to work out fact from opinion.

Building better communities

'We aim to create strong, attractive and thriving communities and neighbourhoods. To do this we help people and local organisations to combat problems like community conflict, extremism, deprivation and disadvantage.'

Source: Communities and Local Government

The government aims to overcome discrimination by making communities more cohesive. People are less likely to behave badly towards each other if they get to know one another better. Often, people are suspicious of those whom they see as being different but, when they meet, they find that they share more than they had expected.

How do we compare?

The EU has its own laws preventing discrimination and member countries are expected to incorporate them into their own law.

In general, the UK meets the EU requirements but we still have a large gender pay gap by European standards. It is a third higher than the EU average and twice that of Ireland. Of the larger member-states, only Germany has a bigger gap.

Check your understanding

1 What types of discrimination are against the law?
2 What evidence is there that pay is becoming more equal?
3 What evidence is there that other forms of discrimination still exist?
4 Find out what is going on in your local community to reduce discrimination. Does your school have any policies to prevent students from discriminating against each other?
5 How can discrimination be reduced?

... another point of view?

'People have more respect for others when they get to know them.'
Do you agree with this statement? Give reasons for your opinion, showing you have considered another point of view.

Attitudes to immigration

Getting you thinking

Keep calm!

Teachers' leaders yesterday appealed for calm at a school where teenagers chanted racist abuse at refugee classmates.

Ten pupils at Parkside Community Technology College, Plymouth, have been suspended after allegedly shouting 'Pakis out' in the playground. Teachers responded by herding 20 of their victims into a classroom for their own safety.

The parents of the refugee children, who were targeted by a mob of about 40 pupils on Wednesday lunchtime, are now refusing to send them back to school.

The Notting Hill Carnival takes place in London every summer. It celebrates Afro-Caribbean culture – its food, music, culture and fashion

The Minister for Borders and Immigration said

'I think the immigration system has been too lenient and I want to make it harder, but I also want to be nice to people who do come to settle here. That's what I have wanted to do all my life since the boy from Uganda came to my school and was called Banana. I was appalled.'

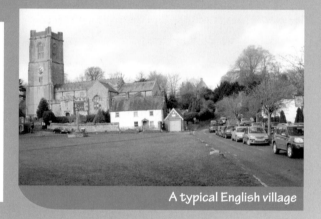

A typical English village

Why do people have different attitudes?

In Unit 1 you discovered that the UK has a diverse population and has had for many years (pages 10–11). Yet people continue to react in different ways to immigrants arriving in the country. There is a number of reasons for this:

- **Fear of change**

  Many people have a fear of difference because new arrivals may change their community. If you are afraid of change you may not know how to deal with people from different backgrounds and cultures.

- **Employment**

  New people may threaten the jobs market, although there is evidence that immigrants take jobs that residents do not want. Many people from new EU countries came to pick fruit, for example. They were brought here because farmers couldn't find enough pickers. When the economy is booming, people are welcome because there are more jobs than people. If unemployment starts rising, the situation may change.

Other people welcome change and enjoy the wide range of cultural activities and choices that a multicultural society offers. The UK has received many ethnic groups over hundreds of years and they have all had an impact on our culture.

Helping people to become self sufficient so they can participate in the local community helps to overcome difficulties. The data on GCSE results shows how some groups are making the most of the opportunities they are offered and can therefore become successful members of the community.

You will explore the reasons why groups of people react differently to new arrivals from other countries.

What's the benefit?

Immigrant workers fill skill gaps and do jobs British workers do not want, but employers and local economies were not reaping the full benefits because many migrants were staying for short periods instead of settling in Britain.

Local economies benefit because migrants can have different skills that could lead to the establishment of new types of businesses and they tended to be more entrepreneurial.

Immigrants could also expand the market for local businesses by establishing links to their countries of origin.

Source: Institute for Public Policy Research

Morrissey said

'Also, with the issue of immigration, it's very difficult because, although I don't have anything against people from other countries, the higher the influx into England the more the British identity disappears so the price is enormous. If you travel to Germany, it's still absolutely Germany. If you travel to Sweden, it still has a Swedish identity. But travel to England and you have no idea where you are. It matters because the British identity is very attractive. I grew up into it, and I find it quaint and very amusing. But England is a memory now. Other countries have held on to their basic identity, yet it seems to me that England was thrown away.'

1 Why do you think the children at Parkside Community College behaved as they did?
2 If you were the Minister, how would you want to 'be nice to people who come to settle here'?
3 Morrissey complains that immigration means that the UK is losing its culture. What aspects of our culture do you think have changed because of immigration? What has stayed the same? What sorts of things have changed for other reasons?
4 How has immigration helped the economy?

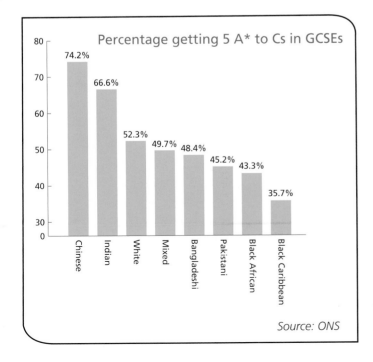

Percentage getting 5 A* to Cs in GCSEs

- Chinese: 74.2%
- Indian: 66.6%
- White: 52.3%
- Mixed: 49.7%
- Bangladeshi: 48.4%
- Pakistani: 45.2%
- Black African: 43.3%
- Black Caribbean: 35.7%

Source: ONS

Check your understanding

1 Why do some people not respond positively to new arrivals?
2 Why do others welcome them?
3 Suggest ways in which problems that might arise can be overcome.
4 How can new arrivals help themselves?

... another point of view?

'We should welcome everyone wherever they come from.'

Do you agree with this statement? Give reasons for your opinion, showing you have considered another point of view.

Working together

Getting you thinking

The Word is a hip-hop group based at Thornhill Business and Enterprise School in Sunderland. Through powerful and highly creative performances, The Word aims to inform young people about cultural, ethnic, racial and religious diversity; to raise awareness of and tackle the problems of discrimination, racism and anti-social issues and, above all, inspire all young people to achieve their ambitions.

In **Leicester**, Sacred Heart Catholic Primary School was twinned with Bridge Junior, 80 per cent of whose pupils are Muslim children. A performance group ran workshops and organised an event for the parents from both schools who met for the first time. The schools carried out work on identity, in which pupils explored their parents' and grand-parents' experiences. Pupils and parents started communicating with each other.

Langport, a small town in Somerset, has recently attracted an increasing number of migrant workers. The local community was offered help to understand that migrant workers – mainly of Polish and Portuguese origin – were arriving to live and work in the area, and why. It offered practical support to help the newcomers to overcome problems with their day-to-day integration. An 'international' sporting event took place, at which new arrivals took part in teams with residents. There were also language classes to help new arrivals learn English.

Radio Salaam Shalom is the UK's first Muslim and Jewish online radio station. It aims to bridge the gap between Jewish and Muslim young people. Radio Salaam Shalom's key success is bringing Muslim and Jewish communities together to consider their shared local values and experiences as residents of Bristol, where it is based, and beyond.

Bradgate Bakery encourages migrant workers to improve their English language skills by giving employees substantial time off to learn English as a wider package of learning and personal development in the workplace.

Sharing Cultural Memories brought 15 older volunteers into ten local primary schools. Volunteers used innovative ways to help pupils with numeracy and literacy. They shared cultural memories and experiences with the children. For example, one volunteer ran a Caribbean Nature project at Rotherfield Primary School, to raise children's awareness about their own and other people's heritage,

1. What is a community? Use Unit 1, page 7 to help.
2. Which groups of people did these projects aim to help?
3. In what way do you think they help communities?
4. Why do you think they are necessary?
5. Are there any activities in your area that aim to help communities work together better?

You will find out why problems of community cohesion exist and look at ways in which they can be resolved.

What is community cohesion?

Community cohesion is the togetherness and bonding shown by members of a community. This can be described as the 'glue' that holds a community together. It might include features such as a sense of common belonging or cultural similarity. You found out about communities and identities in Unit 1 (pages 6–15). Encouraging members of communities to work together better has been part of government policy for a number of years.

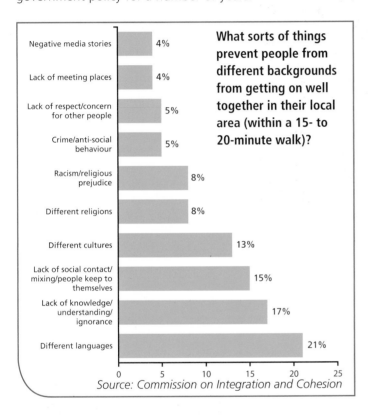

What sorts of things prevent people from different backgrounds from getting on well together in their local area (within a 15- to 20-minute walk)?

Category	%
Negative media stories	4%
Lack of meeting places	4%
Lack of respect/concern for other people	5%
Crime/anti-social behaviour	5%
Racism/religious prejudice	8%
Different religions	8%
Different cultures	13%
Lack of social contact/mixing/people keep to themselves	15%
Lack of knowledge/understanding/ignorance	17%
Different languages	21%

Source: Commission on Integration and Cohesion

What makes communities work together?

- **Lifestyle** is top of the list. People need education, jobs, a reasonable income, healthcare and decent housing if they are to feel secure in their community. If people are in poor health or in debt, have poor skills and bad living conditions, they are likely to have low self-esteem. This often leads to difficulty in getting a job and a sense of insecurity.
- **Social order** is also important. If the community is peaceful and secure, people are more likely to respect each other. Lack of social order can lead to suspicion and lack of respect.
- **Social networks** connect people and organisations, and help people support each other by offering information, trust and friendship.
- **Sense of belonging** is important. It comes from shared experiences, values and identities.
- **Equality** – or fairness – means that people in the community have equal access to jobs, healthcare and education, for example, which affect people's life chances.

When these factors are part of community life, there is more likely to be social inclusion. People who miss out are likely to feel excluded from society and therefore tend to drop out or become disengaged.

Achieving community cohesion

A community that really works needs:
- a common vision and a sense of belonging for all communities
- the valuing of diversity
- similar life opportunities for all
- strong and positive relationships between people from different backgrounds and circumstances in the workplace, in the school and within neighbourhoods.

Check your understanding

1 Why is it difficult for some communities to work together?
2 Explain the factors that make it easier for communities to work together. Explain why each one is important.
3 What sort of activities can help to develop community cohesion?
4 What are the characteristics of a community that works well?

... another point of view?

'Communities need help to be cohesive.'
Do you agree with this statement? Give reasons for your opinion, showing you have considered another point of view.

Key Terms

community cohesion: the glue that holds communities together

Option B: Changing communities: social and cultural identities

207

Changing communities: social

Source A

Active integration

'Immigrants change us, mostly for the better. They don't just bring their labour with them. they create more choice for everyone – of food, of music, of literature – all aspects of the benefits of two-way integration. They compete hard, they lift our standards.

Most immigrants change too. We expect those who come to Britain to play by the rules and to do their best to share in the responsibilities of living together as well as enjoying the rights – for example by learning English so that they can participate fully in the workplace and in the life of the community. And if people want the rules to be different they campaign to change them by the democratic means we have available.

But an integrated society isn't only the sum of what individuals do. It's also what governments and civil society do too. So that means we all – immigrant and home grown – have the right to expect that we will be treated fairly, not exploited and that our dignity is respected.'

Trevor Phillips, Equality and Human Rights Commission

Leave margin blank

Source B

A project called **Sharing Cultural Memories** brought 15 older volunteers into ten local primary schools. Volunteers used innovative methods to help pupils with numeracy and literacy. They shared cultural memories and experiences with the children. For example, one volunteer ran a Caribbean Nature project at Rotherfield Primary School, to raise children's awareness about their own and other people's heritage,

Source C

The Notting Hill Carnival is a celebration of Afro-Caribbean cultures and traditions. The first Carnival took place in 1964. It is held in London every August

1. An immigrant is:

    ☐ A. a British person who leaves Britain.
    ☐ B. a British person who comes back to Britain.
    ☑ C. a non-British person who arrives in Britain.
    ☐ D. a non-British person who leaves Britain.

    (1 mark)

2. A volunteer is usually described as someone who:

☐ A. joins a political party.
☑ B. does something without payment.
☐ C. joins a human rights group.
☐ D. works for pay.

(1 mark)

3 Heritage is:
☑ A. something handed down from one's ancestors or the past.
☐ B. something learnt from people in other countries.
☐ C. a stately home.
☐ D. something old.

(1 mark)

4. In Source A, Trevor Phillips refers to 'the democratic means we have available'. Explain what he means by this statement. (2 marks)

He means that they should use elections to change things.

5. Using Source A and your own knowledge, identify three human rights that Trevor Phillips might be asking to be respected. (3 marks)

Freedom to follow your religion
Freedom from discrimination
Freedom of thought

> There are many others to choose from but these are important in this context.

6. Using Source B, explain the work of Sharing Cultural Memories. (2 marks)

Sharing Cultural Memories brings together older people and young people to discuss their heritage and help the younger to understand their heritage.

7. Using Source B, explain how Sharing Cultural Memories helps to develop community cohesion. (2 marks)

Sharing Cultural Memories helps to develop community cohesion because it brings together old and young and helps people to find out about each other's culture.

209

8. Using Sources A, B and C and your own knowledge, do you agree that meeting people from different communities helps us to become an integrated society?
Give reasons for you opinion and show that you have considered another point of view.

(8 marks)

Many people live in their communities and don't mix with other people from different cultures. When people don't know about each other's cultures, they can be frightened of them. This has led to trouble in some places.

In Source A Trevor Phillips says that we learn from each other and this makes the country and communities stronger. He also says they should try to join in with the British community and not live apart. This is not always easy for people who have been here for a long time and still haven't learnt to speak English.

The student has used information from the first source and puts another point of view.

In Source B the community is becoming more integrated because people are learning about each other's cultures. Young people from the ethnic group of the older people will become more secure in their own background. The older people will also find that as the children grow up, they know them so they don't seem so scary when they hang out.

Source C shows people at the Notting Hill Carnival. People are having fun and getting to know each other better. It has been going a long time and has become part of London's culture.

The student has chosen to go through the sources and show how each one contributes to making a society more integrated. This works well. It would have been just as good to think of the ideas and use the sources to support the argument.

I agree with the statement because we get on better when we get to know each other better. It is not always easy because everyone has to have an open mind and be able to get together.

Extended writing

'To fully experience the benefits of being a British citizen, everyone should learn to speak and write English fluently.'
Do you agree with this view?
Give reasons for your opinion, showing you have considered another point of view.
You could consider the following points in your answer and other information of your own.

- What are the advantages and disadvantages of speaking and writing English?
- What issues do young people and adults face when learning English?

- Is it ethically right to make people speak and write English?
- If a person does not want to learn English should they still be allowed to be a British citizen?

(15 marks)

I think people should learn to speak and write English if they come to live here. It is very hard to play a part in the community if you don't. It is also hard to make the most of everything in England if you can't speak the language.

> A good start. The student had set out a clear point of view and started to address the first bullet point. It is now important to make sure that there is another perspective.

If you don't speak English it is hard to be in education. Most children learn very quickly when they go to school but if they come to school without speaking English, it can take them some time to catch up.

It is very hard to understand what is going on in the country if you don't speak English. There are radio and television programmes in other languages but most is in English. It can be hard to share things if you can't understand the soaps that everyone else follows.

> A good point. It gives a very practical point about life in Britain.

If we think people should learn English, we should make it easy. There should be free lessons for people because people arriving in the country often don't have much money.

> Another good point showing an understanding of the problem.

If people want to be British citizens and be part of the community, they need to speak English if they are to do so. A citizen might have to sit on a jury – and you need to understand what is being said. If you don't understand what the political parties stand for, how can you vote in an election?

I'm not sure which point of view is ethical because it depends on your point of view. People have ethical responsibilities to take part in the activities I just mentioned but then you might be discriminating against people who find it difficult to learn English. It is difficult to decide which decision would be fair. I wouldn't want to deprive people of their culture but they will miss out on a lot if they don't learn the language. I think they should at least make a start so they can go shopping and do ordinary things. Most people will get better just by being here.

> This last point is quite difficult. Try to remember about making ethical decisions. Put your point of view – but make sure you can support it.

Option C: Influencing and

People often say 'the government's got it wrong'. They want to change the decisions that have been made. In Unit 1 you learnt a lot about how government works and now you have a chance to investigate other people's views on the subject. You can then work out the views that you agree with and those you don't and come to your own conclusions.

Topics to investigate

These questions will help you to think about how we can influence and change the way government works. In the exam you will be given a range of points of view on the way democracy works and you will be able to use all the skills and knowledge you have developed in your Citizenship Studies course to answer the questions.

- What are the ethical aspects of representation and levels of benefit?

Getting going

The question to ask yourself is 'What's going on?'. Whatever media you use, you will find lots of useful material. Just Googling a topic will give you masses of information – but how do you know whether it is accurate? How do you know whether the people who run the website have their own mission? There are lots of questions to ask.

Should the supermarket come to town?

Who wants the new supermarket?

At Tesco we are committed to serving new and existing customers. We are also committed to being good neighbours in the communities that we serve. We do this by opening stores that bring fresh, affordable, quality food and greater choice to more people, especially for families and pensioners on low incomes.

Tesco.co.uk

1 Local choice is reduced.
2 Money leaves local communities and goes to shareholders.
3 Traffic congestion increases.
4 Local jobs are lost.
5 Food and packaging waste is generated.
6 Suppliers are exploited and the environment is damaged.

www.birminghamfoe.org.uk

On paper, there are grounds for local authorities to refuse permission for a new supermarket, but they may be reluctant to do so if they think the supermarket will appeal. After all, the resources at the disposal of the big supermarkets are many times greater than those of the local council.

www.gaff.org.uk

We have been pushing for the introduction of stronger policy for town centres that retains the need test and includes a presumption against out-of-town development and a tougher test for diversity to ensure that policy delivers a real choice of where to shop.

Tescopoly.co.uk

1 Why did each organisation hold its point of view?
2 What other questions would you want to ask?
3 Where could you look for the answers?
4 How do you weigh up the different points of view?

212

changing decisions in society and government

- What can individuals and groups do to influence change?
- How can political parties or elections in the UK make a difference?
- Can changing the electoral system change the way Britain and the regions are governed?
- How does the changing pattern of crime affect the way society develops?
- Does the UK send enough or too many people to prison?

- Can matters of civil law be as important or more important than cases involving criminal law?
- What is the impact of the reductions in privacy and civil liberties?
- How is public opinion formed and what influence does this have on decision-making?
- Is government sufficiently responsive to public opinion?
- Do individual countries such as the UK retain any control over their own economies now the global economy is so powerful?

Whose perspectives?

Individual
- How can individuals participate in decision-making either personally or in groups?

Ethical
- What is fair resource allocation and distribution and how are people's contribution to society and government affected?

Community
- How are decisions different and how are they made in different ways in different communities?
- What impact and consequence do individual and collective actions have on communities, including in the voluntary sector?
- What is the impact of identities and diversities?

Social
- Who is responsible for decisions and what redress is there?
- What is the balance between rights and responsibilities?

Political
- Whose opinions matter most?
- Who represents us and who is accountable for decisions?

National
- What are the national influences on public opinion and national decisions and how are these decisions influenced by the impact and accuracy of the media?
- What development and struggle has there been for different rights and freedoms in the UK (speech, opinion, association and the vote)?
- How does parliamentary democracy operate in the UK?

Global
- How do global events and moral considerations influence decisions and the economy?
- How do other forms of government, both democratic and non-democratic, operate beyond the UK?
- What is the impact of democracy and justice in the UK and other countries?

Making ethical decisions

Getting you thinking

The Education Maintenance Allowance is given by the government to young people who want to stay in education after the age of 16. The amount depends on their parents' earnings.

Here are some students' views:

> I get EMA but I don't think it's fair. I have put the majority of it into a savings account ready for university. I know the majority of my friends spend it on alcohol, make-up and that sort of thing. My boyfriend didn't receive any and his parents didn't give him any money at all.

> It should be based on grades or some way of proving that you do really want to be in the sixth form.

> Why can't everyone get paid to stay in school whether your parents earn more or less the 30k?

> I think it's good to give people financial aid, but I think the government should restrict what it is spent on, instead of just giving out money that people can spend on whatever they want.

1 Why do students think the EMA is unfair?

2 One suggests that all students should receive it. Do you think this is fair or unfair? Explain why.

3 What effect would it have on other government spending? Would this be fair?

4 Do you think it is fair to help people to stay in education after 16?

5 What criteria would you use to decide how the money that is available is shared out?

What does 'ethical' mean?

Different people use different words to define 'ethical', but the general view is that it means 'relating to a set of values including compassion, fairness, honesty, respect and responsibility.'

Making an ethical decision means taking all these aspects into account. In order to do this there are some questions to be asked.

- Which action results in the most good and least harm?
- Which action respects the rights of everyone involved?
- Which action treats people fairly?
- Which action contributes most to the quality of life of the people affected?

These questions can be asked of any issue or dispute in order to come to a decision about what to do.

You will find out about the ethical aspects of representation and benefits.

Who's the winner?

Women's No Pay Day

On 30 October, women receive their last payslip of the year and begin working for free thanks to the 17 per cent gender pay gap.  This is called Women's No Pay Day. Members of the Fawcett Society, an organisation that campaigns for equality for women, demonstrates across the country on this day.

Women in Britain earn 17 per cent less than men for full-time work and considerably less than women in other European countries. For part-time work, the difference between men and women rises to 36 per cent. In the course of their working life women earn, on average, £330,000 less than men.

1 Use ethical decision-making to decide whether women should be paid less than men.
2 What else would you need to know before you made a decision?
3 Is equal pay law ethical? Explain your point of view.

Check your understanding

1 What does 'ethical' mean?
2 Use the questions for making an ethical decision to see whether your criteria work for deciding who gets help to stay in education after 16.
3 Why do people's answers to ethical issues differ?

... another point of view?

'Every decision we make should be ethical.'
Do you agree with this statement? Give reasons for your opinion, showing you have considered another point of view.

Does equal pay matter?

Bridget Bodman was financial controller for a large engineering firm. When she left, she was replaced by a man who received a salary of £8,000 more than she had been paid and a car allowance of £8,640.

Bridget took the company to court and won. She said: 'I'm glad I fought the case, although it was very stressful. At first, when I realised there was this pay divide, I went through a lot of doubts – was I not good enough at my job, maybe there was a genuine reason. But then I realised that it wasn't right and that I had to make a stand. Hopefully it will set a good precedent for other women, although I find it amazing that this kind of discrimination is still happening, and on such a wide scale.'

Is everyone's decision the same?

Even when using the ethical decision-making questions, not everyone's answers are the same. It all depends on our personal values and the weight we give to different questions. People may have different opinions on the purpose and value of prison. It often depends on whether they have been affected by serious crime. The evidence shows that everything should be done to keep young people out of prison, but personal experience can influence people's judgement.

Key Terms

ethical: relating to a set of values including compassion, fairness, honesty, respect and responsibility

Influencing change

Getting you thinking

Breaking the law to change the law

Members of a gang involved in campaigning for animal rights were warned today they would be jailed for up to 12 years. They had admitted to blackmail against the owners of a farm breeding guinea pigs for medical research. The owners had faced a six-year campaign of terror ending in the theft of an elderly relative's dead body.

An individual – helping others to help themselves

Emma Triplett went travelling in Nepal and ended up working with girls who had been trafficked and been forced to work in circuses in India. The centre where she worked offered training to these girls, but there was little point because no one would employ them. Emma decided she had to help. She explored the sorts of products they could make and she could sell in England. It turned out to be bags and jewellery. Hatti Trading is now a successful business selling ethically traded products.

Ways to change things

People, by themselves or in groups, can bring about change. It's going on all the time. Just Google 'pressure groups' and you will find all sorts of organisations that are working to change things. You found out how pressure groups work and the range of activities that they use in Unit 1. The stories above show people:

- using individual determination
- being role models
- persuading our elected representatives
- breaking the law to intimidate people.

Whatever strategy you choose, it needs to fit the objective. Emma worked alone because she was doing something she cared about and was dealing with a problem that few others had encountered.

It is often easier to work together because you can make a louder noise and the people you are trying to persuade have to recognise that a large number of people are looking for change.

Change for the better?

Deciding on whether the results of actions make things better or worse often depends on your point of view.

It is hard to dispute that Emma Triplett's actions are making things better for the girls in Nepal. She has also organised them to make products that people want to buy, so consumers in England are better off too.

Aston Villa football club is doing all sorts of things to help the children's hospice as well as bringing it to the attention of everyone who comes to the games or watches them play on the television.

The UK Youth Parliament's actions are more controversial. While many support the government's decision, there are people who think sex education should happen at home and certainly not in primary schools.

The animal rights campaigner firmly believes that we should not use animals in experiments, whatever the benefit to people with health problems. There are many like him, but there are others who think that the laws the government has in place are sufficient to ensure that the use of animals is strictly controlled and is worth the benefits in medical research.

It's all a question of perspective.

You will explore how individuals and groups can influence change.

Campaigning to change the law

The UK Youth Parliament launched a petition calling for the government to ensure that every young person receives sex and relationship education within Personal Social and Health Education by making it a compulsory part of the National Curriculum.

The government has accepted the arguments that PSHE should be compulsory and agreed to undertake a review to consider how to turn the decision into a practicable way forward.

Influencing people to help others

Aston Villa players wear the logo of Acorns Children's Hospice on their shirts. They carry out all sorts of events, including parachute jumps, to raise funds too.

1 Who is influencing change in each of these stories?
2 How are they attempting to do so?
3 Which ones are successful? Explain why.
4 What is a pressure group? Use Unit 1, page 37 to help you.
5 Do you think it is harder or easier to influence change on your own or in groups?
6 Use the ethical questions on page 214 to work out whether the people in these stories have made a positive change.

Check your understanding

1 How can people influence change?
2 Why is change not always welcomed by everyone?
3 Draw spider diagrams for each of the stories to show how different groups of people are affected by the change that that has taken place. Use a black pen for the positive influences and a red pen for the negative ones.
4 Choose a campaigning organisation that has been trying to change things. Select one change they want to make and draw a spider diagram like the ones you did in question 3.

... another point of view?

'Change is always for the better.'
Do you agree with this statement? Give reasons for your opinion, showing you have considered another point of view.

Political change

Getting you thinking

Local and national

Council shuts down speed cameras

Swindon took action against after councillors became frustrated that local residents were having to pay for the upkeep of cameras through their council tax, while central government retained the money from fines. In a single year nearly 30,000 people in Wiltshire received speeding tickets generating £1.76 million, £252,300 in Swindon alone.

Council responds to local needs

The ruling Lib Dem group in Sheffield says that every attempt will be made to replace a centralised council bureaucracy with a system that responds to individual requirements.

'This is a huge sea change in the way the city is run, moving from a one-size-fits-all approach to meeting the needs of the individual, from the Town Hall taking decisions to giving choice to local people and putting business and environment at the heart of what we do.'

'What's right for Burngreave might not be right for Broomhill. What's right for Stocks-bridge might not be right for Southey.'

Local, national or international?

The decisions in 'Getting you thinking' are being made by both local and national government. You found out about how this works in Unit 1 (pages 66 and 78). Local government is making decisions that affect the local area. In London, all the boroughs have their own councils. In other big cities, there is one council that represents the city as a whole. Other parts of the country have county councils or district councils.

International decisions are made by the Council of Ministers of the European Union. These decisions affect all the member countries and national governments have to comply.

Making changes

Political change comes about in a variety of ways – as you found out in Unit 1.

Before a general election, every party writes a manifesto, setting out the plans it will put into action if it wins. Voters can look at the manifestos of the parties to decide which one is closest to their views. They then make a democratic choice, and the party that most people agree with is elected.

Sometimes the winning party can be taken to task because they haven't kept all their promises. This may affect the way people decide to vote at the next election. Sometimes circumstances change, so it would be unreasonable to expect all the promises to be kept. For example, if the economy changes and unemployment goes up, the government will get less income from taxes and it will have to spend more on unemployment benefits. There will be less to spend on other things – so it may be impossible to do everything that was promised.

Once in power, a government can make decisions about all aspects of running the country, but ministers must always remember that they are accountable to the electorate, who can decide whether to re-elect them at the end of the term of office. This can be no more that five years.

A referendum?

Big decisions can be made through a referendum. This does not happen often in the UK. A referendum was held in 1975 to test public opinion on EU membership. There was pressure for another one to decide whether the UK should accept new rules on the running of the EU but the government decided against it.

You will explore how political parties or elections in the UK can make a difference.

Taxes?

Conservatives will cut some taxes and look for more efficient ways of running some government services.

Liberal Democrats will cut 4p off income tax, raise taxes on the rich and cut services.

Labour will raise taxes for some people and some businesses in order to spend more.

Trains?

Conservatives want a new high-speed train network.

Liberal Democrats want a new high-speed train network.

Labour wants 100,000 more train seats.

Hunting?

Conservatives want to repeal the hunting ban.

Liberal Democrats will keep the hunting ban.

Labour will keep the hunting ban.

1 Are the decisions being made at the local or national level?
2 How are decisions made locally and nationally? Pages 66 and 78 in Unit 1 will help.
3 Who wins and who loses from each of these examples of political parties causing change?
4 How can the parties justify making changes?
5 What reasons might each party give for each of the changes? You might want to do a little research.
6 Choose a change that is happening at the moment. Work out who gains and who loses. Use the ethical questions on page 214 to work out whether you think it's a good idea.

Check your understanding

1 How do political parties tell the public about their plans before an election?
2 How does democracy influence change?
3 How can governments test public opinion?
4 Why do governments have to think about the electorate when they decide to make changes?
5 What effect does the media have on people's points of view?
6 How do you think the electorate will measure the success of changes made by the government? Use an example to help you explain.

... another point of view?

'It is important that governments are accountable to the electorate.'

Do you agree with this statement? Give reasons for your opinion, showing you have considered another point of view.

Changing democracy

How local?

Wiltshire's four district councils were replaced with one council for the whole county. The change will save council tax payers £15m a year.

In the past Wiltshire County Council was responsible for areas such as education, social services, highways and libraries. The four district councils were broadly responsible for areas such as leisure, street cleaning, planning and refuse collection. Now they will all be run by one council.

But not everyone was happy ...

> Creating one council would produce an authority too remote to deliver truly local services or community leadership.

How regional?

Wales has an assembly. Scotland has a parliament. Both have powers over some decisions – but not all.

The government wanted to set up regional assemblies to give a voice to regions far from Westminster and return power to local people.

Anti-regional assembly campaigners argued that the new tier of government would be an expensive talking shop with very little real power.

Nearly 80 per cent of voters in a referendum in the North East said 'No'.

Local or national?

The debate over how people should be represented at the local, national and even international level has continued for many years. In Unit 1 (page 87) you found out about devolution and regional government. There are clearly advantages to local representation because people know the environment of the area, what people need and what they don't want.

There are some decisions that cannot be made locally; they need to represent the whole country. A local army clearly wouldn't work. A transport policy needs to make connections across the country.

The drawback of having councils, assemblies and parliaments at many different levels is cost. Running each layer is expensive and the money could be used to provide services that people need or want. Voters must decide how they want to spend the money that is available. One factor in the referendum in the North East was the cost. Wiltshire opted for one large council, to save money by removing the local councils.

The turnout in general elections tends to be higher than in local or EU elections. This is probably related to the amount of media coverage when a general election takes place.

How are the votes counted?

General and local elections in UK are nearly all 'first past the post'. You found out about different ways of running elections in Unit 1 (page 88). 'First past the post' gives the advantage to large parties and makes it hard for small ones to get representation.

There has been pressure, particularly from the Liberal Democrats, to introduce proportional representation, as this gives more seats to smaller parties. The London Assembly elections use a method of proportional representation.

The outcomes give a fairer share of seats to all parties, but can make it hard to govern because there is les likely to be one dominant party in power.

You will explore how changing the electoral system could change the way Britain and its regions are governed.

A new nation?

Scottish Nationalists have campaigned for a long time to cut the ties with England and Wales and become an independent country.

Yes	No
• Scotland would be much wealthier and better prepared than many other independent nations around the world • Revenue from oil and other energy industries could be invested to provide a secure fund to support future generations • Much of ther political and civil framework needed to run the country is already in place, and the people are highly educated	• Without subsidy from the rest of the UK, it is claimed that there would be a tax deficit of up to £11bn • Promises to cut taxes while increasing spending on pensions and higher education would put the country in the red • If the bonds that unite Britain were severed, all the countries of the union would suffer economically and culturally

0

1 What are the advantages and disadvantages of having one council for a whole county to deal with everything?

2 What is devolution? Look at Unit I, page 87 for help.

3 Why did the government want to set up regional assemblies?

4 Why do you think the people of the North East rejected the idea?

5 Why do Scottish Nationalists want to be independent?

6 Why do you think England does not want Scotland to break away?

7 Do you think that electing people to represent you locally is more democratic than if they are in an assembly or parliament further away? Explain your answer.

8 Which government decisions do you think should be made locally, and which nationally?

9 Do you think people are more likely to vote in local, national or international elections? Explain you answer.

The EU system

The UK uses proportional representation to elect MEPs, but EU countries can choose their own system, so they differ widely.

Check your understanding

1 What is meant by 'first past the post'?

2 What is proportional representation?

3 How are decisions made locally and nationally in the UK?

4 What decisions are made locally?

5 What decisions are made nationally?

6 Why can some decisions not be made at a local level?

... another point of view?

'As many decisions as possible should be made locally.'

Do you agree with this statement? Give reasons for your opinion, showing you have considered another point of view.

Crime: fact or fiction?

Getting you thinking

Newspapers say

> **Terrorism a long-term threat**

> **One in seven won't have children from fear of terrorism**

> **New Terrorism Act comes into force**

Liberty, which campaigns for human rights, says

Governments have a duty to take steps to protect citizens from terrorism, but this does not justify side-stepping democratic values.

Since the Prevention of Terrorism Acts of the 1970s, terrorism laws have done little to ensure that we are safe from terrorist attack, but much to infringe the human rights and civil liberties of those living in the UK.

Government ministers want to impose sweeping restrictions on individual freedoms on the basis of secret intelligence and suspicion:

- People can be detained for 28 days without being charged with a crime.
- Laws now restrict our rights to free speech and meeting in non-violent groups.
- Our right to protest has been seriously limited.

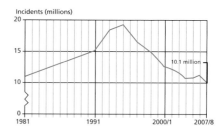

How many children were murdered?

Trends in crime

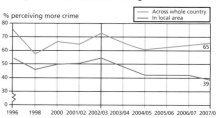

Perception that crime is rising

Source: Home Office

Implant a chip to keep my child safe

Children are being abducted and murdered. You should think about implanting a non-removable permanent chip to keep them safe whatever the ethics.

1 What do the newspaper headlines try to achieve?

2 What is the government doing about terrorism?

3 Why is Liberty concerned about the government's actions?

4 What has happened to the amount of violent crime?

5 What has happened to the number of children who have been murdered since 1995?

6 What is your impression of what is happening to crime? What has influenced your point of view?

7 What impression does the newspaper article give?

8 What motives do newspapers owners have? Check with Unit 1, page 46.

9 Why might ethics be an issue when implanting a chip in a child?

You will explore the changing patterns of crime and their impact on how society develops.

What the data says

We are surrounded by data about all sorts of things. You have to be careful about using it. Even crime statistics can be tricky. Police records don't paint an accurate picture because many crimes are not reported. The government also uses the British Crime Survey, which asks people about their actual experiences of crime.

Organisations, such as pressure groups, which want to persuade us about their beliefs, can choose data carefully to support their point of view.

What sells newspapers?

Many newspapers are sold because of the scandalous and horrific stories on the front page. The more dramatic the story, the higher the sales rise. As newspapers exist to make a profit, editors of papers are likely to select stories that attract most attention and therefore sell more papers.

People make their impressions of the world around them from newspaper headlines and TV news – even if they don't read the paper or listen to the whole programme. We can therefore have a distorted view of the world. The data in 'Getting you thinking' shows how people think that crime is falling where they live but getting worse elsewhere.

The government's point of view

The government always wants to make a good impression in the hope of being re-elected at the next general election. It often chooses the stories that it wants to hit the headlines and promotes them to the media. On the other hand, it has been accused of 'burying bad news' by putting it out on days when important events are taking place, so that the issue won't get much, if any, space in the media.

Challenge what you see!

When you are presented with evidence by any organisation, it is important to ask questions about why the information has been selected.

The government wants you to think that crime is falling. The newspapers want to tell you lurid stories. The papers give us the impression that the number of children who are abducted and murdered is rising, but the data tells us something different.

Remember to look carefully and think about the motives of the people who are giving you the information.

How is society changing?

When exaggerated stories are told, people tend to react more strongly than they need. Many parents are anxious about the safety of their children despite the fact that road accidents and murders are actually declining. On a number of occasions, the media has whipped up a campaign against groups of people and demanded changes in the law, when the evidence contradicts their stories.

Liberty, the human rights campaign group, is concerned about the changes in our detention laws. British law has been based on not locking people up unless they are brought to court and charged with an offence within a few days. The government wanted to extend this to 42 days. Once a law is in place, it can be used for other purposes and can change the culture of the country.

Check your understanding

1 Why is it important to look carefully when data is used as evidence to support a point of view?

2 Why might the government want to persuade the population that it is being successful?

3 Why does the media want to tell dramatic stories?

4 How are changes in the pattern of crime affecting society? Think of some current examples – such as the internet.

... another point of view?

'Crime is rising and we must all be very careful when we go out.'

Do you agree with this statement? Give reasons for your opinion, showing you have considered another point of view.

What's the point of prison?

Getting you thinking

Children in prison are 18 times more prone to commit suicide than children of the same age in the community.

Prison Reform Trust

We must have tougher sentences for – knife crime, rape, shop lifters, computer crimes, firearms offences, dangerous drivers, child offenders

How many?

There are currently over 80,000 men, women and children in prison in England and Wales. The prison population has been rising steadily since 1993, when it was 42,000. This means that there is now a higher percentage of people in prison here than in any other country in Western Europe.

Why does it fail?

It damages family relationships and the chances of successful reintegration back into the community. These are two of the most important factors in reducing re-offending. The size of the prison population means that few prisoners get enough education or constructive activity.

Costs and benefits?

Prisons cost £2.2bn a year. With re-offending rates still at about 60 per cent and over 75 per cent for young offenders, prison is an expensive failure, which has no impact on crime levels or the fear of crime.

Source: Howard League for Penal Reform

What is prison for?

Is prison for:

- punishment – keeping people locked up?
- prevention – keeping people off the streets?
- rehabilitation – helping people deal with the outside world?
- revenge – enabling victims to get their own back?

People hold different views about this, but most would agree that, at the end of a prison sentence, an offender should be able to fit into society again. If they can't they will probably re-offend.

How does the UK compare with other countries?

The UK has more recorded crime per head of its population than any other country in Europe – except Sweden. But it sends nearly twice as many people to prison per head of population as Sweden.

When looking at data like this, it is important to work out what it means. The figures are based on 'recorded' crime, which means that victims think it is worth reporting the crime because something might happen as a result. It may be that, in countries with very low rates, victims don't think it is worth reporting the crime.

Effects of prison

One of the main effects of being in prison is that you are much more likely to go back. And young people are even more likely to go back to prison than older inmates. Prison makes it more difficult to function in the outside world because:

- it breaks contacts with families and friends
- a prison record makes it harder to get a job
- education in prison is often not adequate
- people get out of the work habit
- people lose the skills of organising themselves.

Many people who are in prison are addicted to drink or drugs and, when they come out, they re-offend to pay for the habit.

You will explore whether the UK sends enough or too many people to prison.

Intensive fostering programme

Working with a carer

Instead of being sent to a young offenders' institution, young people on the intensive fostering programme live with a specially trained foster carer for up to 12 months as part of their Supervision Order.

They are expected to cooperate with the conditions of the Order and to comply with the targets set out in their individual programmes.

The programme helps young people to build on skills and knowledge they already have and to develop new ones, which will help them to avoid getting into further trouble.

Intensive foster care is not an easy option and young people may find it difficult at times. However, there is a team of people around to help the young people on the programme to talk about any issues they have a problem with.

Arriving at a young offenders' institution

1 How many people in the UK are in prison?
2 How does this compare with Western Europe?
3 Find out what other penalties a court can impose on an offender. Page 63 will help.
4 What percentage of adults and children re-offend after they have been in prison or a young offenders' institution?

5 Why do so many people re-offend?
6 What is the intensive fostering programme?
7 Explain why it is likely to be more or less successful than prison.

Check your understanding

1 How does the number or people in prison in the UK compare with other European countries?
2 What are the effects of sending people to prison?
3 Why are people likely to find it difficult to fit into the community on leaving prison?
4 Why do some people think that prison works?
5 Draw up a list of the advantages and disadvantages of sending people to prison. On balance, what is your opinion?

… another point of view?

'We should lock up criminals and throw away the key.'

Do you agree with this statement? Give reasons for your opinion, showing you have considered another point of view.

Too many? Too few?

Some people argue that prison works because they see the crime rate is falling. The number of people in prison is rising, so more criminals are locked up and can't offend.

Others, such as pressure groups like The Howard League for Penal Reform, argue that there are too many people in prison. They say prison doesn't work and should be used only for people who are a threat to others.

People have different responses because they think prison serves different purposes – but in the course of coming to a conclusion it is important to consider the evidence of its effectiveness.

Criminal or civil?

Getting you thinking

Damages for downloading

The Central London County Court has ordered four people who illegally downloaded and shared Dream Pinball 3D to pay £2,000 damages to the video games company. They also have to pay the costs of the case, which might reach £1,500.

Sue your school!

Hurstpierpoint College in West Sussex has paid what is believed to be a five-figure sum after Katherine Norfolk took the school to the High Court, claiming that poor teaching had left her with a low grade in her A-levels.

Parents in the private sector pay fees; so there is a direct financial contract with the school, which they could claim is breached by poor teaching.

The cost of libel

The *Daily Star* was ordered to pay 'substantial' libel damages to Italian footballer Marco Materazzi for claiming that he had provoked Zinedine Zidane with 'vile racist abuse'. Zidane head butted Materazzi and was sent off in his last game in a French shirt.

Russell Crowe's civil and criminal liability

Russell Crowe paid damages of $100,000 when he was sued for assault. He got mad when he couldn't get through to his wife on the phone, went to the hotel desk and threw the phone at a member of staff. He later pleaded guilty to a criminal assault charge and was given a conditional discharge.

1 Who was the defendant in each case?

2 Who brought the case in each example?

3 Use Unit 1, pages 58–9 to explain the difference between civil and criminal law.

4 Which are civil and which are criminal cases?

5 Why is it easier to bring a case against a private school?

6 In which case has no criminal activity taken place?

You will explore the ways in which matters of civil law might be as important as or more important than cases involving criminal law.

The difference between civil and criminal

In Unit 1 (pages 58–9) you discovered the main differences between civil and criminal law. Both are important as ways of resolving legal issues, but they have different purposes and outcomes.

Criminal	Civil
• The state prosecutes the defendant	• One person can claim redress from another person
• Defendants have to prove they are not liable	• The defendant is innocent until proved guilty
• The burden of proof for criminal offences is that of 'beyond reasonable doubt'	• The burden of proof is 'the balance of probability', which is much lower than for criminal matters
• The penalties for criminal offences are fines and imprisonment, as well as other non-custodial punishments	• The penalty is paying damages or being prevented from doing something. You can't be sent to prison

Which one?

It depends on the outcome people want.

Criminal law deals with people who have broken the law. The Crown Prosecution Service will look at the evidence and decide whether to prosecute.

Civil law aims to sort out problems between people.

If someone hurts you physically, there is likely to be a criminal charge because the act is against the law. There is also reason for a civil case because you can claim financial payment to make up for the pain and suffering.

If someone has damaged your reputation, you can make a civil case because you want to publicise the fact that they were not right and you are looking for recompense.

If someone is publicising aspects of your life you want to keep from the world at large, you can apply for an injunction to prevent them.

If someone is pestering you and won't leave you alone, you can apply for an injunction to stay away.

Check your understanding

1 What is the difference between the purpose of criminal and civil law?
2 In what circumstances would you use civil rather than criminal law?
3 What are the different outcomes of the two?
4 How might costs affect your decision on whether to go to law?

... another point of view?

'Civil law is only there for the rich to use.'

Do you agree with this statement? Give reasons for your opinion, showing you have considered another point of view.

When you can't get a criminal conviction

It can be very difficult to get a conviction in some criminal cases. Sometimes witnesses can be too frightened to come forward and it is therefore very difficult to produce adequate evidence. On other occasions, it is one person's word against another's and it is impossible to prove beyond doubt.

OJ Simpson's trial in America was an example of this. The criminal trial hadn't proved 'beyond reasonable doubt' that he had murdered his wife, but a civil trial decided that on the 'balance of probabilities' he had. As a result, the victim's family was awarded compensation, but in the criminal case Simpson wasn't found guilty of murder, so he wasn't jailed.

The cost of going to law

If you are the victim of a criminal offence, the state prosecutes and you don't have to pay for the case to take place. If you are the defendant, you will have to pay for your defence – and there is little financial help from the state.

If you are the victim in a civil case, you have to pay for your defence – and again, there is little help from the state. The defendant also has to pay their way. The person who loses will have to pay all the costs of the case. You need to think carefully whether it is going to be worthwhile.

What's happening to freedom?

Britney bans leaks

Britney Spears has obtained an emergency injunction from the High Court in London to stop information about her time in treatment being released.

A number of British tabloid newspapers printed stories claiming to be from 'sources close to Spears' describing her time in rehab.

The Communications Data Bill

This bill allows the authorities to collect and retain details of every phone number we have called or texted, as well as every address to which we have sent emails and internet site we have accessed. The information could be used by government departments, local government and all its agencies.

The Transport Minister said

If they're going to use the internet to communicate with each other and we don't have the power to deal with that then you're giving a licence to terrorists to kill people. The biggest civil liberty of all is not to be killed by a terrorist.

Liberty said

The balance between the privacy of the individual and interests such as national security, crime prevention and freedom of expression is far from settled.

The extent of a right to privacy in the UK and its weight in relation to competing values is unclear. Liberty is concerned with how the state, the press and others strike the balance between privacy and other interests.

Radio Frequency Identification

A tag on everyday products

Right now, you can buy a hammer, a pair of jeans, or a razor blade with anonymity. With RFID tags, that may be a thing of the past. Once you buy your RFID-tagged jeans at The Gap with RFID-tagged money, walk out of the store wearing RFID-tagged shoes, and get into your car with its RFID-tagged tyres, you could be tracked anywhere you travel.

There is no law requiring a label indicating that an RFID chip is in a product.

1 Why did Britney not want the media writing about when she was in rehab?

2 How is the media controlled? Check with Unit 1, page 50.

3 What is a Radio Frequency Identification tag?

4 Why are people concerned about their use?

5 Think of some situations in which they could be useful.

6 What does the government want to be able to look at? Why?

7 Why does Liberty question the government's plan?

You will explore the debate surrounding reductions in privacy and civil liberties.

Contradictions?

In Unit 1 (pages 16–17) you learnt about human rights. The United Nations Declaration on Human Rights (UNDHR) expects that we should have both privacy and security.

The two objectives can be contradictory. The government argues that we need to give up some of our rights if we are going to be safe. Liberty, the human rights pressure group, wants these issues to be looked at very carefully before we decide where to draw the line.

The boundaries on what is acceptable are very difficult to define. On one hand, you have Britney Spears not wanting tabloid publicity about her troubled life. On the other hand, the government wants to have the right to look at any email we send to anyone in order to be able to investigate terror threats.

European Commission on Human Rights
The right to live, as far as one wishes, protected from publicity.

UNDHR Article 12
No one shall be subjected to arbitrary interference with his privacy, family, home or correspondence, nor to attacks upon his honor and reputation. Everyone has the right to the protection of the law against such interference or attacks.

UNDHR Article 3
Everyone has the right to life, liberty and security of person.

Check your understanding

1 What does the UNDHR have to say about privacy and security?
2 Why are there always trade offs when we decide where to draw the line on privacy and security?
3 To what extent do celebrities who generally seek publicity expect to have privacy when they want it?
4 What rules would you set up regarding the government's freedom to look at our emails?
5 What rules would you set up for the use of RFID tags?
6 Explain you reasons for the rules you have devised in questions 4 and 5.

... another point of view?

'The government should have the freedom to do what ever it wants to protect us from terrorism.'

Do you agree with this statement? Give reasons for your opinion, showing you have considered another point of view.

Trade offs

Every decision we make about the level of intrusion into our lives has trade offs. The RFID tag referred to in 'Getting you thinking' could be regarded as snooping on our every move, but there are situations in which it can be useful. If a person who has Alzheimer's disease wanders off and gets lost, it would be good to be able to track their whereabouts.

Whatever the topic, it needs to be investigated carefully before new laws are passed. It is important to look at the ways laws might be used in future. If the government can monitor emails, it might want to do so for reasons other than those related to terrorism in future. It is also important to consider the effect on society in general. Sections of the population, for example, who feel they are being targeted by such laws may be alienated.

We all have different points of view on these issues, but it is important to weigh up the advantages and disadvantages before we come to a conclusion.

Who's listening?

Unit 3: Citizenship in context

Getting you thinking

Government approves plans for third runway at Heathrow

Both the prime minister and transport secretary believe that the new runway is vital to the UK's future economic competitiveness, the *Daily Telegraph* has reported.

'NO 3rd RUNWAY' banner hung on House of Commons

Climate campaigners opposed to Heathrow expansion have scaled the roof of the Houses of Parliament and hung protest banners from the building.

Three villages wiped out by runway

The homes, shops, pubs and school in Sipson will vanish and the neighbouring areas of Harlington and Harmondsworth, will also become uninhabitable.

London Chamber of Commerce says

London competes day-in day-out to attract business from around the world but we are starting to lose ground to other major cities because Heathrow is stretched to breaking point.

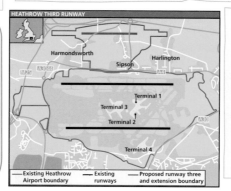

Tories plan £20bn 180mph rail link instead of Heathrow third runway

The Tories would scrap plans for a third runway at Heathrow and instead build a £20 billion high-speed rail line. This could cut more than 66,000 flights a year at the west London airport.

How is public opinion formed?

People receive information from a wide range of sources. In Unit 1, there is information on the role of pressure groups (pages 74 and 82), the media (page 44) and party manifestos (page 66). These all contribute to public opinion.

Pressure groups that have good access to the media are likely to have more influence than others. Some can afford to employ public relations companies to help them to inform people about their objectives. They are likely to have a louder voice and sway people's opinions.

The media itself can take up issues and campaign for change. The issue of NHS top ups in 'Getting you thinking' was given a lot of media coverage both in the papers and on television. In the end the government decided to change its policy.

The government itself does a lot of marketing. A great deal of information is given out in a variety of ways to tell the public about the successes of government policies.

At election time, the main parties are given time on television and radio for campaign broadcasts. These aim to sway the public into voting for them rather than another party.

Does the government listen?

The government doesn't always respond to public opinion. This depends on a variety of factors. As a party's main aim is to be re-elected, it will often respond on issues that it thinks will influence voters. When this is an instant response to an issue, it is not always carefully considered. The media took up the issue of school dinners and the government responded and decided that only healthy food would be available. Unfortunately, many young people don't respond well to this strategy and the numbers eating school dinners fell.

Public opinion does not always have one voice. In the third runway debate, the people living near the airport and the environmentalists had a loud voice. The business community was also powerful because it considered the development of the airport to be crucial to the growth of the economy. The government has to weigh up the different opinions and come to a conclusion.

You will explore how public opinion is formed, the influence it may have on decision making and whether government is sufficiently responsive to it.

You've got cancer, there is a drug that can help, but it's not available on the NHS, what do you do?

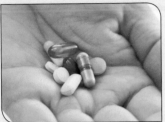

Do you use your life savings or remortgage your house to pay for it?

But – if you want the drug that could lengthen your life you have to become a private patient. That means paying for all your care, as you are not allowed just to top up your care.

NHS drug top-up ban 'to be axed'

Rules banning NHS patients from topping up treatment with drugs that they pay for are to be dropped by the government, according to reports.

1 What were the arguments for and against the third runway at Heathrow?
2 Which stakeholders did the government listen to and why?
3 Why did people want to pay to top up their NHS care?
4 What was the government's view and how did it change?
5 Why do you think it changed?
6 How do you think the government should decide whether to listen to public opinion or not?

Should it always listen?

There are trade offs in any decision. The government has a limited supply of money, as this has comes either from taxation or borrowing. It must therefore decide its priorities. This will influence the decisions.

Public opinion can also call for action that goes against conventions such as the UN Declaration of Human Rights. People often have a gut response to certain offenders. The outcry for information about people on the Sex Offenders' Register, for example, has been resisted by the government.

Check your understanding

1 What are the main influences on public opinion?
2 Why do some organisations have more impact than others?
3 What is the role of the media in forming public opinion?
4 How does the government decide whether to accept pressure from public opinion?

... another point of view?

'We elect the government so it should always follow public opinion.'

Do you agree with this statement? Give reasons for your opinion, showing you have considered another point of view.

Can we control the economy?

Getting you thinking

Where is IKEA?

Europe		Middle East
Austria	Norway	Israel
Belgium	Poland	Kuwait
Cyprus	Portugal	Saudi Arabia
Czech Republic	Romania	United Arab
Denmark	Russia	Emirates
Finland	Slovakia	**Asia Pacific**
France	Spain	Australia
Germany	Sweden	China
Greece	Switzerland	Hong Kong
Hungary	Turkey	Japan
Iceland	United Kingdom	Malaysia
Italy	**North America**	Singapore
Netherlands	Canada	Taiwan
	United States	

Powerful company – powerful country?

Walmart Revenue	$380,000m
Economy of Austria	$377,000m
BP Revenue	$291,000m
Economy of Ireland	$255,000m
HSBC Revenue	$147,000m
Economy of New Zealand	$130,000m
Tesco Revenue	$95,000m
Economy of Morocco	$74,000m
Microsoft Revenue	$51,000m
Economy of Trinidad and Tobago	$20,000m
IKEA Revenue	$18,000m
Economy of the Gambia	$643m

WDR and company reports

What does the economist say?

'The extent to which our economies are coupled together is a shock even to those of us who have worked on globalisation for a long time.'

Paul Krugman, Nobel prize winner for Economics

What does Europe say?

Globalisation is not an option. *It is a fact.*

We live in a *global village*. Information spreads in real-time. Geography is no obstacle to knowledge anymore. Economic views grow together. The same mobile phones and fashion brands are present from Brazil to Beirut.

Globalisation has given us great *opportunities*. Businesses trade more freely, people and goods travel more cheaply and millions of people have been lifted out of poverty.

Yet there is a *dark side*. Increased competition can lead to the outsourcing of jobs. Technological change enables the enemies of globalisation. Inequality breeds discontent.

From a speech by a European commissioner

1 In what parts of the world can you find IKEA?
2 How does this affect the countries where it has shops?
3 The table compares the amount sold by some famous companies with the amount of money in the whole economies of some countries.
 a Which country is IKEA closest to?
 b Do you think this country or IKEA has more influence in the world?
4 What do you think Paul Krugman means when he says countries are coupled together?
5 If countries are 'coupled together', do they need to work together or independently to solve problems?
6 What effect do you think being a 'global village' has on our economies?
7 What are the advantages and disadvantages of globalisation?
8 Why do you think that globalisation is 'a fact'?

You will investigate whether individual countries such as the UK retain any control over their own economy now the global economy is so powerful.

Controlling the economy

In Unit 1 you learnt about how the economy works (pages 104–115) and the influence of big businesses (pages 130–1). Here you can explore the links and connections and think about how businesses and the economy work together.

Who controls the multinationals?

Multinationals have an impact on most countries. They employ people and they sell to people. The two groups are often different. These companies are frequently criticised for the way they treat employees. It is difficult to check their behaviour because they produce goods in many of the poorer countries in the world, where laws are often less strict and it is more difficult to check whether they are being enforced.

Public opinion has had a forceful effect on these enormous companies because, if they hit the headlines for poor working conditions, this affects their reputation. Gap and Nike have both suffered because of public opinion and have made changes in their rules about employing people.

What about the EU?

The UK is a member of the European Union, which means that we keep the laws which are made by the EU and make them part of UK law.

As the UK opted not to join the Euro, our government can put interest rates up if it wants to encourage people and businesses to save more or cut them if it wants them to spend more. Raising interest rates makes money more expensive to borrow, so it tends to reduce spending.

How are countries coupled together?

Trade links countries together. We buy and sell a wide range of products to each other.

What we sell to the world depends on what people and businesses in other countries want to buy. When the economies of the major countries are running smoothly, more people are employed and they tend to grow richer. When people get anxious about the future, they stop buying things, so businesses make less and don't need so many people, and unemployment rises.

All sorts of changes can make people nervous. A rise in oil prices makes most things more expensive, because many use plastics in their manufacture and most have to be transported to the shops and customers.

We have for a long time depended on cheap products from countries such as China and India. These countries have been growing fast, and it is becoming more expensive to make most items. These countries are also wanting to buy more coal, steel and other raw materials that are used in their factories. This is pushing up raw material prices for the rest of the world.

Production in China is on a huge scale

Check your understanding

1 How do multinationals affect countries?
2 Why is it difficult to control multinationals?
3 Why does public opinion influence their behaviour?
4 How does membership of the EU affect the way we can control the economy?
5 How are different countries connected with each other?
6 What sorts of change can affect the economies of countries?

... another point of view?

'The UK should be able to control its economy alone.' Do you agree with this statement? Give reasons for your opinion, showing you have considered another point of view.

Influencing and changing decisions

Source A

The problem with prison

There are currently over 80,000 men, women and children in prison in England and Wales. The prison population has been rising steadily since 1993, when it was 42,000. This means that there is now a higher percentage of people in prison here than in any other country in Western Europe.

Costs and benefits?

Prisons cost £2.2bn a year. With re-offending rates still at about 60 per cent and over 75 per cent for young offenders, prison is an expensive failure, which has no impact on crime levels or the fear of crime.

Why does it fail?

It damages family relationships and the chances of successful reintegration into the community. These are two of the most important factors in reducing re-offending and helping the rehabilitation of offenders. The size of the prison population means that few prisoners get enough education or constructive activity.

Source: Adapted from the Howard League for Penal Reform

Source B

ASBOs become a status symbol

Some teenagers see ASBOs as a badge of pride and a sign of status. According to a Labour Party report, Anti-Social Behaviour Orders (ASBOs) don't work.

The report said:

- ASBOs should no longer be used against children under 12.
- ASBOs should last no longer than two years instead of the current ten years.
- New laws should help parents whose children are drifting into crime.
- Joining youth groups and sports teams would be more likely to prevent crime altogether.

Source: Adapted from: Steve Doughty, ASBOs become 'self-fulfilling prophecy for young people'. www.dailymail.co.uk

Leave margin blank

Source C

Punishment or target for abuse?

Criminals wearing orange jackets while working in the community have been abused and jeered at by members of the public, according to a study by leaders of the probation officers.

Many community and church groups that had been offering Community Payback work placements for offenders have now stopped. They object to offenders having to wear orange jackets bearing the words 'Community Payback'. Opposition is normally on the grounds that wearing the vest humiliated the criminal or that doing unpaid work in the community was punishment itself, without offenders having to wear jackets.

The findings are the first signs of a backlash to the government's policy of making offenders wear fluorescent uniforms when they do work in the community.

Source: Times Online 30 December 2008

1. At what age do children become responsible for criminal acts in England? *(1 mark)*
   - ☐ A. 6
   - ☐ B. 8
   - ☑ C. 10
   - ☐ D. 12

2. The 're-offending rate' in Source A is: *(1 mark)*
   - ☑ A. the percentage of people who are convicted of a crime more than once.
   - ☐ B. the percentage of people who appear in court more than once.
   - ☐ C. the percentage of people who are victims of crime on more than one occasion.
   - ☐ D. the percentage of people who the police think have committed a crime more than once.

3. A newspaper article or television programme is biased if: *(1 mark)*
   - ☐ A. it clearly reports two or more points of view.
   - ☐ B. it uses complicated language.
   - ☐ C. the evidence given is out of date.
   - ☑ D. it leans heavily towards a particular viewpoint.

Leave margin blank

4. Explain what is meant by 'rehabilitation of offenders' in Source A. *(2 marks)*

It means helping people who have been in prison to learn to live and work in the community again and be less likely to reoffend.

5. Using Source B, identify two ways in which young people can be prevented from drifting into crime.
(2 marks)

Method 1

Help from their parents

Method 2

Joining youth groups — Joining sports teams would have been an alternative answer to this question.

6. Using Source C, explain why community and church groups have stopped offering Community Payback placements.
(2 marks)

They don't want to give placements to offenders who have to wear orange jackets because they might be jeered at by the public and this is humiliating. — The student might also have said that doing work in the community is punishment enough.

7. Why do different types of newspaper vary in the way they report stories about crime?

(3 marks)

Newspapers report crime in different ways because they sell papers to people with different views so they are more likely to be biased. Popular papers often have dramatic headlines which make out that crime is worse than it is. Quality papers usually report crime with smaller headlines and less threatening pictures because readers are more likely to read the article than just have a quick look at the headlines and pictures.

Remember that newspapers aim to sell as many papers as they can, so they want to appeal to the customers. The media is often blamed for stirring things up – but they usually do it because they know they will sell more papers. Readers have a responsibility too!

8. Using sources A, B and C and your own knowledge, do you agree that the use of ASBOs and Community Payback can be justified?

Give reasons for your opinion, showing that you have considered another point of view.

(8 marks)

Source A says that prison is not a very effective way of dealing with offenders. 60 per cent of people who go to prison re-offend and 75 per cent of young people do. It is also very expensive. People are split up from their families and don't get a decent education so they don't have much chance of having a normal life. ASBOs have been criticised because they are a status symbol for young offenders. They are difficult to enforce and people are not likely to be caught if they break the rules. If they go on for too long, people start to ignore them.

Unpaid work in the community has been used for a long time. The jackets have been used to make the public see that it is being done. Lots of organisations have taken people to do work for them.

Both ASBOs and unpaid work mean that people don't go to prison so they can keep their jobs or stay in education. If they are sent away, they are more likely to end up going back to prison because they have committed another crime.

Despite some people thinking they are not proper punishment, I think they are justified because it is more important to stop people re-offending.

The student has used all three sources and material about punishments that they would have learnt during the course. There is also an explanation of why it is not a good idea to lock people up.

Extended writing

'The government is more influenced by public opinion than ways of reducing crime and re-offending.'

Do you agree with this view?

Give reasons for your opinion, showing you have considered another point of view.

You could consider the following points in your answer and other information of your own.

- Should the government be interested in reducing crime?
- Is public opinion led by newspapers which have strong views?
- Is there a difference between what the public wants and schemes that might reduce re-offending?
- Why might the government listen to public opinion?

(15 marks)

Leave margin blank

The government wants to reduce crime because the public want to see it going down – so they stay popular with voters.

It is also a good thing to find ways of cutting crime because we need less people to break the law.

> The student has shown that the issue is difficult for the government. It has to balance what works when it is trying to reduce crime and what voters want.

Many people think that offenders should be harshly treated because they should be punished for what they have done. This is a message that newspapers give to please their readers. People want to buy newspapers that agree with their views.

Newspapers also give the opinions of their owners or editors – so they can be very powerful.

> This shows that the student is using the bullets as well as their own knowledge to build an argument.

The government has to balance doing what the public wants and doing things which help to reduce crime. These are not always the same. Schemes which help people to stay out of prison may be better because they help to cut crime. Work in the community means people can keep their jobs or stay in education but the public does not always see the benefit because they want to see public punishment. The government introduced the orange jackets so that the public could see that offenders are being punished. But it makes people feel bad and might mean they don't turn up.

They then might be sent to prison instead.

> This paragraph shows that the student understands the reasons for the argument.

I think that it is better to try to keep people out of prison if we can because it will keep people out of prison in the future. The government wants to win the next election so it listens to public opinion. It must weigh up what is best for the country and explain this to the public. It should not just do what the public wants. This can be difficult because newspapers sometimes only write about what they think the readers want to read.

A good summing up – the student comes to a conclusion but can see the problems that are involved.

Unit 4:

Citizenship

Your campaign: what's the choice 242

Which campaign? 244

Developing your skills: questionnaires 246

Developing your skills: spreading the message 248

campaign

Developing your skills: planning a protest 250

Planning your campaign 252

Participation in action 254

What was the impact? 256

Your campaign: what's the choice?

Students from St Brendan's People & Planet group held a concert to campaign for Fair Trade. They offered all sorts of Fair Trade goodies donated by local supermarkets. To get the message over, the bands had a backdrop that couldn't be ignored.

The slide-show promoted the Fair Trade message and celebrated the group's campaigning. This was just one of many activities they ran to promote their mission. Fair Trade roses sold like hot cakes on Valentine's Day.

1 Why do you think the students decided to campaign for Fair Trade?

2 Why do you think the students decided to hold a concert to campaign for Fair Trade?

3 What do you care about?

4 What campaigns have you seen to be successful?

Citizenship is all about advocacy. The campaign gives you the chance to make your voice heard. There are lots of ways of participating, as you will have found out already.

There are lots of questions to ask before you decide.

When you've worked out the issues, there are two questions to ask.

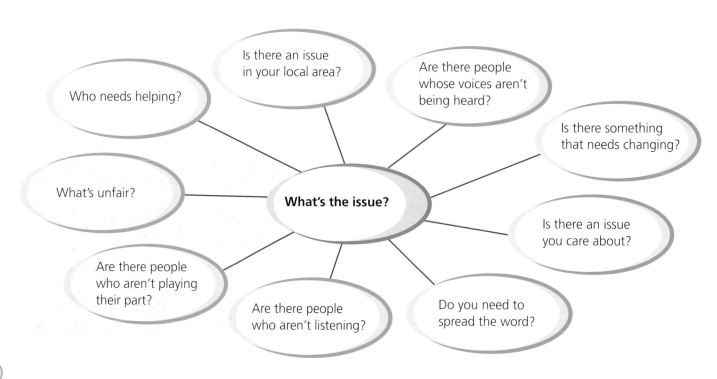

1 How does it fit into Citizenship?

Whatever issue you choose must fit into one of the categories that make up Citizenship (see below). Look through Unit 1 to find an issue you'd like to get involved with. You can't pick the same theme in Units 2 and 4.

You may find that your choice links two or more sections of the list – which is great because Citizenship is all about joined-up thinking. If, for example, you are concerned about sustainable development, you might want to engage the local council or the media to get your message over.

1 Political, legal and human rights and freedoms in a range of contexts, from local to global
2 Civil, criminal law and the justice system – police, youth offending teams, courts, lawyers, prisons and probation
3 Democratic and electoral processes and the operation of parliamentary democracy
4 The development of, and struggle for, different kinds of rights and freedoms (in the UK and abroad)
5 The media
6 Policies and practices for sustainable development
7 The economy in relation to citizenship and the relationship between employers and employees
8 Origins and implications of diversity and the changing nature of society in the UK
9 The European Union, the Commonwealth and the UN

How are we going to make a difference?

What's your issue?
What do you want to change?

What's your aim?
How will you improve things?

What do you need to know?
What information do you need to collect?

Who has the expertise?
Do you have experts in your team? If not, ask others.

What's the threat?
Who are you opponents? Can you persuade them?

What's the plan?
Set a clear plan with a timeline. Stick to it!

2 What's your campaign all about?

There are all sorts of ways of campaigning. It's all about making your voice heard – or helping others to do so. School might be the right place to start.

- Is there something you really care about?
- Where do you want to be heard?
- Who do you want to listen?
- If you want other students to care about your particular issue, you might want to devise a campaign to persuade them.
- There may be others who care about an issue too. Get them together to organise the campaign.
- What's the best way to persuade people to listen?

Perhaps there are issues outside school – is a new supermarket being built, is there a plan for a new runway or are there environmental issues?

Perhaps the issues are further afield – Fair Trade or prisoners who have been locked up without a fair trial?

- A questionnaire might find out what people think.
- A demonstration might get your message over.

Be realistic!

Think carefully about your choice of campaign. You want to be sure you can achieve a result.

Students plant windmills when signing up to their Go Green campaign

Which campaign?

The campaign is an important part of your course. You need to plan, collect evidence and keep a record of what happened at every stage, as it is very important that you show what you and everyone else did. You will also need to work out how well it went. You may already be involved in suitable activities, but if not, you'll need to choose what to do. There are many possibilities for you to consider.

What's the issue?

- Do you care about human rights? Who is being treated badly?
- Do you care about democracy? Who isn't having a say?
- Do you care about things being fair? Who isn't being treated as you think they should?
- Do you care about the law? Does something need changing?
- Do you care about the choices the government is making? What can you do about it?
- Do you care about the environment? What can you change?
- Is something going wrong in your community? Can you change it?
- Are people ill informed about our role in the world? Can you help?

Your campaign could be based on any of these ideas or many others. Remember that being involved in something that really interests you always makes the task easier. For example, does the environment concern you? Are you worried about drugs in your area? Or do you want more facilities for young people in the area?

Young people in Aldbourne campaigned successfully for a BMX track in the village

The right choice

The one really important thing to remember is that your campaign must fit into the Citizenship Studies specification.

If you want:

- to set up a branch of Amnesty International and encourage other students in school to fight for the freedom of those who have been imprisoned without a fair trail – then it's human rights
- to campaign about knife crime in your local area – then it's crime
- to persuade the council to spend more money on activities for young people – then it's the economy
- to persuade your school to go green – then it's the environment
- to help people to understand the work of the UN or the EU – then it's the UK's place in the world

There are endless possibilities.

Take action

Sit down with a blank sheet of paper and think about all the campaigns you might want to carry out.

1 Start by writing down all your ideas.

2 List all the advantages and disadvantages of each idea.

3 Put them in order, from best to worst.

4 Is the one at the top the one you really want to carry out? If so, go ahead. If not, have another look at the list.

Although it's really part of planning, brainstorm how you might go about putting this campaign into action. It will help you to decide whether your idea is realistic.

Check point

Before you make a final decision, check with your teacher that your campaign is suitable for the course requirements.

On the response form, you will need to explain how your plan addresses Citizenship issues. So it's a good idea to think about this right from the start of your activity.

Make sure you are clear about your objectives. You'll be asked what they were and whether you achieved them.

What's the objective?

You may want to save the world – but be realistic! It is much easier to be successful if you start small.

Be very clear and focus on your key message – don't include lots of issues at once.

Think about who you want to persuade:

- How do you want them to be different?
- Identify them clearly so you can work out whether you have been successful.

Young people gather evidence that people support their campaign

How does it link to Citizenship?

Which part of Unit 1 does your issue fit into:

- rights and responsibilities?
- power, politics and the media?
- the global community?

Look carefully at the themes and work out exactly where it fits.

Write four sentences that explain the connections.

Developing your skills: questionnaires

1 Why might you want to find out what people think?
2 Why do you need to be careful when planning the questions?
3 Why do you need to be careful when asking the questions?
4 How do you decide who to ask?

When planning your campaign, one thing you need to think about is what you need to know. You may not have a clear idea of people's views. Once you have found out what people think, you may be able to structure your campaign more effectively.

If you already have a clear idea of what people think, this won't be necessary, but you will need to brainstorm the various possible opinions, so that you are sure of the opposition's views as well as those of your supporters.

Drawing up a questionnaire

Before you begin – make sure you know exactly what you want to find out.

Make the questions very clear – especially if people will fill in the questionnaire on their own.

Make the questions quick – people won't spend long on the questionnaire.

Avoid leading questions (they often start with 'Don't you think that … ?') – they give you the answer you want to hear but it may not be what people really think.

Is the order of the questions important? If so, work out which should come 1st, 2nd, 3rd …

Do you need to know:
- how old people are?
- what gender they are?
- how much they earn?
- whether they are healthy?

These are sensitive questions, so ask them carefully.

Do you want short, sharp answers? If so, use closed questions – they often have yes/no/don't know answers.

Do you want more thoughtful answers? If so, use open questions – you will find out about people's opinions and why they hold them.

Avoid obvious questions – no one will answer 'Yes' to 'Would you be cruel to animals?'

Work out the results

When you have used your questionnaire to carry out a survey, you need to work out what the answers mean.

Closed questions are easy. You simply have to add up the number of each different response. Draw up a tally sheet showing the possible answers for each question. Count up how many people gave each answer and put the number in the box.

Question 1: How often do you go swimming?

Once a week or more	Once every two weeks	Once a month	Less often
卌	|||	卌	||

The line drawn across 4 makes it 5. This makes counting easy.

Open questions ask people for their opinions and ideas.

Read them carefully in order to decide how to divide them up.

Many people come up with fairly standard views, so you can put them into separate groups.

Work out how many you have in each group and note any ideas that stand out from the others.

Jot down some good examples of what people were thinking. They will help your report. Sometimes people offer very strange ideas.

These can also be noted in order to show the range of answers.

Displaying your results

Very often you want other people to know your findings, so you need to make them as clear as possible. Graphs and charts will help you to do this. Bar charts and pie charts are good ways of showing data.

If you put the results into a spreadsheet, you can choose a wide variety of different sorts of graph to show your evidence. Be careful to choose the one that suits your data.

Check point

Try out your questionnaire on someone like the people you are planning to ask. If some questions don't work, change them. Using duff questions is a waste of time!

Take action

Do you need to find out what people think? If so, set about writing a questionnaire. Think carefully about the guidelines provided here. You might start with closed questions and have an open question or two at the end. Make sure you are not asking leading questions. This can be quite hard when you really believe in something.

Key Terms

closed questions: ask for short factual answers

open questions: ask people to express a point of view or longer answer

Developing your skills: spreading the message

1 How can the local radio station help with your campaign?
2 What other media might you use?
3 What would you need to think about before talking to the media?

How to spread your message

What's your message?

What is the single most important point that you want your target audience to remember?

This is your 'message'.

Your message should now be the focus for every conversation that your pressure group has with the public.

What's the evidence?

What facts support your argument?

You must give the target audience a reason to believe you.

Who is your target audience?

A target audience is the group of people you are trying to reach with your message. Who is most interested in your point of view? Why?

For example, if an issue will have an impact on the environment, you might choose young parents as a target audience. They may be concerned about how the issue affects their children's future.

Presenting your message

Present your message in an interesting and emotive way. What headline could you use to grab the attention of the reader?

What sort of words could you use to stir their emotions? Destroy, hopeless, saved, heroic or desolate? These words are often used for the impact they have on a reader.

How to persuade people

Put across your point of view

Begin by asking questions and using the answers as a starting point. You may even provide the answer yourself – it will start them thinking. This gets people interested in what you have to say, and helps them to agree with your point.

Try:

- Why should we be interested?
- Haven't we heard enough?
- Why do they oppose/propose this?
- What will we gain from this?

Make it easy for people to agree with you

If you want people to agree with your point of view, show them that you have lots in common. If you like the same things, you are more likely to get on!

You need to do this before starting to talk about the topic you want to discuss.

Try:

- As a member of this community for many years …
- We all want the best solution …

Think about the opposition

Consider the opposition's point of view before you start. You'll be able to answer their questions if you are prepared. This shows everyone that you have a balanced point of view.

Always have a short, snappy ending

End your argument on a high note using a short, snappy sentence, such as 'We need the skate board park NOW!'

How to approach the local media

The local media is very important to the success of a local campaign because:

- it affects the local community
- it's a great way of getting free publicity and attracting support from other people.

Preparing a press release

A press release should tell the journalists who work at the local paper, radio or TV station all they need to know about your campaign:

- what the issue is
- why it is of interest to the local community
- contact details for you and your group
- suggestions of interesting pictures for newspaper and television.

It should be written in snappy language, like a newspaper article, and be aimed at your target audience. Press releases are sometimes printed in a newspaper with very little editing, so try to use a catchy headline.

When your press release is ready, find out the name and address, telephone number or email of local newspapers, radio and television stations.

Write a letter or send an email to the contact name that you have been given. The letter should explain why you feel so strongly about the issue and ask the journalist to contact you for any further information.

Take action

Work out:

- What's your message?
- Who is your target audience?
- Why will your message appeal to your target audience?
- How will you sell it to them?
- Who do you need to talk to in your local area? Remember that they are probably people of power and influence – so their evidence will be helpful.

Check point

Discuss making contact with the local media with your teacher first.

Ask for a copy of any interviews. It will all add to your evidence.

Developing your skills: planning a protest

SAVE LIVES – STOP KNIVES!

More than 1,000 people joined the families and friends of knife and gun crime victims in a protest march across London.

Vanessa Hyman and her daughter Cheyna protest over the murder of Anton their son and brother

The idea for the People's March was started on Facebook by Sharon Singh and Gemma Olway from south-west London. It received the backing of several national newspapers, which promoted it to the public.

The marchers chanted 'Stop the knives, save lives' as they walked through London. Onlookers clapped and some motorists beeped their horns in a show of support.

The minister responsible for the police spoke to the crowd, saying: 'If your local community isn't doing enough, speak to your local councillor and if they don't do enough sack them at the next election or get hold of your MP and if they don't do anything sack them.'

1 Why do you think Sharon and Gemma decided to organise a protest march?

2 What effect do you think the backing of national newspapers offered?

3 What reception did the marchers get from passersby?

4 Why do you think the minister responsible for the police spoke to the crowd?

5 What advice did he give them? Why do you think he said this?

Why protest?

Protest and marches are very powerful because they attract the attention of the public and offer them the opportunity to join in or show their support in other ways. They are often used:

- when controversial decisions are being made
- to draw attention to an issue
- to commemorate an anniversary.

A march or protest should not be organised lightly. If badly planned, a protest can be a flop, upset the general public and even break the law. Making life difficult for ordinary people should be avoided. Truck drivers blocked motorways and city centres because the price of diesel was too high. Even though many people supported their cause, the resulting traffic jams upset just as many.

Whether to protest

It is only worth organising a march or a protest if:

- public opinion is so strong that a fairly good turnout can be guaranteed
- it can be planned sufficiently far in advance to meet the legal requirements
- it can be well publicised and promoted
- it can be well managed on the day.

If a full-scale march or protest is too large a project, smaller events might be easier to organise. A demonstration before a council meeting or at a supermarket that is not doing enough for the environment are much simpler to organise and can have a direct effect.

Questions to ask

Any event needs to be carefully targeted and set up to have maximum effect, so there are some questions that must be asked before you begin.

- Who are you trying to reach?
- What are you trying to achieve?
- What needs to be done and who will do it?
- Are there any costs? How will they be paid?
- Whatever the event, the police should be informed – and you must check with the school that they are happy for you to go ahead.
- Have you checked the health and safety regulations?
- Is there likely to be opposition? If so, work out how you will deal with it.
- Can we get the media interested? The whole point of a protest is to be noticed!

Take action

Plan the action carefully. Ask yourself:

- What are you trying to achieve?
- Who is going to do what?
- Who do you need to contact?
- Who is on your side? Will they help?
- How will you work out whether it has been a success?

Check point

Before you think about planning an event outside school, check with your teacher.

Publicising the event

The grand finale

The event mustn't just fizzle out at the end. The knife crime march ended in Hyde Park. The crowd was addressed by the Metropolitan Police Commissioner, a government minister and a video message from the Prime Minister. Not many events can attract such high status people, but finding a high profile person who believes in your issue will help to get the message across.

A protest can have a big impact – particularly when it has media coverage

Planning your campaign

The People & Planet Group

'We've spoken to the school about switching to renewable light bulbs and they've agreed if we find a price which will mean that within five years it's benefitting the school economically, so we're researching that. They've also said they're happy that we look into renewable energy sources for the school's electricity, and might be happy to switch if we find them a good price. We're sending a petition to various governments to encourage them to sign up to Kyoto, and we're planning a green themed mufti day to raise money for People & Planet.'

On top of that, the group gave an assembly to the younger students at their school on how they can help to stop climate change, and they are currently trying to get more of them involved in their group.

1 What was the People & Planet Group's objective?
2 Draw a spider diagram to show their range of activities.
3 What planning do you think was needed to organise these activities?

What are the stages?

> **Stage 1** What is our objective?

> **Stage 2** Who are we targeting?

> **Stage 3** Who is involved in organising?

> **Stage 4** What are our roles?

> **Stage 5** What do we need to do?

> **Stage 6** What resources do we need?

> **Stage 7** When must things happen?

> **Stage 8** Have we got a back-up plan if things go wrong?

> **Stage 9** When are the deadlines?

> **Stage 10** Draw up the timeline.

Planning

Planning means setting out what must be done and making sure that everyone knows their responsibilities. By following the stages above you will be on the right track. You will need to gather evidence and be able to explain the links to Citizenship, so you need to build this into your plan. The following pages will help you with the stages of organising your campaign and gathering the evidence you need.

What will you need to collect?

- A statement of the objectives of your campaign
- An explanation of how it links to Citizenship
- Your plan – showing how you managed time and resources
- The methods of campaigning you used – and an explanation of how they helped
- Evidence of what you did
- Evidence of how you aimed to meet your objectives
- Evidence that you have tried to persuade people in positions of power or influence and found out what they thought
- Evidence of the views of others
- An explanation of the outcomes – and whether you met your objectives
- Your thoughts on whether you made a positive impact on your issue – using your evidence

Making your plan

Brainstorm all the things that need to be done. Can you divide these things easily into groups? Who has the skills needed for each activity? Should people work in pairs or on their own? Then, when you have made these decisions, draw up a list to explain exactly what everyone has to do.

You will need it throughout the campaign, to check whether everything has been done and to put in your records.

You will need to add the plan to your report form – so make it very clear and keep it safe.

Planning your timeline

Look carefully at your plan and draw up your timeline and put the name of the person responsible beside every point.

This will give you markers to check whether everything is on track. It will also give everyone target dates for getting things done.

Remember that dealing with people outside school can take time, so make it a priority.

Example: Planning your campaign

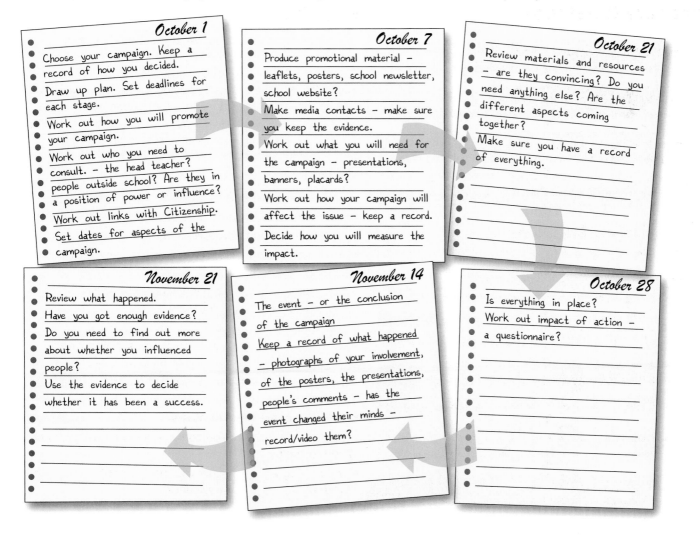

October 1
Choose your campaign. Keep a record of how you decided.
Draw up plan. Set deadlines for each stage.
Work out how you will promote your campaign.
Work out who you need to consult. – the head teacher? people outside school? Are they in a position of power or influence?
Work out links with Citizenship.
Set dates for aspects of the campaign.

October 7
Produce promotional material – leaflets, posters, school newsletter, school website?
Make media contacts – make sure you keep the evidence.
Work out what you will need for the campaign – presentations, banners, placards?
Work out how your campaign will affect the issue – keep a record.
Decide how you will measure the impact.

October 21
Review materials and resources – are they convincing? Do you need anything else? Are the different aspects coming together?
Make sure you have a record of everything.

November 21
Review what happened.
Have you got enough evidence?
Do you need to find out more about whether you influenced people?
Use the evidence to decide whether it has been a success.

November 14
The event – or the conclusion of the campaign
Keep a record of what happened – photographs of your involvement, of the posters, the presentations, people's comments – has the event changed their minds – record/video them?

October 28
Is everything in place?
Work out impact of action – a questionnaire?

Participation in action

Save my school!

Aimee said: 'I was racing to save my school. It's such a good school – it is really unfair to close it down.

'I tried to use the success of the triathlon to highlight what I see as a failure of the council in their decision to shut the school.'

1 How is Aimee showing her citizenship skills?
2 Why does she want to make a difference?
3 Why did she pick this strategy?
4 What do you think she had to do to plan this activity?
5 What sort of evidence do you think she collected?
6 How does this activity relate to the content of the course?

How you aimed to meet your objectives

Aimee really didn't want her school to close. She worked out how she could communicate the issue to as many people as possible. As a triathlete, she knew that the press would cover her next race – and she was right, as the picture above shows.

In your campaign plan you set out how you planned to meet your objectives. What strategies did you use?

Did you:
- produce leaflets, posters, banners or placards?
- run an assembly?
- put on a play?
- set up a website?
- hold a meeting?
- send letters or emails?
- talk to local radio or newspapers?
- hold a protest?
- lobby your councillors, MP, or MEP?
- use any other strategy?

Whichever strategies you have used, you need to know why you selected them and how you participated.

How did you communicate with others?

Who were you trying to persuade:
- the general public?
- people in positions of power?
- other school students?
- parents?

What strategies did you use for each group?

When you set about persuading people, you need to be able to present a good argument. There are moments when making a lot of noise can be useful. If you want to raise the issue with a lot of people, a demonstration might work well. If you want to persuade people in power, you need to have very good arguments on your side. If you are going to persuade them, you also need to know their point of view. It is much easier to fight if you know how the opposition thinks.

Think about how your participation meets theses needs.

Gather evidence of your action and how you made a contribution

There are all sorts of ways in which you can submit your supporting evidence. It doesn't just have to be in writing.

- Photos are great because they can show you were involved. Placards and banners are too big, but you can take pictures of them being used – as evidence of participation and communication.
- A video can show the work involved in your campaign. An audio recording of a meeting or a presentation about carrying out your activity gives a clear picture of how you were working.
- A PowerPoint presentation that explains or persuades people of your point of view makes a good piece of evidence.
- A website that lets people know your plans or persuades them to support you is helpful evidence as it shows just what you were trying to do and how you went about it.
- If you investigate what people think, you may use a questionnaire. This, together with the results, shows the way you worked and what you found out.
- You might write letters or emails to explain, persuade or justify your point of view. These are useful pieces of supporting evidence, as they give people a good picture of the campaign.

Gathering all the information as you go along will help you to put it all together. It's very easy to forget exactly what happened and when!

What views did others hold?

You need to keep a record of other people's views, but, rather than writing about it, you can use other forms of evidence.

- The local media can be a useful source of other people's points of view. If you are campaigning about something local, you can be sure that they will be involved. Look out for press cuttings.
- Has the opposition got a website? This can be an easy source of evidence – but make sure that you only include what is relevant.
- You could interview people and record the conversation.

... another point of view?

When Oxford University built a new centre for medical research, animal rights protestors tried to prevent it happening. Supporters of the development took to the streets as well.

What was the impact?

When St Brendan's had such great success with their Fair Trade gig (see page 242), they decided more needed to be done.

The students realised that they needed to make Fair Trade an integral part of their college. They wrote a policy, which went to the governors for approval – and it was passed.

1 Why do you think the students thought Fair Trade should be integral to the college?

2 How did they decide to go about it?

3 Are the governors people in a position of power?

4 What was the impact of the St Brendan's students' campaign?

5 Have they changed people's minds?

6 Were governors important in your campaign? If so, explain how.

What were the outcomes?

Whatever the topic of your campaign, things will have happened. Your evidence will help you to explain the effects of your campaign. Go through your evidence and explain the outcomes.

What were the reasons?

If it all went according to plan, just explain what happened. You might include a mention of who helped and why it was straightforward.

If things went wrong or you had to change your plans, explain why and how you sorted things out.

Were there things you did particularly well, or would do better next time?

Did you achieve your objectives?

The objective of a campaign is to change things – but you can't expect to get your way all the time. Negotiation is a part of most political activity.

If you changed your objectives during the campaign, explain how and why. Did it make your objectives more achievable?

Don't worry if you weren't successful. There are always two sides to an argument and not every campaign makes change happen immediately – but it might have an effect at a later date. If you didn't win, did you change people's ideas? Very often the outcome is a compromise.

- A new supermarket might want to cut down trees to build an access road. Perhaps they changed the line of the road and saved some of the trees.
- The council wants to close the skate park. Perhaps it might just be opened at the weekend instead.
- The school wants students to wear a more formal uniform. Perhaps it might be redesigned to keep everyone happy.

Explain what happened and what elements of your campaign were achieved.

Evidence that you made an impact

Your evidence might be letters or emails that show how people have accepted your point of view. The students from St Brendan's would have had the minutes of the governors' meeting and their Fair Trade policy to show what they had achieved.

Perhaps you have pictures to show what you achieved. A pedestrian crossing outside your school? Some lights in the underpass – or at least agreement that the council will install them. Look back at the examples on previous pages and think about the sort of evidence that other students might have had to show their achievements.

Recording it all

You can write up your activity in stages. There is quite a lot to think about, so this is probably the best way. Your teacher will let you know how it's planned. The most important things are:

- knowing how your action fitted into Citizenship
- that you have collected the evidence for each stage and know what it shows
- that you have worked out the impact you made.

Once this is clear, the writing up should be straightforward. Remember that the coursework is worth 60 per cent of the whole GCSE, so you can get lots of marks for doing things rather than just taking an exam.

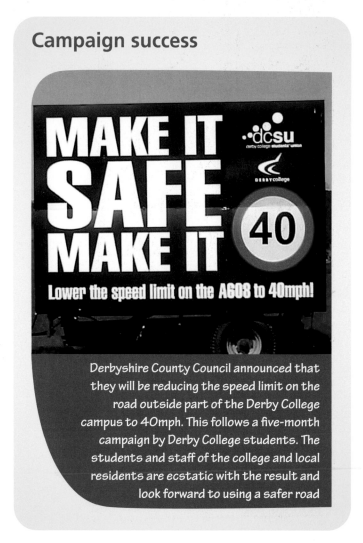

Campaign success

MAKE IT SAFE MAKE IT •dcsu DERBYcollege 40
Lower the speed limit on the A608 to 40mph!

Derbyshire County Council announced that they will be reducing the speed limit on the road outside part of the Derby College campus to 40mph. This follows a five-month campaign by Derby College students. The students and staff of the college and local residents are ecstatic with the result and look forward to using a safer road

Index

accountability 80–1
Activities 154–65
Acts of Parliament 18–19, 80–1
    see also individual Acts
advertising 47
advocacy 84–5, 160–1, 242
agencies of UN 127
Agenda 21 100–1, 181
aid 142–3, 184–5
AIDS/HIV 140–1
Amnesty International 118–19
assemblies 87, 220
asylum seekers 29, 195–7
attitudes see points of view

barristers 61
belonging, sense of 207
biased views 47
bills (laws) 80–1
borrowing money 112–15
boycotts 133
British nationals 8–9
the Budget 114–15
bullying 202
business rates 71
businesses 106–9, 111, 117, 130–1

CAB (Citizens Advice Bureau) 33
the Cabinet 79
cabinet of councils 68–9
campaigning 240–57
    see also Citizenship Activities
canvassing by MPs 76–7
car transport 138–9, 176
carbon footprint 171, 175
censorship 49
Chancellor of the Exchequer 115
change
    communities 190–211
    environmental 136–7, 168–89
    fear of 204
    influencing 212–39
    prices 110–11
Chief Executive (councils) 68–9
children 143, 194, 222
Chinese community 7, 12
Christian community 7, 12–13
Citizens Advice Bureau (CAB) 33
Citizenship Activities 154–65
    see also campaigning
civil law 58–9, 226–7
civil liberties 228–9
climate change 136–7, 172–85
closed questions 246–7
collective action 118

Commonwealth of Nations 124–5
Communications Data Bill 228
communities 6–13, 96–151, 181, 190–211
Community Champions 174–5
community cohesion 206–7
compensation cases 23
competition 105
congestion charges 138–9, 176
constituencies 76–7
consulting the public 84–5
consumers 32–3, 103, 130, 174
contracts of employment 35–7
Convention on the Rights of the Child (CRC) 17, 25
costs
    controlling 111
    law cases 227
    prisons 224
Council of Europe 147
council tax 71
councillors 26–7, 66
councils 66–75, 218, 220
county court 59
courts 59, 62–3, 144–7
CRC see Convention on the Rights of the Child
crime 144–5, 222–5, 250–1
criminal law 58–63, 226–7
crown court 59, 63
cultural diversity 9–13, 201
    see also race
cultural identities 190–211
customers see consumers
customs duty 122–3

data, crime 223
Data Protection Act 52–3
debt and poverty 128–9
decisions
    ethical 170–1, 177, 192–3, 214–15
    influencing/changing 212–39
Declaration of Human Rights 17–18, 28, 229
deflation 110–11
democracy 26–7, 64–91, 220–1
development see sustainable development
devolution 87, 220–1
dictatorships 91
Disability Discrimination Act 19, 22–3, 35
discrimination 19–23, 35, 51, 190, 202–3
dismissal from employment 37
diversity 9–13, 190, 200–1
division of labour 107
dual heritage 15

ECHR (European Convention on Human Rights) 28
economic growth 98–9, 108–9, 184
economic migrants 194–5, 197–8, 204–5

economy 98–9, 104–15, 117, 184, 232–3
  see also money matters
editors (news) 46–7
education 21, 214
elections 26–7, 65, 76–7, 218, 220
  see also voting
electorate 88–9
emigration 10–11, 198–9
emissions reductions 179, 181
employment laws 34–7, 193, 202–3
  see also economic migrants; labour issues
energy sustainability 99, 101
environmental change 136–7, 168–89
equal pay cases 35, 193, 202, 215
equality 202–3, 207
ethical decisions 170–1, 177, 192–3, 214–15
ethnic minorities 9–13, 201
  see also race
EU see European Union
Euro currency 122–3
European Convention on Human Rights (ECHR) 28
European Court of Human Rights 146–7
European ombudsman 123
European Parliament 26–7, 121
European Union (EU) 6, 35, 120–3, 196–7, 203, 232–3
evidence 157–8, 161–3, 248, 252, 254–5, 257

Fair Trade 132–3, 159–60, 164, 242, 256
fear of change 204
first past the post system 88–9, 220
food miles 171
food stocks 99
footprint see carbon footprint
Forward Plan, councils 72–3
fossil fuels 136–7
fostering programmes 225
free trade 132–3
freedom 27, 48–9, 228–9

gender issues 31, 193, 202–3, 215
general elections 76, 77, 220
Geneva Convention 145
genocide 144–5
global community 96–151
global economy 232–3
global warming 136–7, 172–3
  see also climate change
globalisation 131, 232–3
  see also global community
government
  decisions 212–39
  revenue 114–15
  see also local government
Green Papers 80–1
greenhouse gases 173, 178–9, 181

see also climate change
growth, economic 98–9, 108–9, 184

Health and Safety laws 35
hereditary peers 87
High Court 59
HIV/AIDS 140–1
homophobia 21
House of Commons 78–9, 81
House of Lords 81, 87
human rights 13, 16–19, 28–9, 124, 143, 146–7, 229
humanitarian aid 142–3, 184–5
humanitarian crimes 144–5

identity 8–9, 14–15, 161, 190–211
  see also communities
identity cards 14–15, 82
IMF (International Monetary Fund) 134–5
immigration 10–11, 193–201, 204–5
inclusive education 21
inflation 110–11
influencing decisions 212–39
  see also decisions; persuasion; power
integrated society 200, 208
intensive fostering programme 225
interdependency 106–7
interest charges 111, 113
international courts 144–5
international debt 128–9
international decisions 218
International Monetary Fund (IMF) 134–5
international organisations 118–19, 134–5
internet 33, 45

journalists 47
judges/judiciary 59–61
juries 59–60
justice systems 56–63, 144–5
  see also laws; legal rights

Kyoto Protocol 137, 179

LA21 see Local Agenda 21
labour issues 107, 183
  see also employment laws
language factors 198
laws 56–61, 226–7
  changing 216–17, 223
  employment 34–7, 193, 202–3
  European courts 147
  humanitarian crimes 145
  making laws 80–1
  media 50–1
  see also justice systems; legal rights
LEDCs see less economically developed countries

legal rights 18–19, 22–3, 32–7, 203
  see also laws
less economically developed countries (LEDCs) 98–9, 128, 182–3
libel 50–1, 226
Liberty group 222–3
lobbying 82–3
Local Agenda 21 (LA21) 100–1, 181
local economies 205
local government 26–7, 66–75, 218, 220

magistrates 59–60, 62–3
majority party, councils 68–9
manifestos 66–7, 218
marches 250–1
markets 108–9, 122
mass media *see* media
mayors 69
MEDCs *see* more economically developed countries
media 44–55, 222–3, 230, 249
 'melting pots' 200–1
member states of EU 121
Members of Parliament (MPs) 26–7, 76–9
Members of the European Parliament (MEPs) 26–7, 121
message-spreading 248–9
micro-credit 125
migration *see* immigration
Millennium Goals, UN 102, 127
Ministers of State 79
minority groups 9–13, 201
minutes of meetings 72–3, 163
mitigating factors 63
money matters 70–1, 112, 114–15
  see also economy
more economically developed countries (MEDCs) 98–9, 128, 182–3
MPs *see* Members of Parliament
multicultural communities 9, 201
  see also cultural diversity
multinationals 130, 233
Muslim community 7, 12–13, 200

nations
  decision-making 218, 220
  identity 8–9
  power 130
  sustainability agendas 180–1
neighbourhoods 6–7
news media 46–7, 50–1, 222–3
  see also media
not in my backyard (NIMBYs) 176–7

Office of Fair Trading 33
ombudsmen 72–3, 123
open questions 247
opinion polls 53, 84
Opposition party 79

Parliament 80–1, 87, 220
  see also Acts of Parliament; European Parliament; Members of Parliament
participation 152–65, 254–5
peacekeeping role of UN 127, 142–3
people's peers 87
perspectives *see* points of view
persuasion 52, 160, 179, 249, 254
  see also influencing decisions
planning stages 158–9, 250–3
points of view 160–1, 165, 190–1, 212–13, 223
  campaigning 249, 255
  environmental change 168–9
  immigration 197, 204–5
police 61
political parties 46–7, 66–9, 76–9, 83, 89, 218
political rights 26–7
politics 42–95, 218–19
polling stations 67
pollution 136–7, 182–3
  see also climate change
poverty 113, 128–9
power 42–95, 130–1
prejudice 20
Press Code 50–1
press freedom 48–9
press releases 249
pressure groups 34–5, 74–5, 82–3, 134–5, 216, 230
price changes 110–11
Prime Minister's role 79
prisons 224–5
privacy rights 228–9
private sector 104–5
probation officers 61
producer power 130
profit 104–5
proportional representation 89, 220
protests 134–5, 250–1
public consultation 84–5
public opinion 44–55, 84–5, 230–1, 233
public sector 104–5
public transport 139

questionnaires 163, 246–7

race 31, 202
  see also cultural diversity; ethnic minorities
Race Relations Act 18–19, 22–3, 35
racism 11, 21
Radio Frequency Identification (RFID) tags 228
rate of inflation 111
 'recorded' crime 224
recorders in court 63
recording work 165, 257
redistributing income 113

redundancy 37
referendum vote 86–7, 218, 220
refugees 118–19, 142–3
regional decisions 220
religious diversity 12–13, 190, 200
renewable resources 99
representation 65–7, 89, 160–1, 220
resource sustainability 99, 103
respect 25
responsibilities 24–5, 36–7
  see also rights/responsibilities
retraining schemes 109
RFID tags 228
rights/responsibilities 4–41, 123, 203, 228–9
  see also human rights
road pricing 138–9, 176
Royal Assent 81

school councils 64–5
Scotland 220–1
Secretaries of State 79
Security Council, UN 127, 142
sellers' rights 33
sense of belonging 207
Sex Discrimination Act 22–3, 35
Shadow Cabinet 79
shareholders 104–5
single currency 122–3
skills development 160–1, 246–51
slander 50–1
small businesses 106
small claims court 59
social identities 190–211
social networks 207
social order 207
society 152–65, 212–39
  see also social...
solicitors 61
Speaker of the Commons 78–9
specialised businesses 107
spin doctors 47
stakeholders 53
student immigrants 199
suffrage 26–7, 30–1
suffragettes 31
sustainable communities 181
sustainable development 98–103, 168–89
sweatshops 132–3

target audiences 248
targets, environmental 178–9, 181
taxation 114–15, 179
teamwork 157
tolerance 13
torture 119
trade 132–5, 184–5, 233
  see also Fair Trade
trade-offs 177, 229, 231
trade unions 34–5
Trading Standards Department 33
transport 101, 138–9, 176
tribunals (employment) 36–7, 202

UDHR *see* Universal Declaration of Human Rights
UN *see* United Nations
UNAIDS projects 140–1
UNDHR (United Nations Declaration on Human Rights) 229
UNICEF projects 126–7, 140
United Nations (UN) 126–7, 142–3
  debt relief 129
  HIV/AIDS projects 140–1
  human rights 13, 17, 28–9, 229
  Millennium Goals 102, 127
Universal Declaration of Human Rights (UDHR) 17–18, 28

viewpoints *see* points of view
voluntary organisations 85, 118–19
volunteers 117
voting
  general elections 77
  referendum vote 86–7, 218, 220
  rights 26–7, 30–1
  systems of 88–9, 220

wards of councils 66–7
warnings (employment) 37
WDM (World Development Movement) 134
White Papers 80–1
women *see* gender issues
workplace responsibilities 36–7
  see also employment laws
World Bank 134–5
World Development Movement (WDM) 134
World Trade Organization (WTO) 132, 134–5

young offenders 224–5
youth councils 72–3

William Collins' dream of knowledge for all began with the publication of his first book in 1819. A self-educated mill worker, he not only enriched millions of lives, but also founded a flourishing publishing house. Today, staying true to this spirit, Collins books are packed with inspiration, innovation and practical expertise. They place you at the centre of a world of possibility and give you exactly what you need to explore it.

Collins. Do more.

Published by Collins
An imprint of HarperCollinsPublishers
77 – 85 Fulham Palace Road
Hammersmith
London
W6 8JB

Browse the complete Collins catalogue at
www.collinseducation.com
© HarperCollinsPublishers Limited 2009
ISBN-13 978 0 00 731264 1

British Library Cataloguing in Publication Data
A Catalogue record for this publication is available from the British Library

This high quality material is endorsed by Edexcel and has been through a rigorous quality assurance programme to ensure that it is a suitable companion to the specification for both learners and teachers. This does not mean that its contents will be used verbatim when setting examinations nor is it to be read as being the official specification – a copy of which is available at www.edexcel.org.uk.

Commissioned by C Evans
Picture research: Suzanne Williams
Cover design: Angela English
Cover image: istock Photo
Internal design: Thomson
Illustrations: Yane Christensen, Sylvie Poggio Artists; Aetos Ltd.
Index: Indexing Specialists (UK) Ltd.
Production: Simon Moore
Printed and bound by Printing Express, Hong Kong

Acknowledgements

The publishers would like to thank the following for permission to reproduce photographs. The page number is followed, where necessary, by t (top), c (centre), b (bottom), l (left), or r (right):

p.4 (l) Still Pictures/Tim Page; p.4 (c) Rex Features; p.4 (r) Corbis; p.5 (l) PA Photos/Dominic Lipinski/PA Wire; p.5 (c) PA Photos/Denis Farrell/AP; p.5 (r) PA Photos; p.6 (tl) Alamy/Tim Pannell/Corbis Super RF; p.6 (tc) Alamy/TravelStockCollection – Homer Sykes; p.6 (tr) Alamy/David Hoffman Photo Library; p.6 (bl) Redferns Picture Library/Stefan M. Prager; p.6 (cm) Alamy/Alexandra Carlile/Elvele Images Ltd; p.6 (cr) Alamy/Paul M Thompson; p.6 (bc) Alamy/Yavuz Arslan/Black Star; p.6 (br) Rex Features/Fotex Medien Agentur GMBH; p.8 (l) Rex Features; p.8 (tr) Alamy/nagelestock.com; p.8 (br) Rex Features/Mauro Carraro; p.11 Alamy/Graham Oliver; p.12 (tl) Alamy/Neil Holmes/Holmes Garden Photos; p.12 (tc) Alamy/Adina Tovy/Robert Harding Picture Library Ltd; p.12 (tr) Alamy/Sally and Richard Greenhill; p.12 (bl) Alamy/Paul Doyle; p.12 (br) Alamy/Guy Somerset; p.13 Telegraph & Argus, Bradford; p.14 (tl) Photofusion/David Montford; p.14 (bl) Getty Images; p.14 (m) Magnum Photos; p.14 (r) Photofusion; p.16 (tl) Alamy/Lucinda Marland/Janine Wiedel Photolibrary; p.16 (tc) Still Pictures/Hartmut Schwarzbach/argus; p.16 (tr) Still Pictures/Joerg Boethling; p.16 (bc) Alamy/Ton Koene/Picture Contact; p.16 (br) Corbis/Steven Clevenger;

p.17 (l) Still Pictures/Tim Page; p.17 (r) Rex Features/Sipa Press; p.18 (tl) Corbis/Bettmann; p.18 (tr) Corbis; p.18 (b) Photofusion/Jackie Chapman; p.20 (b) Photofusion/Brian Mitchell; p.21 (l) Rex Features/Sipa Press; p.21 (r) Sally & Richard Greenhill; p.22 Campaign for Racial Equality; p.24 Science Photo Library/Alex Bartell; p.25 Sally & Richard Greenhill; p.26 (l) Alamy/Jenny Matthews; p.26 (tc) Alamy/Buzz Pictures; p.26 (tr) Alamy/Purestock; p.26 (bl) Rex Features/David Hartley; p.26 (br) Getty Images/Daniel Sambraus/STOCK4B; p.27 (l) Courtesy of Aldbourne Youth Council /www.4children.org.uk; p.27 (r) Wikimedia/Heinz-Josef Lücking (Authorisation/Wikimedia/Creative Commons/Attribution-Share Alike 2.5 Generic); p.28 (l) Mary Evans Picture Library; p.28 (r) Rex Features/Denis Cameron; p.29 Alamy/Friedrich Stark; p.30 (t) Getty Images/George Cruikshank/Photo by Spencer Arnold/Hulton Archive; p.30 (bl) PA Photos; p.30 (br) photo courtesy of the votes at 16 coalition 2009; p.31 (tr) Library of Congress; p.31 (cr) Rex Features/Sipa Press; p.31 (bl) PA Photos/Denis Farrell/AP; p.32 (b) Alamy/Harriet Cummings; p.34 (tl) Alamy/Alex Segre; p.34 (tc) Alamy/Neil McAllister; p.34 (tr) Alamy/Martin Jenkinson; p.34 (cm) Getty Images/Colorblind/Stone; p.34 (b) PA Photos/Dominic Lipinski/PA Wire; p.36 PA Photos/Empics; p.37 Alamy/Malcolm Case-Green; p.38 Still Pictures/Sean Sprague; p.42 (l) Getty Images/AFP; p.42 (c) Sally & Richard Greenhill; p.42 (r) PA Photos/Peter Jordan; p.43 (l) Alamy/Maggie Murray/Photofusion Picture Library; p.43 (c) Alamy/Jeff Morgan education; p.43 (r) Sally & Richard Greenhill; p.44 (tl) Alamy/Helene Rogers; p.44 (tc) Alamy/Mark Boulton; p.44 (tr) Getty Images/Tom Grill/Photographer's Choice RF; p.44 (bl) Rex Features/Chris Ratcliffe; p.44 (bc) Alamy/Rex Argent; p.44 (br) Corbis/Comstock Select; p.46 Reuters/Rebecca Cook; p.48 Getty Images/AFP; p.49 (l) Corbis; p.49 (r) Getty Images/AFP; p.50 (l) Getty Images/George Pimentel/WireImage; p.50 (c) Rex Features; p.50 (r) Rex Features/Tim Rooke; p.55 PA Photos/Peter Jordan/PA Archive; p.56 (b) Sally & Richard Greenhill; p.57 Alamy/snappdragon; p.58 (tl) Rex Features/Nikos Vinieratos; p.58 (tr) Getty Images/Chris Jackson; p.58 (b) Getty Images/Gareth Cattermole; p.60 Rex Features; p.64 John Walmsley Education Photos; p.65 Alamy/Maggie Murray/Photofusion Picture Library; p.66 Jenny Wales; p.67 (l) Photofusion/Paula Solloway; p.67 (r) Alamy/Maggie Murray/Photofusion Picture Library; p.68 Jenny Wales; p.70 (t) Alamy/Peter Titmuss; p.70 (cl) Alamy/Stuart Rimmer; p.70 (cr) Alamy/Neil McAllister; p.70 (bl) Alamy/Neil McAllister; p.70 (br) Alamy/David Hoffman Photo Library; p.72 Courtesy of IMPACT – Warrington Youth Council; p.73 Alamy/Jeff Morgan education; p.74 Alamy/Shout; p.75 (l) Alamy/Peter Marshall; p.75 (r) Photofusion/Ulrike Preuss; p.76 (t) Courtesy of Jo Swinson MP; p.76 (b) Courtesy of Jo Swinson MP; p.77 Sally & Richard Greenhill; p.78 Paul Hackett; p.79 PA Photos/Empics; p.80 (l) Alamy/Lawrence Wiles; p.80 (c) Rex Features/Richard Gardner; p.80 (tr) Rex Features/Loop Delay/WestEnd61; p.80 (br) Getty Images/Ron Levine/Digital Vision; p.81 Rex Features; p.82 (l) NO2ID; p.84 (l) Rex Features/Alisdair Macdonald; p.84 (r) Rex Features/E. M. Welch; p.85 Courtesy of The Point, Scope West Sussex; p.86 (l) Getty Images; p.86 (c) Sally & Richard Greenhill; p.86 (r) Photofusion/Gary Parker; p.87 PA Photos/Adam Elder/PA Archive; p.88 National Youth Agency; p.89 Getty Images/Fred Duval/FilmMagic; p.90 (t) Getty Images/Vano Shlamov/AFP; p.90 (b) Getty Images/Desmond Kwande/AFP; p.91 Alamy/Joe Sohm/Visions of America, LLC; p.96 (l) Getty Images/Melanie Stetson Freeman/The Christian Science Monitor; p.96 (c) Courtesy of The SMASH Youth Project / www.smash-youth-project.co.uk; p.96 (r) PA Photos; p.97 (l) Still Pictures/Friedrich Stark/Das Fotoarchiv.; p.97 (c) Rex Features/Top Photo Group; p.97 (r) Science Photo Library/NASA; p.98 (tl) Alamy/Glyn Thomas; p.98 (tr) Alamy/Sally and Richard Greenhill; p.98 (cm) Alamy/Motors; p.98 (br) Getty Images/Melanie Stetson Freeman/The Christian Science Monitor; p.100 (tl) Alamy/Grantly Lynch/UK Stock Images Ltd; p.100 (cl) Alamy/Joe Fox; p.100 (tc) Rex Features/Jeff Blackler; p.100 (cr) Rex Features/Jeff Blackler; p.100 (bc) Alamy/Paula Solloway/Photofusion Picture Library; p.100 (br) Alamy/Peter L Hard; p.100 (b) Getty Images/Tim Boyle; p.100 (tr) PA Photos/John Birdsall; p.101 (tl) Rex Features/Shout; p.101 (tr) Alamy/David J. Green; p.101 (br) Wikimedia/Nikola Gruev; p.102 (l) Alamy/Steve Morgan; p.102 (r) Science Photo Library/Victor De Schwanberg; p.103 (tl) Design: Surya Graf for Snack On/Björn Rust; p.103 (tc) copyright Total Merchandise Ltd 2008; p.103 (tr) Alamy/Mark Boulton; p.103 (b) PA Photos/Clara Molden/PA Wire; p.104 Getty Images/Digital Vision; p.105 (l) Alamy/Dave Bowman; p.105 (r) Alamy/Justin Kase...; ...Michalke/imagebroker; p.107 (tc) Ala...; p.107 (tr) Alamy/David Williams; p.10...; (br) Alamy/geogphotos; p.108 Alamy...; Alamy/Horizon International Images L...; Museum/Motoring Picture Library; p.1...; (bl) Alamy/IS046/Image Source Pink; p...; p.112 (br) Alamy/Dan Atkin; p.114 (tl)...; Peterson/Photodisc; p.114 (tc) Getty Ir...; (tr) Getty Images/Barbara Penoyar/Pho...; Peterson/Photodisc; p.116 Courtesy of...

/www.smash-youth-project.co.uk; p.117 Courtesy of Costain.com and Katesgrove Primary School; p.118 courtesy of PumpAid/ www.pumpaid.org; p.119 Amnesty International; p.120 Getty Images/AFP; p.122 (t) Stewart Golf; p.122 (b) iStockphoto/villiers; p.123 Getty Images/Mychele Daniau/AFP; p.124 (l) Rex Features/Veronica Garbutt; p.124 (r) Camfed/Mark Read; p.126 UNICEF/Sri Lanka/Beatrice Progida/October 2006–118; p.128 Alamy/fine art; p.129 UN Photo by Mark Garten; p.130 Getty Images/Don Farrall/Photodisc; p.131 Still Pictures/Mark Edwards; p.132 (l) Still Pictures/Friedrich Stark/Das Fotoarchiv.; p.132 (r) Fairtrade; p.133 Still Pictures/Harmut Schwarzbach; p.134 PA Photos/Michel Spingler/AP; p.135 PA Photos/Chris Radburn/PA Wire; p.136 (l) Science Photo Library/NASA; p.136 (r) PA Photos/PA Wire; p.137 (t) Getty Images/Carlo Allegri; p.137 (b) Still Pictures/Shehzad Noorani; p.138 Rex Features/Steve Williams; p.139 (l) Rex Features/Top Photo Group; p.139 (r) Rex Features/Sipa Press; p.140 Still Pictures/Jorgen Schytte; p.142 UN Photo; p.143 (l) UN Photo by R LeMoyne; p.143 (tr) UN Photo by Marie Frechon; p.143 (br) Coalition to Stop the use of Child Soldiers provided our copyright is acknowledged (please ensure our full name is used) and the following caption is used: Drawing by a former child soldier of the armed group, National Liberation Forces, Burundi, 2006.; p.144 ICC-CPI; p.145 Rex Features/Sipa Press; p.146 iStockphoto/geopaul; p.147 PA Photos/Cathal McNaughton/PA Wire; p.148 Alamy/David Noton Photography; p.152 (l) copyright of the image is Wiltshire County Council Development Service for Young People; p.152 (c) Courtesy of Stoke-on-Trent City Council; p.152 (r) Photofusion/Christa Stadtler; p.153 (l) John Walmsley Education Photos; p.153 (c) iStockphoto; p.153 (r) John Walmsley Education Photos; p.154 copyright of the image is Wiltshire County Council Development Service for Young People; p.155 (l) Courtesy of Stoke-on-Trent City Council; p.155 (r) Courtesy of the Young Co-operatives /www.youngco-operatives.coop; p.155 Courtesy of the Young Co-operatives /www.youngco-operatives.coop; p.156 (t) Photofusion/Christa Stadtler; p.156 (b) Alamy/Paula Solloway; p.160 iStockphoto/diane555; p.160 Jenny Wales; p.161 (tl) John Walmsley Education Photos; p.161 (c) John Walmsley Education Photos; p.166 (l) PA Photos/Greg Baker/AP; p.166 (c) Photofusion/Peter Marshall; p.166 (r) Alamy/Chris Pearsall; p.167 (l) Alamy/David Frazier/Corbis Premium RF; p.167 (c) Rex Features/Mauro Carraro; p.167 (r) Rex Features/Stuart Atkins; p.168 (t) Alamy/David Frazier/Corbis Premium RF; p.168 (c) Alamy/Robert Canis; p.168 (b) Alamy/Jenny Matthews; p.169 (t) Getty Images/David McNew; p.169 (b) BNPS.co.uk; p.170 Getty Images/George Doyle/Stockbyte; p.171 Getty Images/Peter Macdiarmid; p.173 (t) Alamy/David Noton Photography; p.173 (b) Alamy/Jim Zuckerman; p.174 Alamy/Dynamic Graphics 29/Jupiterimages/Creatas; p.176 (t) Alamy/Bill Brand; p.176 (b) BNPS.co.uk; p.177 Getty Images/David McNew; p.179 Alamy/David Frazier/Corbis Premium RF; p.180 (t) Corbis/Ragnar Schmuck/zefa; p.180 (c) Alamy/keith morris; p.180 (b) PA Photos/TJO; p.181 Alamy/Grantly Lynch/UK Stock Images Ltd; p.182 (t) iStockphoto/fotoon; p.182 (b) PA Photos/AP; p.183 PA Photos/Greg Baker/AP; p.184 Cartoonstock/Nilsson-Maki, Kjell; p.185 Alamy/isifa Image Service s.r.o.; p.190 (t) Photofusion/Peter Marshall; p.190 (b) Getty Images/Daniel Berehulak; p.191 (t) Rex Features/Mauro Carraro; p.191 (b) Alamy/Janine Wiedel Photolibrary; p.192 (t) Alamy/Angela Hampton Picture Library; p.192 (b) PA Photos/Gareth Fuller; p.194 Photofusion/Peter Marshall; p.196 Getty Images/Louai Beshara/AFP; p.197 Alamy/Alan Wylie; p.198 Getty Images/Steve Baccon/Riser; p.199 (t) Alamy/Mike Booth; p.199 (b) Getty Images/Scott E Barbour/The Image Bank; p.200 Rex Features/Tony Buckingham; p.202 North News & Pictures; p.203 Alamy/Janine Wiedel Photolibrary; p.204 (t) Rex Features/Mauro Carraro; p.204 (b) Jenny Wales; p.205 (l) Alamy/Phovoir/FCM Graphic; p.205 (r) Getty Images/Louise Wilson; p.206 (t) Courtesy of The Word/www.respect-theword.com; p.206 (c) Western Gazette/Len Copland; p.206 (b) Courtesy of RADIO SALAAM SHALOM "Muslims and Jews Talking Together"; p.208 Rex Features/Mauro Carraro; p.212 (t) Alamy/Chris Pearsall; p.212 (b) Alamy/Simon Holdcroft; p.213 Rex Features/Richard Jones; p.214 (bl) Alamy/Lisa Pines/UpperCut Images; p.214 (tc) Alamy/Purestock; p.214 (tr) Alamy/Redchopsticks.com LLC; p.214 (bc) Alamy/Stephen Ramsey/UpperCut Images; p.215 The Fawcett Society; p.216 Jenny Wales; p.217 Rex Features/Glyn Thomas; p.218 Rex Features/Stuart Atkins; p.219 Alamy/Mark Bourdillon; p.220 Alamy/David Williams/The Photolibrary Wales; p.225 (l) Alamy/Angela Hampton Picture Library; p.225 (r) Alamy/Adrian Sherratt; p.226 (l) Rex Features; p.226 (r) Corbis/Nancy Kaszerman/ZUMA; p.228 (l) PA Photos/Jackson Lee/Starmax/EMPICS Entertainment; p.228 (r) Alamy/Stuart Atkins; p.231 Getty Images/Tetra Images; p.232 (l) Rex Features/Rob Schoenbaum; p.232 (r) Alamy/blickwinkel; p.233 Rex Features/Richard Jones; p.235 Rex Features/Richard Gardner; p.240 (l) www.peopleandplanet.org/St Brendan's College People & Planet group with band members; p.240 (c) www.peopleandplanet.org/Sibford School People & Planet group launching their Go Green campaign; p.240 (r) Courtesy of Aldbourne Youth Council /www.4children.org.uk; p.241 (c) Manchester Evening News; p.241 (r) Derby College Students' Union; p.242 www.peopleandplanet.org/St Brendan's College People & Planet group with band members; p.243 www.peopleandplanet.org/Sibford School People & Planet group launching their Go Green campaign; p.244 Courtesy of Aldbourne Youth Council /www.4children.org.uk; p.245 Sally & Richard Greenhill; p.250 Jenny Wales; p.251 Photofusion/David Hoffman; p.252 www.peopleandplanet.org/Oxford High school students take part in a People & Planet Fairtrade workshop; p.254 Manchester Evening News; p.255 PA Photos/Tim Ockenden; p.255 PA Photos/Tim Ockenden; p.256 www.peopleandplanet.org/St Brendan's College People & Planet group with band members; p.257 Derby College Students' Union.

Photos sourced by Pictureresearch.co.uk

The publishers gratefully acknowledge the following for permission to reproduce copyright material. Every effort has been made to trace copyright holders, but in some cases this has proved impossible. The publishers would be happy to hear from any copyright holder that has not been acknowledged.

Thanks to:
Crown copyright material is reproduced with the permission of the Controller of HMSO and the Queen's Printer for Scotland: p. 9, 10, 11, 12, 24, 45, 71;
Oxford University Press for the use of statistics from the Human Development Report 2007/8: p. 128, 130;
Population Reference Bureau for use of HIV/AIDS statistics: p. 146.